CW00686442

Close-up

TEACHER'S BOOK

B2

Katrina Gormley

SECOND EDITION

NATIONAL GEOGRAPHIC
LEARNING

Australia · Brazil · Mexico · Singapore · United Kingdom · United States

NATIONAL GEOGRAPHIC
L E A R N I N G

Close-up B2 Teacher's Book, Second Edition
Katrina Gormley

Publisher: Sue Trory

Development Editor: Kayleigh Buller

Editorial Assistant: Georgina McComb

Cover Designer: Ken Vail Graphic Design

Text Designer/Typesetter: Wild Apple

Content Project Manager: Cathy Reay

For product information and technology assistance, contact us at
Cengage Learning Customer & Sales Support, cengage.com/contact

For permission to use material from this text or product,
submit all requests online at **cengage.com/permissions**
Further permissions questions can be emailed to
permissionrequest@cengage.com

ISBN: 978-1-4080-9852-3

National Geographic Learning
Cheriton House, North Way, Andover, Hampshire, SP10 5BE
United Kingdom

National Geographic Learning, a Cengage Learning Company, has a mission to bring the world to the classroom and the classroom to life. With our English language programs, students learn about their world by experiencing it. Through our partnerships with National Geographic and TED Talks, they develop the language and skills they need to be successful global citizens and leaders.

Locate your local office at **international.cengage.com/region**

Visit National Geographic Learning online at **NGL.Cengage.com/ELT**
Visit our corporate website at **www.cengage.com**

Cover image: (front cover) © WLADIMIR BULGAR/Science Photo Library/Corbis, (back cover) Paul Sampson/Alamy

The Publisher has made every effort to trace and contact copyright holders before publication. If any have been inadvertently overlooked, the publisher will be pleased to rectify any errors or omissions at the earliest opportunity.

Printed in Greece by BAKIS sa
Print Number: 03   Print Year: 2018

Contents

Contents

Introduction to Close-up

Welcome to *Close-up Second Edition*, an exciting intermediate and upper-intermediate course which brings English to life through spectacular National Geographic photography and facts carefully selected to appeal to the inquisitive minds of students.

Course Components

Close-up B2 Student's Book with online student zone

The Student's Book is divided into twelve topic-based units. Each unit starts with a stunning photograph linked to the theme of the unit and a summary of the contents of the unit. There are five two-page lessons in each unit covering reading, vocabulary & grammar, listening & speaking, grammar & Use your English and writing. The unit ends with a video page to accompany the National Geographic video clips found on the online student zone. The video clips are designed to expand students' knowledge of the world they live in, and the tasks in the Student's Book aid comprehension and further discussion of the topic.

Each unit also contains:

- tasks that actively develop students' reading, listening, speaking and writing skills.
- *Exam close-up* boxes and *Exam Tasks* that provide step-by-step advice and strategies for how to best to approach exam tasks and have the opportunity to put the advice into practice.
- *Useful Expressions* boxes in the speaking & writing sections that provide students with appropriate language when doing communicative tasks.
- plenty of opportunity for discussion of the topics in the *Ideas Focus* sections.

Close-up B2 Student's Book also contains six reviews, one after every two units, which consolidate the vocabulary and grammar taught within those units.

At the back of the Student's Book, there is a wealth of reference material. The Grammar Reference and Irregular Verbs List support the Grammar Focus within each unit. The Writing Reference provides a summary of the important points to remember for each genre of writing as well as a check list. There is also a Speaking Reference, bringing the *Useful Expressions* presented throughout the course together in one place. In addition, the collocations, expressions, prepositions and phrasal verbs actively taught in the Student's Book are also listed for easy reference.

The online student zone includes the Student's Book audio and video, and the Workbook audio available to download.

Close-up B2 Workbook

The Workbook accompanies *Close-up B2 Student's Book*. Like the Student's Book, it is divided into twelve units and six reviews. Each unit consists of reading, vocabulary, grammar, listening, Use your English and writing. The reviews include multiple-choice grammar and vocabulary items. The audio on the online student zone contains the recordings for use with the listening tasks.

The Workbook's clear and simple format means that it can be used at home as well as in class. The Workbook is available with or without the *Online Workbook*.

Close-up B2 Teacher's Book

Close-up B2 Teacher's Book provides clear lesson plans with detailed instructions and tips for teachers on how to make the best of the material in the Student's Book. The key to all tasks in the Student's Book and Workbook are included, along with the Student's Book transcripts with justification for the answers to the listing tasks underlined.

Close-up B2 online teacher zone

The online teacher zone contains a comprehensive testing package in printable PDF format. The multiple choice quizzes, one for each unit of *Close-up B2 Student's Book*, focus on the key vocabulary and grammar items presented in the unit. Progress Tests, one for use after every two units of *Close-up B2 Student's Book*, include a reading comprehension task, a writing task as well as vocabulary and grammar tasks. There is also a Mid-Year Test (*Units 1-6*) and an End-of-Year Test (*7-12*) that provide a written test covering reading comprehension, Use of English and writing, as well as a listening test. There is a section of photocopiable vocabulary and grammar tasks which can be used with students who finish early in class, as a way of revising prior to a test, or as extra practice of the vocabulary and grammar. All keys to these tests are included.

The *Close-up B2 online teacher zone* also includes the Student's Book audio and video along with the Workbook audio and transcripts, plus the Workbook transcripts with justification for the answers to the listing tasks underlined. In addition, there is a Student's Record document, which can be printed for each student, where test results can be recorded.

Close-up B2 Interactive Whiteboard Software is downloadable from the online teacher zone.
Close-up B2 Interactive Whiteboard Software includes content from the Student's Book, plus the audio and video. The Interactive Whiteboard has easy to navigate, interactive tasks, word definition functions, grammar animation and a series of games for further practice.

Justification for reading comprehension and listening tasks is available at the touch of a button, as is the key to all tasks. *Close-up B2 Interactive Whiteboard Software* also contains the Content Creation Tool, which allows teachers to create their own interactive tasks to use in class, and is compatible with any interactive whiteboard hardware.

1 Personally Speaking

Reading:	multiple-choice, identifying key information
Vocabulary:	emotion-related words, transforming words
Grammar:	present simple & present continuous, present perfect simple & present perfect continuous
Listening:	multiple-choice, highlighting key words
Speaking:	talking about free-time activities, answering personal questions, linking words, time expressions, tenses
Use your English:	phrasal verbs, prepositions, completing gapped texts
Writing:	informal letter / email, using the correct tone, planning your reponse

Unit opener

- Ask students to look at the title of the unit and to guess what it might mean (giving your opinion on a certain subject/explaining how you feel about something).
- Ask students to come up with as many adjectives related to feelings and emotions that they can think of. Then ask them to say if each word describes a positive or negative feeling, or whether it is neutral.
- Ask students to look at the picture and the caption and ask them how the man might be feeling and why she might be feeling this way.
- Ask them how they would feel if they were in this situation.

Reading

A

- Ask students to look at the picture in the top right-hand corner and to say how the person is feeling. Ask them to come up with as many ideas as to why the person is reacting in this way.
- Ask them to look at the words in the yellow box in A to pick the best word to describe what the man is feeling (fear).
- Ask students to say each of the words after you and elicit their meanings. Correct their pronunciation where necessary.
- Ask students to read the instructions in A and the question after the yellow box. Check that they understand what they have to do. Ask them to work in pairs and then check as a class.
- Ask them to suggest various situations in which someone would feel these emotions.

B

- Ask students to look at the picture on the left of the article and ask them how they would feel if they saw this girl running and what they think they might do as a result of seeing her (possibly look to see who or what is chasing her, or run in the same direction). Ask them where they think she might be and why.
- Ask students to read the title of the article and elicit how it relates to the picture. Ask them if they believe fear can spread from person to person. Encourage them to talk about personal experiences they may have had where fear spread among the people present.

- Ask students to read the definition of *neuroscientist* in *Word Focus* and correct their pronunciation of the word if necessary.
- Ask students to read the instructions in B and check that they understand what they have to do.
- Ask them to skim read the text and to note down the ways neuroscientists say fear spreads. Explain that they don't have to read in detail as they will have another opportunity to read the text.
- As a class, ask students to tell you the points they noted down.

Answers

Neuroscientists have been concentrating on people's reactions to body language rather than facial expressions to find out how fear spreads. They scan people's brains while they are looking at still images of frightened-looking actors in various situations. However, the actors' faces have been blocked out, so responses to the images depend on the body language of the actor.

New studies are also being conducted to investigate how participants react to moving images which show frightening scenes.

Word Focus

- Ask students to look at the words in red in the text and to re-read the sentences they are found in. Remind students that when they don't know the meaning of a word, they should look carefully at the sentence it is found in to work out its meaning. Ask students to work in pairs to decide what each of the words mean.
- Ask students to read the *Word Focus* box to compare their answers with the definitions.

C

- Draw students' attention to the *Exam Close-up* and tell them that these boxes are used throughout the book to give them tips about how to do specific tasks.
- Ask students to read the box here and ask a student to explain what it says in his or her own words. Explain that they should work out which facts questions 1-6 ask about and identify the parts of the text that deal with them. Explain that underlining information in the sentence stems and the text will make it easier for them to compare the information in the text with the options in the questions.

D

- Ask students to read the instructions and items 1-6 with their options. Explain anything the students don't understand.
- Remind students to underline the parts of the text that refer to each of the items.
- Ask students to do the task individually, but check as a class.

Answers

1 a *(Now a new study has shown that body language may be just as important as facial expressions for communicating fear.)*
2 b *(It shows that fearful body postures are processed in the emotional part of the brain ...)*
3 b *(... we also communicate through our bodies without our conscious minds being much aware of it.)*
4 c *(Unlike earlier studies, ... fearful body posture can create fear in observers. Participants ... were shown video stills ... the actors' faces were blocked out.)*
5 a *(There was a lot more going on in the brain than when the neutral images were shown.)*
6 d *(It is an extremely important evolutionary mechanism because any bird left behind may become prey.)*

E

- Ask students to look at the words in the yellow box here and to scan the text again to find and underline them. Ask them to say each of the words after you and elicit that they are all verbs. Correct their pronunciation where necessary.
- Remind them that they should always try to work out the meaning of a word from its context and ask them to read the sentences in the text each word is in.
- Ask students to read the instructions and check that they understand what they have to do. Encourage them to read all the sentences in E once before writing in any answers. Ask them to do the task individually, but check as a class.

Answers

1 react	4 process
2 evaluate	5 carry out
3 communicate	6 focus

Ideas Focus

- Explain to students that they are going to answer some questions about fear. Ask students to read the questions and explain anything they don't understand.
- Ask students to answer the questions in pairs and encourage them to draw on their personal experience as much as possible.
- Go round the class monitoring students to make sure they are carrying out the task properly. Don't correct any mistakes at this stage, but make a note of any problems in structure and pronunciation.
- Ask students at random to answer each of the questions and encourage the other students to give their opinions. If students are willing to discuss scary experiences with the class, allow them to do so.

- Write any structural mistakes that students made on the board without saying who made them, and ask them to correct them. Deal with any problems in pronunciation that came up.

Answers

Students' own answers

Teaching Tip

Allowing students time to discuss their own experiences helps to improve their fluency and gives them a real reason to communicate in English. Try to be aware of any sensitivities students may have, however, in talking about themselves and don't insist when they seem reluctant to talk about particular subjects.

Vocabulary

A

- Ask students to look at the picture on the right ask them to describe it. Ask them why the man might be reacting in this way and what might have happened to him. *(He has broken his leg and is in pain).*
- Ask students to read the instructions and check that they understand what they have to do.
- Read the prepositions in the yellow box to students and explain that they will use each of them once.
- Read the words and phrases in bold in the sentences to the students and ask them to say them after you. Correct their pronunciation where necessary. Point out that these are idiomatic phrases which take certain prepositions.
- Ask students to do the task individually, but check as a class.

Answers

1 in	4 at
2 out	5 with
3 on	6 under

B

- Ask students to read the instructions and check that they understand what they have to do.
- Say each of the words in the yellow box to the students and ask them to repeat them after you. Correct their pronunciation where necessary. Elicit that they are all nouns which refer to emotions and elicit which ones are positive *(amazement, confidence, joy)* and which are negative *(anxiety, disgust, fury, misery, shame).*
- Ask students to read through all the sentences once to decide whether the words in bold are positive or negative. Tell them to bear this in mind when choosing the correct word from the yellow box.
- Ask students to do the task individually, but check as a class.

Answers

1 joy	5 anxiety
2 fury	6 confidence
3 amazement	7 disgust
4 misery	8 shame

Teaching Tip

You could expand on this task by asking students to note down the adjectives that can be formed from these nouns (amazing/amazed, anxious, confident, disgusting/ disgusted, furious, joyous/joyful, shameful/shameless/ ashamed, miserable).

C

- Read the words in the yellow boxes to the students and ask them to repeat them. Correct their pronunciation where necessary.
- Elicit which words are verbs (affect, express, convey), which is a noun (effect), which is an adjective (lonely) and which is an adverb (alone).
- Ask students to read the instructions and check that they understand what they have to do. Ask them to read each sentence for gist and to work out what part of speech the missing word is.
- Ask students to do the task individually, but check as a class.

Answers

1	effect	4	lonely
2	affect	5	convey
3	alone	6	express

D

- Ask students to read the *Exam Close-up* and tell them to follow these guidelines when transforming words for the *Exam Task*. Ask students to read the instructions and check that they understand what they have to do.
- Read the words in bold at the end of each sentence to the students and ask them to repeat them. Correct their pronunciation where necessary. Then ask them what part of speech each word is. Explain that they will have to fill in the sentences with a different part of speech.
- Ask students to read the sentences for gist and to work out what part of speech is needed to complete them.
- Ask students to do the task individually, but check as a class.

Answers

1	disgusted	5	loneliness
2	frightening	6	enthusiastic
3	pride	7	annoyance
4	optimistic	8	eagerness

Grammar

- Ask students to look back at the article in Reading and to find and underline verbs in the Present Simple and Present Continuous.
- Ask students which tense appears more often in the text and to say why (*Present Simple is used more often as it's a factual article which discusses scientific facts and general truths.*).
- Revise the affirmative, negative, question forms and short answers of these two tenses with the class. Then elicit the adverbs of frequency and time expressions that are used with each tense.

A

- Ask students to read the instructions and check that they understand what they have to do.
- Ask students to focus on any time expressions or adverbs of frequency.
- Ask students to do the task individually, but check as a class.

Answers

1	PC	7	PC
2	PC	8	PS
3	PS	9	PS
4	PC	10	PC
5	PS	11	PS
6	PC		

B

- Ask students to read the instructions and check that they understand what they have to do. Explain that they should only match the present simple sentences in A.
- Ask students to read uses a-e and explain anything they don't understand. Then encourage them to read back through the sentences in A.
- Ask students to do the task individually, but check as a class.

Answers

a5 b3 c9 d8 e11

C

- Ask students to read the instructions and check that they understand what they have to do. Explain that they should only match the present continuous sentences in A.
- Ask students to read uses a-f and explain anything they don't understand. Then encourage them to read back through the sentences in A.
- Ask students to do the task individually, but check as a class.

Answers

a6 b10 c2 d7 e1 f4

Now read the Grammar Reference on pages 161 & 162 (1.1 to 1.3) with your students.

D

- Ask students to look at the picture above the text and to describe what is happening in it. Ask them what they notice about the child's hand. (*He or she is painting with their left hand.*).
- Ask students to skim read the text to find out how the picture relates to the text (*The text presents some facts about people who are left-handed.*).
- Explain to students that they should think about which use of each tense is being used in each item, whether verbs are stative and to look out for time expressions and adverbs of frequency that are used with these tenses.

- Ask students to do the task individually, but check as a class.

Answers

1	are reading	6	find
2	believe	7	works
3	pass	8	are discovering
4	have	9	controls
5	tend	10	makes

E

- Ask students to read the instructions and check that they understand what they have to do.
- Ask students to look at item 1 and elicit what the subjects of the missing verbs are *(Grandma, It)*. Ask them which of the verbs in brackets is stative *(smell)* and elicit that they will need the Present Simple here.
- Ask students to read the rest of the sentences carefully and to think about what the subjects are, whether verbs are stative or not and to underline any time expressions or adverbs of frequency in the sentences.
- Ask students to do the task individually, but check as a class.

Answers

1 are you baking, smells
2 look, are you thinking
3 want, Do you like
4 am/'m having, do not/don't understand
5 seems, is/'s working
6 is not/isn't coming, has
7 is/'s talking, do not/don't recognise
8 are they running, is chasing

Listening

A

- Ask students to read the instructions and check that they understand what they have to do.
- Ask students to read the pairs of sentences and to underline key words. Ask them to work with a partner to discuss other ways of saying the main ideas in each sentence.
- Remind students that in listening tasks, ideas are often paraphrased and that it's a good idea to get into the habit of reading questions before listening and to think of other words and phrases that they might hear on the recording.
- Play the recording all the way through and ask students to mark their answers. Then ask students to discuss their answers with a partner and to justify any answers that are different.
- Play the recording again and ask students to check their answers and to complete any answers they haven't already completed.
- Check the answers as a class and ask students to justify their answers using the words and expressions they heard on the recording.

Answers

1b 2a 3a 4b

B

- Ask students to read the instructions and check that they understand what they have to do.
- Ask them to read the situations and the options and elicit that they will hear two different extracts. Ask students to work with a partner to discuss what they think each conversation will be about. Point out that they will hear information relating to all three options on the recording.
- Play the recording all the way through and ask students to mark their answers. Play the recording again and ask students to check their answers and to complete any they haven't already completed.
- Ask students at random to say what questions they wrote. Accept any logical answer at this stage and explain to students that there may be differences in the questions they have written.

Suggested answers

1 What job doesn't the boy like doing?/What job does the boy's sister do?
2 What is the head teacher worried about?/What does the head teacher think is the cause of the problem being discussed?

C

- Ask students to read the information in the *Exam Close-up* about highlighting key words.
- Give students time to read through 1-6 in the *Exam Task* and to underline key words in the questions and in the options. Ask them to think of other words that could say the same thing and answer any questions they may have about them.
- Point out that as all the options will be related in some way to information on the recording, it is a good idea to note down what is said about each option. This will help them decide which one answers the focus of the question.

D

- Ask students to read the instructions in the *Exam Task* and check that they understand what they have to do.
- Play the first situation on the recording once and ask students to note down their answers to question 1 before playing it again. Check the answer to question 1 and ask students to justify it before playing the rest of the recording.
- Play the recording once all the way through and ask students to mark their answers. Then ask students to discuss their answers with a partner and to justify any answers that are different.
- Play the recording again and ask students to check their answers and to complete any answers they haven't already marked.
- Check the answers as a class and ask students to justify their answers.

Answers

1b 2c 3b 4b 5a 6a

E

- Ask students to read the instructions and check that they understand what they have to do.
- Ask students to swap books and to quickly look at the answers their partner chose in the *Exam Task* before listening to the recording.
- Play the recording again all the way through and ask students to check each other's answers.
- Once they have checked their partner's answers, ask them to swap books again and see how well they did. Answer any questions they might have.

Extra Class Activity

If time allows, you could ask students to write a conversation between two of the passengers in the picture. Then ask them to write down a question and three possible options on a separate piece of paper. Go round the class giving students any help they may need with their conversations and their questions.
Then ask students to swap questions and options with a partner. Each student should take it in turn to read their conversation while the other student answers the question.
At the end, you could ask a few students to read out their conversations to the class.

Speaking

A

- Ask students to read the prompts they will use to make questions and answer any queries they may have about them.
- Ask students to work in pairs to make questions from the prompts..
- Go round the class monitoring students to make sure they are carrying out the task properly. Don't correct any mistakes at this stage, but make a note of any problems in question formation.

B

- Ask students to look at the five pictures and read the topics for each one.
- Ask them to match the topics and pictures with the questions in A. Ask students to do this individually and then compare their answers with a partner.
- Check answers as a class. Ask students to justify their answers if there are any different answers amongst the students.

Answers

1 everyday activities
2 holidays and travel
3 personal experiences
4 education and work
5 media and communication
6 personal experiences/everyday activities
7 holidays and travel
8 education and work

C

- Ask students to read the instructions and check that they understand what they have to do.
- Give students time to read questions 1-8 in A again.
- Play the recording once all the way through and ask students to make a note of their answers. Then ask students to discuss their answers with a partner and to justify any answers that are different.
- Check answers as a class.

Answers

Speaker A 4 Speaker B 8 Speaker C 7 Speaker D 1 Speaker E 3

D

- Read the *Useful Expressions* to the students and explain that we use these structures in order to talk about ourselves. Point out the linking expressions are used to add further information.
- Ask students to read the questions. Explain that they will answer these as they listen to the recording again.
- Check the answers as a class and ask students to justify their answers. Point out to students that listening to others can help them improve their own performance in speaking tasks. Tell them to bear their answers in mind when they come to do a similar task to the one the students were given.

Answers

a Speakers A, C and D b Speaker C *(and, because)*, Speaker D *(usually, Because)* c Speaker D *(then, after that)* d Speaker B, e Speaker A and Speaker C

E

- Ask students to read the information in the *Exam Close-up*. Remind them to think about which tense they should be using in response to each question.
- Go round the class monitoring students to make sure they are carrying out the task properly. Don't correct any mistakes at this stage, but make a note of any problems in tenses and pronunciation. Also make a note of any answers that do not add extra information.
- Ask some pairs to ask and answer the questions in front of the class.
- Write any structural mistakes that students made on the board without saying who made them, and ask them to correct them. Deal with any problems with tenses and pronunciation that came up.

Ideas Focus

- Ask students to read the questions quickly and deal with any queries they may have.
- Ask students to work in pairs to take turns to answer the questions.
- Go round the class monitoring students to make sure they are carrying out the task properly. Don't correct any mistakes at this stage, but make a note of any problems with structure and pronunciation.
- Ask a student from each pair to answer one of the questions until each pair has had a turn. Ask other students if they agree or if they have something else to add.

- Write any structural mistakes that students made on the board without saying who made them, and ask them to correct them. Deal with any problems in pronunciation that came up.

Answers

Students' own answers

Grammar

- Write the sentences below on the board and ask students how they differ in meaning and which tenses have been used in each one.
  - She has studied hard for the physics exam, so she should do well.
  - She has been studying all day for the physics exam, so she's tired.

  (The first sentence talks about a completed action that has an effect on the present, whereas the second sentence focuses on how long the action has lasted. The Present Perfect Simple is used in the first sentence and the Present Perfect Continuous is used in the second sentence.)
- Revise the affirmative, negative, question forms and short answers of these two tenses with the class.
- Then elicit the time expressions and adverbs of frequency that are used with them.

A

- Ask students to read the instructions and check that they understand what they have to do.
- Ask students to read the sentences 1-8 and to put a tick or a cross depending on which tense is used.
- Ask students to do the task individually and compare their answers with a partner.
- Check answers as a class.

Answers

1 ✗	5 ✓
2 ✓	6 ✗
3 ✗	7 ✓
4 ✓	8 ✓

B

- Read the uses of the tenses a-h with the students and explain anything they don't understand.
- Explain they only need to write the name of the tense that each set of uses refers to.
- Ask students to complete the rules individually, but check as a class.

Answers

Present Perfect Simple - sentences a-e
Present Perfect Continuous - sentences f-h.

C

- Ask students to read the two sentences and to underline the words that are different. Elicit that both *gone* and *been* are past participles of the verb *go*.
- Ask students to discuss the difference in meaning between the sentences with a partner and decide where Pam is for both sentences.
- Check answers as a class.

Answers

Sentence *a* means that Pam is still at her friend's house, whereas sentence *b* means that she went to her friend's house at an indefinite time in the past and has since returned.

Be careful!

- Write the words *yet, before, lately, still, ever, just, already* and *never* on the board. Then write the following sentences and ask students to complete them using the time expressions.
  - She ____ hasn't explained why she was crying. *(still)*
  - I have ____ been so upset in my life! *(never)*
  - Have they finished the assignment ____? *(yet)*
  - You don't have to lock the door because I've ____ done it. *(just/already)*
  - I haven't eaten Chinese food ____. *(before/lately)*
  - Have you ____ been in a frightening situation? *(ever)*
- Ask students to read the information in *Be careful!* and explain anything they don't understand.
- If necessary, give students extra practice by asking them to write their own sentences with these words.

Now read the Grammar Reference on pages 162 & 163 (1.4 to 1.6) with your students.

D

- Ask students to read the first sentence and to decide which of the uses from B it matches *(for something that happened at an indefinite time in the past)*. Ask them which tense the correct option is *(Present Perfect Simple)*.
- Remind students to look back at the uses in B as they do the task and to pay attention to time expressions in the sentences.
- Ask students to do the task individually, but check as a class.

Answers

1 Have you ever had
2 It's been raining
3 haven't spoken
4 I've been waiting
5 haven't finished
6 have visited

E

- Ask students to read the instructions and the incomplete sentences. Check that they understand what they have to do.
- Encourage students to look back at the uses of the tenses in B in order to decide which tense should be used.
- Ask students to do the task individually, but check as a class.

Answers

1 have you been doing
2 Haven't you finished
3 has Kim been, have been looking
4 have they been studying
5 Have you been waiting
6 Has Karen made

F

- Ask students to read the instructions and check that they understand what they have to do.
- Ask students to read the dialogue all the way through, without filling in any answers at this stage.
- Ask a student to say in his or her own words what the dialogue is about.
- Remind students that they should only write one word in each gap. Encourage them to look at the words immediately before and after each gap in order to work out what kind of word is missing.
- Ask students to do the task individually, but check as a class.

Answers

1	ever	6	for
2	never	7	lately
3	just	8	still
4	ever	9	since
5	before/yet		

Use your English

A

- Read the phrasal verbs 1-6 to the students and ask them to repeat them. Correct their pronunciation if necessary.
- Ask students to read the definitions a-f without filling in any answers at this stage.
- Ask students to do the task individually, but check as a class.

Answers

1c 2d 3b 4a 5e 6f

B

- Ask students to read the instructions and check that they understand what they have to do.
- Ask students to read through the sentences and to pay attention to the words that are immediately before and after the gap. Encourage them to look for clues as to the tense the verb should be in and point out that they may have to change the form of the verb in some cases.
- Ask students to do the task individually, but check as a class.

Answers

1	bottle up	4	freaked out
2	chickened out	5	burst into
3	Cheer up	6	calm down

C

- Read the prepositions in the yellow box to the students and explain that they will have to use some prepositions more than once.
- Ask students to read the sentences, without filling in any answers at this stage, and to underline the verbs before the gaps and circle the adjectives. Explain that the preposition they will use depends on these words.

- Ask students to do the task individually, but check as a class.

Answers

1	to	4	to
2	to	5	for
3	on	6	on

D

- Ask students to read the instructions and check that they understand what they have to do.
- Ask students to read the information in the *Exam Close-up* and explain anything they don't understand.
- Stress how important it is to read the text all the way through first so that they know what it is about and what tenses have been used. They should also look carefully at the words before and after the gap.
- Ask students to read the text in the *Exam Task* and decide what type of word goes in each gap. *(1 auxilary verb 2 adverb 3 preposition 4 modal verb 5 verb 6 conjunction 7 noun 8 verb)*

E

- Ask students to read the text through again and remind themselves of what type of word goes in each gap.
- Ask students to complete the task individually, read the text through again, and then compare their answers with a partner. They should discuss any differences.
- Check answers as a class.

Answers

1	is	5	avoid
2	most	6	If
3	in	7	health
4	can	8	have

Writing: an informal letter / email

- Ask students to read the information in the *Learning Focus* on using the correct tone in letters and emails. Ask them if they write emails regularly and if so ask them who they write to and whether they write friendly, informal emails or formal emails. Ask if they ever write letters and if so, who to.
- Ask students what kind of language can help them achieve a nice, chatty style in their informal letters or emails *(informal phrasal verbs, idiomatic expressions, question tags, etc)*.

A

- Ask students to read the instructions and check that they understand what they have to do.
- Ask students to read 1-10 and answer any queries they might have about them.
- Give students time to write their answers and go round checking their answers as they write and giving them any help they may need.

- Ask each student to read out one of their answers, and ask for class agreement before confirming an answer is correct.
- After checking the answers, ask students to tell you which of 1-10 is inappropriate for an informal letter or e-mail, and why. *(Number 8, because it is language that would be used in a text message.)*

Answers

1F 2I 3F 4I 5I 6F 7F 8I 9I 10I

B

- Ask students to read the instructions and check that they understand what they have to do.
- Ask them to read the email from Tom in the small box.
- Ask students to do the task individually, but check as a class.

Answers

Tom wants to know about his friend's new town, new school and new friends.
Students have to answer four questions.

C

- Ask students to read the instructions and check that they understand what they have to do. Make sure they understand they should write phrases from A and not their own ideas.
- Give students time to write their answers and go round checking their answers and helping them where necessary.
- Ask each student to read an answer, but ask for class agreement before confirming an answer is correct. If any students have a different answer, ask them to justify their choice.

Answers

1 It was great to hear from you!
2 Oh well, you can't have everything!
3 Got any advice for me?
4 Anyway, how about visiting?
5 Hope to hear from you soon.

D

- Ask students to read the instructions and check that they understand what they have to do.
- Give students time to read through the email and to underline the parts which deal with the statements.
- Ask students to decide if the statements are true or false and compare their answers with a partner.
- Check answers as a class.

Answers

1 F *(She is getting ready for her music exam and feels stressed.)*
2 T *(The town is full of tourists in the summer.)*
3 F *(She hasn't made any friends yet because she's shy.)*
4 F *(She asks for Tom's advice.)*
5 T *(Anyway, how about visiting?)*

E

- Ask students to read the instructions and check that they understand what they have to do.
- Ask students to read the questions and explain anything they don't understand.
- Ask students to do the task individually, but check as a class.

Answers

1 yes
2 yes
3 yes
4 yes - use of informal language and phrases, use of exclamation marks and contractions

F

- Ask students to read the instructions and check that they understand what they have to do.
- Ask students to read the *Useful Expressions* and explain anything they don't understand. Ask students to practise using these expressions by writing sentences of their own with them.
- Then ask them to read the email and complete the gaps using the words from the *Useful Expressions*.
- Ask students to do the task individually and then compare their answers with a partner.
- Check answers as a class.

Answers

1 Hi/Hello,
2 Thanks
3 hear
4 well
5 Sorry
6 busy
7 Why
8 Bye

G

- Ask students to read the information in the *Exam Close-up*.
- Ask students if Emma did all of these things in her email in C *(yes)*.
- Ask students to use the bullet points here as a checklist when they come to write their own emails.
- Ask students to read the instructions and check that they understand what they have to do.
- Now ask them to read the task they will have to do and ask them the following questions.
  - What do you have to tell Jim? *(what you have been up to)*
  - What questions do you have to answer? *(how you got on with your exams; any subjects your're worried about; how you coped with the stress of the exams)*
- Ask students to think about the plan that they should follow when writing their email. If time allows, ask students to note down ideas that they might use in each paragraph.
- Set the writing task for homework.
- Encourage students to use the Writing Reference and checklist for informal emails on page 178.

Suggested answer

Hi Jim,

I'm well, thanks. I've been really busy with studying for my exams, which took up a lot of my time. I think I did OK, too, though I'm a bit worried about my maths exam. It was tough!

I coped with the stress by trying to be organised. I planned what revision to do each day and I had regular breaks through the day. Each night before an exam I went to bed early to get a good night's sleep. Dad helped me too, by asking me questions from the notes I'd made. I'm glad they're over now and I can relax. I've been listening to music and catching up with friends and all their news. Maybe we can get together soon and have a nice long chat!

Bye for now.

Jade

General Note

The National Geographic videos can be used as an interesting way to introduce your students to other cultures. They are authentic National Geographic videos, and it is not necessary for students to understand everything they hear to benefit from them. The videos have the option to play English subtitles so that students can read on screen exactly what is said in the documentary. This feature may help students with some of the tasks in the worksheets. The videos are also a good way to encourage your students to watch TV programmes and films in English so that they can get used to the sound of the language. The more students are exposed to English, the easier it will be for them to pick up the language.

Background Information

The Chinese art of calligraphy dates back to around four or five thousand years ago. It is considered to be an art form because of the intricate painting techniques needed to produce it, and also because each artist has individual differences in his or her brushstrokes. However, it is not only taught as a medium of artistic expression, but also as a form of discipline.

Before you watch

A

- Explain to students that in this lesson they are going to watch a video about a special kind of artist. Ask them to look at the globe and to tell you which part of the world the person lives in. Elicit what they know about New York and its population.
- Read the words a-d to the students and ask them to repeat them. Then ask students to read the meanings 1-4 and explain anything they don't understand.
- Ask students to do the task individually, but check as a class.

Answers

1d 2c 3a 4b

While you watch

B

- Tell students that they will now watch the video and do a task based on the information they hear.
- Ask students to read the statements 1-6 and ask them who the documentary will be about (an artist called Ming who lives in New York).
- Explain anything in the statements that the students don't understand. Then play the video all the way through without stopping and ask students to mark their answers. Ask students to compare their answers with a partner's and to justify any answers that are different. Play the video again so that they can check their answers.
- Ask students to do the task individually, but check as a class.

Answers

1	T		(00.11)
2	F	(... from his father.)	(00.45)
3	F	(... portraits of tourists)	(01.19)
4	T		(01.41)
5	T		(03.20)
6	T		(04.01)

After you watch

C

- Explain to students that this is a summary of the information they heard on the video.
- Read the words in the yellow box to the students and ask them to repeat them. Ask them to write N, V or Adj beside each of the words depending on whether it is a noun, verb or adjective.
- Explain to students that they should read the whole summary before writing any answers first to work out what part of speech is missing.
- Tell students to read back through the text once they have finished to check their answers.
- Ask students to do the task individually, but check the answers as a class.

Answers

1 cosmopolitan
2 differences
3 tourists
4 benefits
5 practises
6 ethnicity
7 artist
8 introduces

Ideas Focus

- Ask students to read the three questions and answer any queries they might have.
- Ask students to work in pairs and explain that they should both give their opinions on all three queries.
- Go round the class monitoring students to make sure they are carrying out the task properly. Don't correct any mistakes at this stage, but make a note of any problems in structure and pronunciation.
- Ask each pair to answer one of the questions and repeat until each pair has had a turn.
- Write the advantages of living in a cosmopolitan city and how we can learn about other people's cultures on the board as they give answers.

Answers

Students' own answers

2 One World?

Reading: multiple matching, finding similar words and phrases in the text
Vocabulary: culture-related words, countries, adjective form of countries, looking at text around a gap
Grammar: past simple & past continuous, *used to* & *would*, past simple vs present perfect simple
Listening: gapped text, predicting content
Speaking: talking about cultures and lifestyles, decision making, talking together, managing a discussion
Use your English: phrasal verbs, collocations & expressions
Writing: an opinion essay, organising your essay, writing topic sentences, planning your opinion essay, introducing points, introducing your opinion, concluding & summarising

Unit opener

- Ask students to look at the title of the unit and to guess what kind of things they expect to learn about in this unit (*different cultures of the world, globalisation and its effects on local cultures and customs*).
- Ask students to look at the picture and the accompanying caption. Ask them what the person is doing and why he might be doing it in this location. Ask them what benefits modern technology can offer people in remote locations and how the picture makes them feel.
- Ask students if they can think of any other ways in which technology can help people in remote places.

Reading

A

- Ask students to read the instructions and check that they understand what they have to do.
- Give students time to read the five changes and then ask them to discuss them with a partner.
- As a class, ask students what changes have taken place and how the culture of their country has been influenced by these changes. Encourage students to give examples and to comment on whether these influences have been beneficial to their country or not. You could also ask them which aspects of their own culture have become popular in other countries.

B

- Ask students to read the instructions and check that they understand what they have to do.
- Ask students to read the four sentences and explain anything they don't understand.
- Give students a short amount of time to read the article and decide which sentences are true. Remind them that they don't have to read in detail as they will have another opportunity to read the text.
- Ask students to do the task on their own and then to compare their answers with a partner.
- Check answers as a class.

Answers

Students should tick sentences **1** and **4**

C

- Ask students to read the information in the *Exam Close-up* and ask a student to explain what it says in his or her own words.
- Explain that in multiple-matching tasks it's very important to read the questions and underline key words so that you can look out for related ideas as you read. Point out that as the questions aren't in the order of the text, it isn't practical to take each question at a time and look for relevant information. In order to save time, students need to have studied all questions and answer them as they come across relevant information.
- Ask students to read the *Exam Task* and underline key words in the questions, but stress that the ideas will be paraphrased in some way.

Word Focus

- Ask students to look at the words in red in the text and to re-read the sentences they are found in. Remind students that when they don't know the meaning of a word, they should carefully look at the sentence it is found in to work out its meaning. Ask students to work in pairs to decide what each of the words mean.
- Ask students to read the *Word Focus* box to compare their answers with the definitions given. Explain anything they don't understand.

D

- Ask students to read the instructions again and check that they understand what they have to do. Explain that the task is multiple-matching and that they should answer A, B, C or D to show the paragraph where they find the information. Explain anything they don't understand.
- Remind students to underline information in the paragraphs related to the questions as they read the text.
- Ask students to do the task individually, but check as a class.

Answers

1. B *(Now, we are able to look after our families and send our children to school. We used to feel so bad about our lives, but now we are happy.)*
2. D *(Globalisation is destroying the uniqueness of different lifestyles and cultures ...)*
3. C *(I believe a global culture will lead to more tolerance and respect for other people, and make the world a more peaceful place.)*
4. A *(There used to be five factories in this town, and they were the biggest source of employment for miles around.)*
5. D *(Personally, I feel threatened by globalisation.)*
6. B *(A foreign company opened a clothing factory there a few years ago.)*
7. A *(The factory owners make bigger profits and get richer, but the unemployed workers are left with no jobs and no future.)*
8. C *(Also, in a global village, we will be able to solve global environmental problems by discussions.)*
9. D *(Before American style fast food caught on, people here in Japan used to eat more rice and vegetables and a lot less red meat, bread, dairy products and sugary food.)*
10. C *(For some people, this creates fears about losing their national identity ... and make the world a more peaceful place.)*

Teaching Tip

Always give students plenty of time to discuss their opinions on the theme of reading texts. This not only helps their fluency, but also helps them to understand better the key ideas of the text. The photos that accompany the texts provide a good starting point for discussion. Before moving on to the next task, ask students to look at the pictures accompanying the text here. Ask them what aspects of the people's lives they show and if they can work out anything about their lives from the pictures.

E

- Ask students to read the instructions and check that they understand what they have to do.
- Ask students to read the first sentence and the word in brackets. Elicit that they will find the correct form of the word to make grammatical sense in the sentence in paragraph A.
- Ask students to scan paragraph A to find the answer and check it as a class. Then ask students to find the other answers in a similar way.
- Ask students to do the task individually, but check as a class.

Answers

1 beneficial	4 poor
2 unemployed	5 peaceful
3 cultural	6 traditional

Ideas Focus

- Explain to students that they are going to have a discussion about globalisation. Ask them to read the two questions. Explain anything they don't understand.
- Ask students to work in pairs to take turns to answer the questions.
- Go round the class monitoring students to make sure they are carrying out the task properly. Don't correct any mistakes at this stage, but make a note of any problems in structure and pronunciation.
- As a class, ask students at random to answer the questions. Ask the other students if they agree or have anything else to add.
- Write any structural mistakes that students made on the board without saying who made them. Deal with any problems in pronunciation that came up.

Answers

Students' own answers

Vocabulary

A

- Ask students to read the instructions and check that they understand what they have to do.
- Read the sets of words in 1-6 to the students and ask them to repeat them. Correct their pronunciation where necessary.
- Ask students to work in pairs to encourage discussion, but check the answers as a class. Ask students to explain why one of the words is the odd one out in each item.

Answers

1. local *(The others are used to talk about things that happen on a worldwide level, but 'local' refers to a specific place.)*
2. knowledge *(The others are related to customs and how people live in particular places, but 'knowledge' means the information and understanding you have about something.)*
3. experience *(The others are feelings, suggestions or opinions that we have in mind, but 'experience' is something that happens to us.)*
4. aspect *(The others are things that happen or exist, but 'aspect' is a particular part of something.)*
5. demand *(The others mean that something is made bigger or takes place over a larger area, but 'demand' means to insist that you are given something or that something happens.)*
6. provide *(The others mean that goods are passed from one person to another either for money or for other goods, but 'provide' means that something is simply given to someone or made available for them to use.)*

B

- Ask students to write down as many things that they can think of that people from other countries might associate with their country and its people (eg Spain – tapas, bullfighting, beaches, etc). Ask them why these things have become associated with their country and whether they give an accurate picture.

- Read the countries in the yellow box to the students and ask them to repeat them. Correct their pronunciation where necessary.
- Ask students what things they associate with each of these places.
- Ask students to read the instructions and check that they understand what they have to do.
- Read the words in 1-8 to the students and ask them to repeat them. Correct their pronunciation where necessary.
- Ask students to do the task on their own, but check as a class.

Answers

1	Sweden	5	Egypt
2	The Netherlands	6	Switzerland
3	China	7	India
4	Brazil	8	America

C

- Elicit the adjective form from the countries in B and ask students to write them in their vocabulary notebooks.
- Ask students to read the instructions and check that they understand what they have to do.
- Encourage students to read through all the sentences before they fill in any answers. Tell them to look for cultural clues to each of the countries.
- Ask students to do the task individually, but check as a class.

Answers

1	American	5	Indian
2	Dutch	6	Swedish
3	Egyptian	7	Swiss
4	Chinese	8	Brazilian

D

- Ask students to look at the picture and its accompanying caption and ask them why camels are an important commodity to the people in the picture (*The Bedouins are nomadic desert people who use camels to transport their belongings and goods from place to place in the desert.*).
- Explain to students that they are going to read a text about the early history of international trade. Ask them what, if anything, they know about this subject.
- Ask students to read the information in the *Exam Close-up* about looking at the text around a gap and explain anything they don't understand.
- Then ask students to read the *Exam Task* instructions and check that they understand what they have to do.
- Read the words in the yellow box to the students and ask them to say them after you. Correct their pronunciation where necessary.
- Ask students to read the text for gist, without filling in any answers at this stage. Ask students how the picture relates to the text (*Caravans of camels used to transport goods over land. This led to trade routes being established in the 7th and 8th centuries. Towns were even established at places where camels stopped to rest.*).

- Ask students to do the task individually, but check as a class.

Answers

1	roadways	5	civilisations
2	networks	6	influence
3	export	7	customs
4	ports	8	homelands

Grammar

- Ask the questions below at random round the class. Make sure each student answers at least one question.
  - When did you last go on a long journey?
  - How did you travel the last time you went on holiday?
  - Which country interested you most when you were younger? Why?
  - How old were you the first time you visited an archaeological site?
- Ask students which tense the questions and their answers were in (*Past Simple*) and elicit how this tense is formed. Revise affirmative, negative, question forms and short answers of this tense. Remind students that the Past Simple has the same form for all persons, apart from the verb *be*.
- Write the following sentences on the board and ask students which tense has been used this time (*Past Continuous*).
  - The camel was carrying a heavy load.
  - Jane was boarding the plane this time yesterday.
  - They weren't speaking in Spanish.
  - We were sitting by the harbour having a drink.
- Elicit that the first and third person singular (*I, he, she, it*) form the Past Continuous with *was* followed by the main verb with *-ing*, and that the second person singular/ plural, and first and third person plural (*you, we, they*), form it with *were* followed by the main verb with *-ing*. Revise the affirmative, negative, question forms and short answers.

A

- Ask students to read the instructions and check that they understand what they have to do.
- Ask students to read sentence *a* and tell you which tense is used in the sentence (*Past Simple*). Check they have the correct answer before they do the rest of the task. Ask them to tell you why the Past Simple is used (*for completed actions that happened one after the other in the past*).
- Ask students to do the task individually, but check as a class.

Past Simple sentences
1, 2, 5, 8
Past Continuous sentences
3, 4, 6, 7, 9

B

- Ask students to read the instructions and check that they understand what they have to do. Then ask them to read the uses of the Past Simple and Past Continuous. Explain anything they don't understand. Then encourage them to read back through the sentences in A.
- Ask students to do the task individually, but check as a class.

1 Past Simple
2 Past Continuous

C

- Read the information to the students and elicit that we can't use *would* with stative verbs to talk about habits, but that we can use it with active verbs.
- Ask students to read the three sentences and to decide which is wrong. Ask them to justify their answer.
- Ask students to look back at sections A, B and D of the Reading text to underline examples they can find of *used to* for past habits (*A – used to be five factories, B – used to feel bad, D – used to eat*). Ask them if *would* could be used instead of *used to* in these instances (*- in A and B, it would be wrong because we cannot use* would *with past states*).

The second sentence is wrong because we cannot use *would* with past states.

Now read the Grammar Reference on page 163 (2.1 to 2.3) with your students.

D

- Ask students to look at the picture and ask them the questions below. Accept any logical answers.
  - Why do you think this sculpture was made?
  - What was the warrior doing?
  - What was he wearing?
  - What does the sculpture tell us about his civilisation?
- Explain to students that they are going to read a text about the civilisation this warrior was part of. Ask them to read the text without filling in any answers at this stage, and to guess which civilisation mentioned this warrior was part of (*Mesopotamian*).
- Explain to students that they should pay attention to the context each missing verb is in to help them decide which tense is appropriate in each case. Encourage them to look back at A while doing the task. Remind them that they should check they have the correct form of *be* if a gap requires the Past Continuous.
- Ask students to do the task individually, but check as a class.
- If students seem interested give them more information using the Background Information box.

1 were	6 were springing up
2 contributed	7 developing
3 creating	8 became
4 using	9 coming up with
5 established	10 led

Background Information

Mesopotamia is the land mass between the Euphrates and Tigris rivers. It stretched from present-day Iraq, north eastern Syria, south eastern Turkey to south western Iran. The Assyrians inhabited the area in northern Mesopotamia *(northern Iraq)* from around the 24th century BC to 608 BC.

E

- Ask students to read the instructions and check that they understand what they have to do. Explain that they should consider the verbs in italics in each sentence and correct the ones that are wrong.
- Point out to students that they should pay attention to time references in the sentences as these will help them to decide if a tense is correct or not. Also, they should check to see which other tenses are used in the sentences and whether verbs are active or stative. Remind them that stative verbs can't be used in the continuous tenses or with *would* to talk about a past habit.
- Ask students to do the task in pairs to encourage discussion, but check as a class.

1 was digging (*longer action interrupted by a shorter action*)
2 correct
3 discovered (*a completed action in the past*)
4 always used to get (get excited *is a state so* would *can't be used*)
5 Did you use to listen (*wrong past form of* used to)

Listening

A

- Ask students to read the instructions and check that they understand what they have to do.
- Ask students to work in pairs to discuss what type of word could go in each gap, eg *noun, verb, determiner, adjective*. Tell them not to write anything at this stage, but make notes of their decisions in a notebook.
- Ask students to now guess the actual word or words that could complete each sentence. Allow them time to reach a decision in their pairs about the words..
- Check their answers as a class and accept any logical answers, without revealing what is said on the recording at this stage.
- Play the recording once all the way through and ask students to listen to see if they were correct. Then ask students to discuss their ideas with another pair and to compare them with their own guesses.

Answers

1 place
2 adjective
3 a number
4 dates
5 verb

B

- Explain to students that they are going to listen to the recording again and that they should fill in the blanks in the sentences in A.
- Play the recording all the way through and ask students to write their answers. Ask students to discuss their answers with a partner and to justify any answers that are different.
- If necessary, play the recording once more to allow students to check their answers and fill in any missing answers.
- Check as a class and ask students to justify their answers.

Answers

1 Berlin
2 cultural
3 5/five
4 1824, 1930
5 became

C

- Ask students to read the information in the *Exam Close-up*. Point out that in A, they predicted what kind of words were missing and that in B, they filled in the gaps with the exact words they heard on the recording. Explain that this will always be the case in this type of task.
- Ask students to think read the sentences in the *Exam Task* and underline the important words (usually before or after the gap) before they listen to the recording.

D

- Ask students if there are any cultural festivals in their country and/or local area. If so, ask them what sort of events take place during the festivals and if they have ever attended one. If not, ask them what sort of events they think such a festival might have and if they would enjoy such events.
- Explain that they are going to listen to a radio report about such a cultural festival. Ask students to read the instructions and check that they understand what they have to do.
- Then ask students to read the sentences 1-8 to find out what the cultural festival is (*The Berlin Long Night*). Ask them to guess why it's called the *long night* and what kind of events it involves.
- Play the recording all the way through once and ask students to write their answers. Then ask students to discuss their answers with a partner and to justify any answers that are different.

E

- Play the recording again and ask students to check their answers and to complete any answers they haven't already marked.
- Check the answers as a class and ask students to justify their answers.

Answers

1 important role
2 1997
3 January, August
4 (special) pass
5 dance performances
6 common occurrence
7 White Nights Festival
8 10 pm

Teaching Tip

If students have problems with listening, suggest that they make time to listen to English more outside the class. Suggest that they watch films and TV programmes in English, preferably without subtitles, whenever possible. If your school has a multimedia library, suggest that students borrow DVDs or CDs to listen to. Point out that it's not necessary to understand every word as long as they understand the general idea of what is being said. Explain that they must listen as often as possible to the language being spoken naturally for their ears to become accustomed to it.

Speaking

A

- Ask students to read the two questions and answer any queries they may have about them.
- Ask students to work in pairs to take it in turns to ask and answer questions about themselves.
- Go round the class monitoring students to make sure they are carrying out the task properly. Don't correct any mistakes at this stage, but make a note of any problems in structure and pronunciation.
- Ask each pair to ask and answer one of the questions and repeat until each pair has had a turn.
- Write any structural mistakes that students made on the board, without saying who made them, and ask them to correct them. Deal with any problems in pronunciation that came up.

B

- Ask students to think of a foreign culture that interests them. Ask them what they know about this culture and how they learnt these things. Ask them if there are any aspects of the culture that they would like to find out about.
- Ask students to read the instructions and check that they understand what they have to do.
- Give students time to write down as many ways they can think of and then ask them to work in pairs in order to answer the questions based on their ideas.
- Go round the class monitoring students to make sure they are carrying out the task properly. Don't correct any mistakes at this stage, but make a note of any problems in structure and pronunciation.

- Ask each pair to ask and answer one of the questions and repeat until each pair has had a turn.
- Write any structural mistakes that students made on the board, without saying who made them, and ask them to correct them. Deal with any problems in pronunciation that came up.

C

- Ask students to read the information in the *Exam Close-up*. Stress the importance of discussing all the options as fully as possible. Point out that this will help them to choose the most logical options and it will also help them to understand how the other person feels about each option. You might also like to point out that in an exam situation, the examiner won't be able to assess their language level properly if they don't discuss each option in detail.
- Ask students to read the *Exam Task* and to underline the two things they are asked to do *(talk about how useful each of the suggestions would be in learning about other cultures and then deciding which two would be best for your class and age group)*. Elicit that in decision-making tasks, they should have a two-way conversation, so they should encourage each other to give opinions and ask for reasons to justify them.

Useful Expressions

- Read the *Useful Expressions* to the students and ask them to repeat them. Correct their pronunciation and intonation where necessary.
- Explain to students that in the type of task they will do in the *Exam Task*, it's important to use expressions such as these in order to manage their discussion. These expressions will help them to begin and carry out the task smoothly and in a polite manner.

D

- Ask students to read the instructions again and check that they understand what they have to do.
- Ask students to look at the six photos and read the captions.
- Ask students to do the task in pairs and remind them that it is a discussion. Remind them to use the *Useful Expressions*, to discuss all the options and to reach an agreement at the end.
- Go round the class monitoring students to make sure they are carrying out the task properly. Don't correct any mistakes at this stage, but make a note of any problems in structure and pronunciation.
- Ask each pair to tell the class which two options they choose and to say why and repeat until each pair has had a turn.
- Write any structural mistakes that students made on the board, without saying who made them, and ask them to correct them. Deal with any problems in pronunciation that came up.

Ideas Focus

- Ask students to read the questions quickly and deal with any queries they have.
- Ask students to work in pairs to take turns to answer the questions.
- Go round the class monitoring students to make sure they are carrying out the task properly. Don't correct any mistakes at this stage, but make a note of any problems in structure and pronunciation.

- Ask a student from each pair to answer one of the questions and repeat until each pair has had a turn. Ask other students if they agree or if they have something else to add.
- Write any structural mistakes that students made on the board, without saying who made them, and ask them to correct them. Deal with any problems in pronunciation that came up.

Answers

Students' own answers

Grammar

- Ask the questions below at random round the class. Make sure each student answers at least one question.
  - Have you ever been to another country?
  - What food have you tasted from other countries?
  - Have you ever spoken in English to a visitor to your country?
  - Has it snowed lately where you live?
- Ask students which tense the questions were in *(Present Perfect Simple)* and ask them if all their answers were in the same tense *(Some answers may have been in the Past Simple.)*.
- Elicit that we form the Present Perfect Simple using the verb *have* in the correct form, ie *has* for third person singular *(he, she, it)* and *have* for all other persons. The auxiliary verb is then followed by the past participle of the main verb.

A

- Ask students to read the instructions and check that they understand what they have to do.
- Ask students to do the task in pairs to encourage discussion, but check as a class.
- Explain that the Past Simple is used for completed actions or actions that happened at a specific time in the past. The Present Perfect Simple is used for actions that happened at an indefinite time in the past and have some effect on the present.
- Ask students to read the rule and elicit that they have to complete it with the appropriate tenses. Encourage them to look back at the sentences above to decide on the answers.
- Ask students to do the task individually, but check as a class.

Answers

Past Simple: went, ~~Past~~ Present Perfect Simple: have never been

Past Simple, ~~Past~~ Present Perfect Simple

B

- Ask students to read sentences 1 and 2 and to underline the words that are different. Elicit that the Present Perfect Simple is used in 1 and the Past Simple in 2.
- Ask students to read the questions and elicit that they should write *1* or *2* in the boxes provided.
- Ask students to do the task individually, but check as a class.

Answers

> a2 b1

Now read the Grammar Reference on pages 163 & 164 (2.4) with your students.

C

- Ask students to read the instructions and check that they understand what they have to do.
- Ask students to read sentence 1 and circle the correct answer. Elicit that the Present Perfect Simple has been used here as it refers to an action that has an effect on the present. Ask students to read the second sentence and ask them to underline any time references it contains *(for days)* and ask them what this tells them *(The Present Perfect Simple should be used.)*.
- Ask students to do the task individually, but check as a class.

Answers

> | 1 | hasn't seen | 5 | taught |
> |---|---|---|---|
> | 2 | looked | 6 | for |
> | 3 | last went | 7 | yet |
> | 4 | hasn't found | 8 | developed |

D

- Ask students to read the instructions and check that they understand what they have to do.
- Ask students to look at sentence 1 and elicit what the subject of the missing verb is *(I)*. Ask them if the verb in brackets is stative or active *(active)* and elicit that they need the Present Perfect Simple here.
- Ask students to read the rest of the sentences carefully and to think about what the subjects are, whether verbs are stative or not and to underline any words that help them choose the tense, such as *just, yet, already, since.*
- Ask students to do the task individually, but check as a class.

Answers

> 1 have already eaten
> 2 left, haven't seen
> 3 have never eaten
> 4 hasn't started
> 5 hasn't been, was
> 6 A has bought
>   B bought
> 7 A Have you ever flown
>   B flew
> 8 overslept, missed, hasn't done

Use your English

A

- Write the verb *call* on the board and ask students if they know any phrasal verbs with this verb.
- Ask students to read the instructions and check that they understand what they have to do.

- Read the phrasal verbs in the yellow box to the students and ask them to repeat them. Correct their pronunciation where necessary.
- Ask students to read through the sentences before working out any answers. Encourage them to rewrite the sentences they are sure about first. Explain that in some cases they may have to split the verb and particle so that the object of the sentence comes directly after the verb.
- Ask students to do the task individually, but check as a class.

Answers

> 1 They called on the manager to make a speech.
> 2 I can't talk now, so I'll call you back.
> 3 Tina called round yesterday, but I wasn't at home.
> 4 We called in an electrician/called an electrician in to come to fix the broken heater.
> 5 Let's call up Tom and Jerry/Tom and Jerry up and ask them to join us.
> 6 The job calls for honesty, responsibility and hard work.
> 7 Mr Jones called out the names/called the names out and then the lesson started.
> 8 We had to call off our trip/call our trip off due to bad weather.

B

- Write *do/make* and *a mess of something* on the board and ask students which verb completes the collocation *(make)*. Explain that in English we call this a collocation, which means that certain words can be used beside other words to form a common expression.
- Ask students to read the instructions and check that they understand what they have to do.
- Ask students to do the task in pairs to encourage discussion, but check as a class.

Answers

> The following should be crossed out:
> 1 a mistake
> 2 an impression
> 3 a word
> 4 control

Teaching Tip

You could extend this task by asking students to come up with verbs that could collocate with the words they crossed out in B. For example, *make/correct a mistake, make an impression/give the impression, have a word, take/lose control.*

C

- Ask students to read the instructions and check that they understand what they have to do.
- Point out that they should look for clues in the sentences regarding the tense and form the verbs should be in. In particular, they should look for other verb tenses in the sentences and the subjects before the gaps.

- Ask students to read sentence 1 and to underline the subject (*Alexander the Great*) and any verbs (*stretched*) and to say which tense the verb is in (*Past Simple*). Ask them to look back at B to find a suitable collocation to complete the gap and ask them to write it in the appropriate tense and form. Check their answer before moving on.
- Ask students to do the task individually, but check as a class.

Answers

1	built an empire	5	do you good
2	save space	6	save money
3	do business	7	build a reputation
4	played a joke on	8	played a role

D

- Ask students to read the instructions and check that they understand what they have to do.
- Read the words in bold at the end of each sentence to the students and ask them to repeat them. Correct their pronunciation where necessary. Then ask them what part of speech each word is. Explain that they will have to fill in the sentences with a different part of speech and might need to add a prefix as well as a suffix, or make internal changes to a word.
- Ask students to read the sentences for gist and to work out what part of speech is needed to complete them.
- Ask students to do the task individually, but check as a class.

Answers

1	classified	5	succeed
2	prove	6	apologise
3	relieved	7	terrorise
4	encourage	8	criticise

Writing: an opinion essay

- Ask students to read the information on organising essays and explain anything they don't understand. Ask students why they should write in paragraphs (*so that their ideas are organised and dealt with in a logical manner*) and why each paragraph should contain a topic sentence (*to let the reader know what the main idea of the paragraph is*).
- Explain to students that they need to start their essay with an introductory paragraph which gives the reader a clear idea of your opinion on the essay topic. It's equally important to finish your essay with a concluding paragraph which summarizes your opinion in one or two sentences.

A

- Ask students to read the instructions and to glance at the paragraph in the box. Ask them why they think there is a line at the beginning (*something is missing that they should fill in*) and then to read the questions next to the box. Elicit that it is the topic sentence that is missing and that they will have to choose the best one to complete the paragraph.

- Ask students to read the options a-c and then to read the paragraph in the box to decide which sentence best completes it. Encourage them to think about the content as well as the level of formality. Ask them to discuss their answer with a partner and to justify their choices.
- Check the answer as a class and ask students to explain why the option they choose is the best and to say why the others aren't as good.

Answers

The best answer is 'b' because it includes a topic (*learning a foreign language*) and a main idea (*how important it is*). The rest of the paragraph goes on to develop this main idea.
The others are not as appropriate because a is too informal and too personal and c because the paragraph is about travel not free time.

B

- Ask students to read the instructions and check that they understand what they have to do.
- Ask them to read the first paragraph in A again and think about how the essay will continue. Ask them to work with a partner and discuss their ideas.
- Ask several students for their ideas as to what else will be in the essay and ask the other students to say what other ideas they had.

C

- Ask students to read the instructions and the writing task and check that they understand what they have to do.
- Ask them to underline the key words in the writing task and ask them what they would have to write (*an essay on the reasons why it is important to learn a foreign language*).
- Ask students to read the two notes and explain they are going to complete 3 with their own idea.
- Give students a few minutes to decide what they would include in the essay. Give students any help they might need as they complete the notes.
- Ask several students to read out their ideas to the class.

D

- Ask students to read the model essay and to pay particular attention to paragraph 4.
- Ask students to comment on what ways it is similar or different to their own ideas. Ask them what the topic of the paragraph is (*cultural knowledge*) and if they agree with the writer's views. Encourage everyone to give their opinion.

E

- Ask students to read the instructions and explain anything they don't understand.
- Ask students to read the essay again and underline the topic sentence of each paragraph (*the first sentence in each paragraph*).
- Ask students to say if they think each one summarises what is written in each paragraph (*yes, they do*).
- Invite students to say whether the topic sentences made it easier for them to read the essay and understand it.

F

- Ask students to read the instructions and explain anything they don't understand.
- Remind students they have to think of reasons why learning another language is useful for study, not just business or pleasure.
- Ask them to individually brainstorm some ideas and write the in the space provided, and then write a topic sentence.
- Monitor and help if necessary. When finished, ask students to compare their ideas and topic sentence with a partner.
- Ask students to tell you their ideas and read their topic sentence to the class.

Useful Expressions

- Read the *Useful Expressions* to the students and ask them to repeat them. Correct their pronunciation where necessary.
- Check that students understand the differences between the expressions and why we use them.
- Ask students to write sentences of their own using two or three expressions.

G

- Ask students to read the instructions and explain anything they don't understand.
- Elicit that we use linking words and phrases between paragraphs to show how one paragraph follows on from the previous one and between sentences to show how ideas relate to each other. Revise some of the most common linking words and phrases before students look at the essay in D again.
- Ask students to underline examples in the essay and then to compare them with a partner. Once they have done that, ask them to circle the correct words and phrases in the text in G.
- Check the answers as a class.
- Once the answers have been discussed, ask students to work in pairs to come up with as many linking words and phrases as they can think off.
- Ask a student to come up to the board and to make a list of the phrases the others have come up with. Discuss what the function of each example is (*ie to introduce ideas, to contrast with a previous idea, to add another point, to conclude, etc*).

Answers

1 mind
2 Apart
3 addition
4 consider
5 Finally

H

- Ask students to read the information in the *Exam Close-up*.
- Ask them to quickly read the instructions in H and elicit that the correct style for this task would be formal.
- Remind students that they should introduce examples using the linking words and phrases they saw in *Useful Expressions*. Remind them to think carefully about their topic sentences that should introduce the topic of the paragraph.
- Ask students to read the instructions for the *Exam Task* and explain anything they don't understand.
- Ask students if they or anyone they know have ever studied abroad. If so, ask them what their experience was like and what benefits they gained from it. If not, ask them to imagine what it would be like and what they think they could gain from such an experience.
- Ask students to think about statements 1 and 2 and what they would write. They should then add their own idea in the space provided.
- Ask students to make a plan before writing their essay. If time allows, ask students to note down ideas that they might use in each paragraph.
- Set the writing task for homework.
- Encourage students to use the Writing Reference and checklist for opinion essays on page 185.

Suggested answer

Many students nowadays choose to study abroad rather than in their own country. Globalisation means that more young people want to find out more about the world at the same time as getting a good education.

To begin with, universities overseas are often of a better standard than those in a student's own country. There is also a bigger choice of courses to take, as well as the opportunity to meet people of the same age from all over the world.

Another advantage of studying abroad is the cultural aspect of it. You not only improve your language skills, but make friends and learn more about the traditions, food and customs of the country.

Finally, another reason to study abroad is that it teaches you independence and how to be responsible. For most students, it is the first time they have had to budget and manage their own money. Paying bills and rent, shopping and entertainment all have to be budgeted for.

To sum up, there are many good reasons for studying in another country. These include standard of education, learning about the culture and learning to be a responsible person. Whatever the reasons for studying overseas, a few years living in another culture can only enrich your life and help you become an independent adult.

2 A Special Type of Neighbourhood

 Video

General Note

The National Geographic videos can be used as an interesting way to introduce your students to other cultures. They are authentic National Geographic videos, and it is not necessary for students to understand everything they hear to benefit from them. The videos have the option to play English subtitles so that students can read on screen exactly what is said in the documentary. This feature may help students with some of the tasks in the worksheets. The videos are also a good way to encourage your students to watch TV programmes and films in English so that they can get used to the sound of the language. The more students are exposed to English, the easier it will be for them to pick up the language.

Background Information

San Francisco got its name from Spanish colonists who arrived there in 1776. For over 2,000 years prior to that, it had been inhabited by Native Americans. The Spanish colonists set up a fort and a mission in honour of St Francis of Assisi in the area of the present-day Golden Gate Bridge. The mission was moved to another area in 1783, and the original building is still standing in the neighbourhood now known as The Mission. In the 19th century, the city experienced a wave of immigration from Germany, Italy, Ireland and Scandinavia. From the 1950s on, most new immigrants were from Mexico. Their cultural influence is still very predominant in this neighbourhood today.

Before you watch

A

- Explain to students that in this lesson they are going to watch a video about immigrants in San Francisco, California. Ask them to look at the globe to see where California is. Elicit what they know about California and ask them why people from other countries and cultures might decide to go there to live.
- Ask students to answer the questions in pairs. Encourage them to draw on their own experience from immigrants to their own country.
- Go round the class monitoring the students to make sure they are carrying out the task properly.
- Elicit the different cultural influences that immigrants can bring to a host culture and ask them which ones they find most interesting.
- Write any structural mistakes that students make on the board, without saying who made them, and ask them to correct them. Deal with any problems in pronunciation that came up.

While you watch

B

- Explain to students that they are now going to watch the video. Ask them to read sentences 1-6 and explain anything they don't understand.
- Ask them to think about which words may be correct before watching.

- Play the video all the way through without stopping and ask students to circle their answers. Ask students to compare their answers with a partner's and to justify any answers that are different. Play the video again so that they can check their answers.
- Check the answers as a class.

Answers

1	central	(00.34)
2	recent	(01.03)
3	relatives	(01.31)
4	organisation	(02.13)
5	murals	(02.51)
6	feelings	(03.08)

After you watch

C

- Explain to students that this is a summary of the information they heard on the video.
- Read the words in the yellow box to the students and ask them to repeat them. Correct their pronunciation where necessary. Ask students to write *N*, *Adj* or *V* beside each of the words depending on whether it is a noun, adjective or verb.
- Explain to students that they should read the whole summary before writing any answers first to work out what part of speech is missing.
- Tell students to read back through the text once they have finished to check their answers.
- Ask students to do the task individually, but check the answers as a class.

Answers

1	means	**5**	life
2	immigrants	**6**	stays
3	raise	**7**	famous
4	cares	**8**	reflects

Ideas Focus

- Ask students to read the instructions and make sure they understand what they have to do. Then ask them to read the three questions and answer any questions they might have.
- Ask students to work in pairs and explain that they should both give their opinions on all three questions.
- Go round the class monitoring students to make sure they are carrying out the task properly. Don't correct any mistakes at this stage, but make a note of any problems in structure and pronunciation.
- Ask each pair to answer one of the questions and repeat until each pair has had a turn.
- Write the kinds of art, food and music that immigrants have brought to the students' communities on the board. Encourage the students to discuss other ways in which immigrants enrich their community and country.

Answers

Students' own answers

Objectives

- To revise vocabulary and grammar from Units 1 and 2
- To practise exam-type tasks

Revision

- Explain to students that there will be a review after every two units in *Close-up B2*. Tell them that Review 1 revises the material they saw in Units 1 and 2.
- Explain that students can ask you for help with the exercises or look back at the units if they're not sure about an answer, and stress that the review is not a test.
- Decide how you will carry out the review. You could ask students to do one task at a time and then correct it immediately, or ask students to do all the tasks and correct them together at the end. If you do all the tasks together, let students know every now and again how much time they have got left to finish the tasks.
- Ask students not to leave any answers blank and to try to find any answers they aren't sure about in the units.
- When checking students' answers to the review tasks, make a note of any problem areas in vocabulary and grammar that they still have. Try to do extra work on these areas so that your students will progress well.

Vocabulary Revision

- Say the words *respond, reply, concentrate, connect, focus, lead, interested* and *based* one by one to the students and ask them which prepositions follow them.
- Ask students to write down the names of as many European countries as they can think of. Then ask them to write down the adjective from the names of the countries. Make sure they revise *Spain* and *Spanish*.
- Elicit from students the phrasal verbs they learnt in Unit 1 which are related to emotion (*bottle up, burst into, calm down, cheer up, chicken out, freak out*) and ask them to write sentences of their own with these phrasal verbs.
- Ask students to explain the difference between the following pairs of words: *effect/affect, adventurous/dangerous, optimistic/enthusiastic, basically/eagerly, frightening/frightened, exciting/excited.*
- Ask students to work in pairs to tell each other about situations in which they:
  - were in agony
  - were at a loss for words
  - felt great pride
  - were kept in suspense.

Grammar Revision

- Write these sentences on the board and ask students to say which tenses have been used and why.
  - I go to France every year.
  - They're cutting the grass this morning.
  - She has never been abroad.
  - We have been studying ancient Egyptian civilisation this month.
  - Pat went on an expedition to the Himalayas two years ago.
  - Jan was boarding the plane when her hat blew off.
  - Revise the affirmative forms of these tenses as a class. Then ask individual students at random round the class to tell you the negative and question forms. Revise the uses of the Present Simple, Present Continuous, Present Perfect Simple, Present Perfect Continuous, Past Simple and Past Continuous and the time expressions used with them.
- Write the sentences below on the board and ask students to complete them with *used to* or *would*, or their negative forms. Explain that if both structures can be used then they should write in both options.
  - Jack ____ be scared of rollercoasters. *(used to)*
  - Sue ____ love watching horror movies. *(used to)*
  - When I was young I ____ run away when I saw the school bully. *(would/used to)*
  - My mum ____ swim in the sea because she was afraid of deep water. *(wouldn't/didn't use to)*
  - Then revise as a class the rules for *used to* and *would* to talk about repeated actions in the past.
- Write the following sentences on the board and ask students to explain the difference between them.
  - I've been to Paris twice. *(an action that took place in the past, but we don't know when)*
  - I went to Paris twice last year. *(a completed past action which took place at a time mentioned)*
  Ask students to explain the difference in use between the Past Simple and the Present Perfect Simple tenses.

Part 1

- Ask students to read the instructions and check that they understand what they have to do.
- Ask students to read the title of the text and ask them what they think the text will deal with. Then ask them to skim read the text, without circling any answers at this stage, to find out which aspects of fear it deals with (*how some people enjoy the sensation of fear and how this can be used in treating phobias*).
- Point out to students that they should read all four options for each item before deciding which word best fits each gap. Remind them to pay attention to the whole sentence each gap is in as the general context will help them understand what word is missing.
- Remind students to read back through the text once they have finished to check their answers.

Answers

> 1C 2B 3B 4A 5C 6B 7D 8A

Part 2

- Ask students to read the instructions and check that they understand what they have to do.
- Ask students what they know about Halloween and how people usually celebrate this holiday. Ask them which countries they think it is popular in and whether people celebrate it in their country.
- Ask students to skim read the text, without filling in any answers at this stage, to find out when Halloween is and which aspect of this holiday the text deals with (*October 31, the history of Halloween and how the way it is celebrated has changed over the years*).
- Encourage students to pay particular attention to the words immediately before and after each gap to work out what part of speech is missing, however, remind them that they have to take into consideration the general context of the sentence so that they understand which structure is being used.
- Remind students to read back through the text once they have finished to check their answers.

Answers

9	the
10	all
11	thought
12	would
13	became
14	until
15	have
16	forward

Part 3

- Ask students to read the instructions and check that they understand what they have to do.
- Ask students to read the title of the text and ask them what it might mean. Ask them to skim read the text, without filling in any answers at this stage, to find out where this event takes place and what it involves (*Pamplona, Spain, running through the streets with bulls chasing after you*). Ask students if they would consider taking part in this event and to say why/why not.
- Read the words at the side of the text to the students and ask them to repeat them. Correct their pronunciation where necessary.
- Ask students to read back through the text and to decide which part of speech is missing from each gap, and to complete the gaps using the correct form of the words given.
- Remind students to read back through the text once they have finished to check their answers.

Answers

17	adventurous	21	optimistic
18	Basically	22	enthusiastic
19	dangerous	23	eagerly
20	frightening	24	pride

Part 4

- Ask students to read the instructions and check that they understand what they have to do.
- Ask students to read both sentences in each item and to underline the information in the first sentence that is missing from the second sentence. Then ask them to look at the word given to decide how the missing information could be inserted into the second sentence using this word. Remind students that they will have to use a different structure in order to keep the meaning the same.
- Remind students that they mustn't change the word given in any way.
- Encourage students to read back through the completed sentences once they have finished to check their answers.

Answers

25	are going/are planning to go
26	used to believe
27	have not celebrated Halloween since
28	seven hours ago
29	has gone to
30	I was taking/having a

3 Star Quality

Reading:	missing sentences, choosing the right sentences
Vocabulary:	words related to the entertainment business & celebrities
Grammar:	past perfect simple & past perfect continuous, past simple vs past perfect (simple & continuous)
Listening:	multiple matching, identifying synonyms
Speaking:	talking about celebrities, comparing photos
Use your English:	phrasal verbs, prepositions, gapped text, completing missing words in a text
Writing:	story, thinking about the details, using prompts, time, dramatic and concluding phrases

Unit opener

- Ask students to look at the title of the unit and ask them to guess what this unit will be about (models, celebrities, the star system).
- Ask students what kind of people they consider to be celebrities and then ask them to think of as many words as possible related to celebrities and make a list of them on the board.
- Ask students to look at the picture and its accompanying caption and ask them what aspect of being famous is shown here (loneliness/always travelling) and ask them how they think the celebrity shown here might be feeling.
- Ask them how the picture makes them feel.

Reading

A

- Ask students to look at the picture of the bronze statue and ask them if they know who it is of. If they mention Cleopatra, ask them what they know about her and how she might be linked to the unit theme.
- Ask students to look at the picture and accompanying caption in the top right-hand corner, and ask them why archaeologists are interested in Cleopatra.
- Ask students to read the instructions and check that they understand what they have to do.
- Ask students to work in pairs to encourage discussion, but check as a class.

B

- Ask students to skim read the text to find relevant information to the statements in A. Explain that they should concentrate on these details and that they don't have to read in detail as they will have another opportunity to read the text.
- Ask students to do the task individually, but check as a class.
- Ask students which information surprised them most and why.

Answers

1T 2F 3T 4F

Word Focus

- Ask students to look at the words in red in the text and to re-read the sentences they are found in. Remind students that when they don't know the meaning of a word, they should look carefully at the sentence it is found in to work out its meaning. Ask students to work in pairs to decide what each of the words mean.
- Ask students to read the Word Focus box to compare their answers with the definitions given.

C

- Ask students to read the information in Exam Close-up and ask a student to explain what it says in his or her own words.
- Tell students to look out for phrases that express the sequence of events (firstly, secondly, furthermore, in addition, etc) and explain why they should pay attention to pronouns (Pronouns are used to refer back to something that has already been mentioned, so if the sentence after the gap contains a pronoun, the missing sentence should contain the noun it refers to and vice versa.). Explain to students that it's a good idea to get into the habit of underlining these clues in missing sentences when they read through them for the first time.
- Ask students to read the instructions and check that they understand what they have to do.
- Ask students to read the sentences A-G in the Exam Task and underline the clues that will help them understand what information they can follow on from (A – the real Cleopatra, was not actually such a beauty, B – she, the site, she, there, C – Alexandria, lies under about 6 metres of water, D – However, paid Cleopatra much less attention, E – In the twentieth century, she, F – She, her beloved Mark Antony, G – When the victorious army, Cleopatra was in danger). Point out that the sentences should also make sense before the sentence that follows after the gap.

D

- Ask students to read the article again and to decide where each missing sentence goes.
- When they have finished tell them to read back through the text to make sure the sentences make sense and to check the sentence they haven't used doesn't fit anywhere.
- Ask students to do the task individually, but check as a class.

- Once the answers have been checked, ask students to explain the title of the text and to say how it relates to the pictures that accompany the text (*Archaeologists want to find the place where Cleopatra is buried. The pictures show sites where archaeological excavations have taken place in hope of finding her tomb.*).
- If students seem interested, give them further information using the Background Information box below.

Answers

1E 2A 3G 4C 5B 6F

Background Information

Cleopatra was born in 69 BC and died on August 12th 30 BC. She was of Greek ancestry and belonged to the Ptolemaic dynasty. Unlike previous Ptolemaic rulers who spoke only Greek, Cleopatra learnt to speak Egyptian, the language of her subjects. There were many queens of Egypt who bore the name Cleopatra, but the one we refer to today as Cleopatra was Cleopatra VII Philopator. Cleopatra's son with Caesar was called Caesarion; with Mark Antony she gave birth to twins Cleopatra Selene II and Alexander Helios, and another son Ptolemy Philadelphus. Her son Caesarion was declared Pharaoh on her death, but he was soon killed by Caesar's heir Gaius Julius Caesar Octavius.

E

- Ask students to look at the words in the yellow box and to scan the text again to find and underline them. Read the words to the students and ask them to repeat them. Correct their pronunciation where necessary.
- Remind them that they should always try to work out the meaning of a word from its context and ask them to read the sentences each word is in.
- Ask students to read the instructions and check that they understand what they have to do.
- Ask students to do the task individually, but check as a class.

Answers

1 location	4 royal
2 inspiration	5 attention
3 reputation	

Ideas Focus

- Explain to students that they are going to answer some questions about celebrities. Ask students to read the questions and explain anything they don't understand.
- Ask students to answer the questions in pairs and encourage them to draw on their personal feelings about celebrities and who they like and dislike.
- Go round the class monitoring students to make sure they are carrying out the task properly. Don't correct any mistakes at this stage, but make a note of any problems in structure and pronunciation.
- Ask students at random to answer each of the questions and encourage the other students to add their opinions.
- Write any structural mistakes that students made on the board without saying who made them, and ask them to correct them. Deal with any problems in pronunciation that came up.

Answers

Students' own answers

Vocabulary

A

- Ask students to read the instructions and check that they understand what they have to do.
- Ask students to read each of the sentences carefully and to read the three options to think about the differences in meaning.
- Ask students to do the task individually, but check as a class. Elicit the meanings of each of the options.
- When answers have been checked, ask students to write sentences of their own with the words that don't fit the sentences.

Answers

1a 2b 3b 4c 5c 6a 7c 8b

B

- Explain to students that the options in each sentence may be similar in meaning in some way, and that they have to circle the one which is correct in the context of the sentence.
- Ask students to read through the sentences again once they have finished, to check their answers.
- Ask students to do the task individually, but check the answers as a class. Correct their pronunciation where necessary.

Answers

1 eyes
2 publicity
3 sites
4 winner
5 fan

C

- Ask students to look at the picture under the text and ask them what this map might symbolise (*how social networking services have taken over the world*).
- Ask students which social networking services they know about and whether they use any of them. If so, ask them how often they use them and what they use them for.
- Read the words in the yellow box to students and ask them to repeat them. Correct their pronunciation where necessary.
- Ask students to read the title of the text and ask them how it might be related to social networking services. Ask them to skim read the text, without filling in any answers at this stage, to work it out (*Celebrities are turning to services like Twitter in order to become more popular.*).
- Ask students to do the task individually, but check as a class.

Answers

1	PR	5	account
2	sites	6	comments
3	fans	7	stars
4	publicity	8	privacy

Grammar

- Write the sentences below on the board and ask students what the difference in meaning between them is.
  - They had rehearsed the song many times, so it sounded great live. (The act of rehearsing was a completed action in the past which took place before they played it live.)
  - They had been rehearsing the song for hours when they decided to take a break. (The act of rehearsing was in progress for some time before it was interrupted by them taking a break.)
- Ask a student to come up to the board and underline the verbs in both sentences. Elicit that the tenses are Past Perfect Simple, Past Simple and Past Perfect Continuous, Past Simple.
- Revise the affirmative, negative, question forms and short answers of the Past Perfect Simple and Past Perfect Continuous.

A

- Ask students to read the sentences 1-4 and ask students to look at the words in bold.
- Ask them to write which tenses they are and compare their answers with a partner.
- Check answers as a class.
- Once the answers have been checked, ask students to look back at the Reading text about Cleopatra to find examples of these two tenses (Paragraph 1 – she had already been, Paragraph 3 – had been fighting, had died, Paragraph 4 – it had been affected, Paragraph 5 – it had been, she had managed, she had walked, Paragraph 6 – had missed, she had prepared, Sentence B – she had walked, Sentence F – she had prepared, she had planned).

Answers

1 Past Perfect Simple
2 Past Perfect Simple
3 Past Perfect Continuous
4 Past Perfect Continuous

B

- Ask students to read the questions about the sentences in A and point out that one question has two answers. Check that students understand that they should write 1, 2, 3 or 4 in the boxes provided depending on which sentence(s) correctly answer(s) each question.
- Ask students to do the task in pairs to encourage discussion, but check as a class.

Answers

a1, 2 b3 c4

Now read the Grammar Reference on page 164 (3.1 & 3.2) with your students.

C

- Ask students to read the instructions and check that they understand what they have to do.
- Encourage them to read the sentences carefully to look for clues as to whether the sentence talks about a finished action in the past that happened before another past action, an action that was in progress when another past action interrupted it or an action that was still in progress at a point in the past.
- Ask students to read back through the sentences once they have finished to check their answers.
- Ask students to do the task individually, but check as a class.

Answers

1	hadn't been singing	6	Had you been waiting
2	had already given		
3	had been waiting	7	had left
4	hadn't been	8	had started out
5	had been going		

D

- Ask students to look at the title of the text and the picture and ask them what the text might be about. Ask them who the woman might have been and what she might have been doing when she fell to Earth.
- Ask students to read the instructions and check that they understand what they have to do. Then ask them to read the verbs in the yellow box.
- Ask students to read the text all the way through without filling in any answers at this stage. Ask students to think about which verb fills each gap and to look for clues in the surrounding sentences as to which tense they should use.
- Remind students to read back through the text once they have finished to check their answers.
- Ask students to do the task individually, but check as a class.

Answers

1	hadn't been	5	had been working
2	had found	6	had made
3	had flown	7	had been training
4	had reached	8	had finished

Listening

A

- Ask students what kind of celebrities they have read about so far in the unit. Ask them to think of today's celebrities and ask them what they are usually famous for.
- Then ask students what kind of people they think become celebrities. Tell them to think of the celebrities they have heard of and think about what type of person they are. Encourage everyone to give their opinion and then work with a partner to discuss what kind of person becomes a celebrity.
- Invite students to tell the class what they discussed with their partner. Ask other students if they agree or disagree with their opinion.
- Ask students if they would like to be a celebrity and if so, why.

B

- Ask students to read the instructions and check that they know what they have to do.
- Ask students to read the three statements and underline the key words.
- Remind students to make notes on what they hear. Ask them to read the three statements again.
- Play the recording through for the students to listen and make notes. If necessary, play the recording a second time.
- Ask students to chose the statement that best summarises what they heard and compare their choice with a partner.
- Check the answer as a class. Ask students to justify their choice with examples of what was said on the recording.

Answers

Sentence b

C

- Ask students to read the information in the *Exam Close-up*. Point out also that the topic of conversation may be the same as what is written in an answer choice, but the point being made may be slightly different or the opposite of what the speaker says.
- Write on the board: *People don't want to see members of the royal family.* and *People can't get enough of the royal family.* Elicit that the negative verb forms in both can mislead them as it seems they both deal with the topic in a negative way. Point out, however, that although the verb is in the negative in *can't get enough* the phrase actually has a positive meaning, ie *they want more.*

D

- Ask students to read the instructions and check that they know what they have to do.
- Ask students to look at the *Exam Task* and remind them they have to underline the key words and think of synonyms or words to express the same thing in a different way.
- Point out the example A in Task D that uses synonyms for the sentence in A in the *Exam Task*.
- Ask students to work with a partner to think of synonyms or other words for items B-H in the *Exam Task*.
- Monitor and help with vocabulary as necessary. Check their ideas as a class.

E

- Ask students to read the instructions and check that they know what they have to do.
- Elicit that the general topic here will be about meeting celebrities. Ask students to come up with different ways that people might react when they meet someone famous and what situations they may be in.
- Ask students to read the sentences A-H and explain anything they don't understand. Make sure students understand that three of the sentences don't match with any of the speakers.
- Elicit that they should write a letter A-H in the boxes next to each of the speakers.
- Play the recording once all the way through and ask students to mark their answers. Then ask students to discuss their answers with a partner and to justify any answers that are different.

F

- Play the recording again and ask students to check their answers and to complete any answers they haven't already completed.
- Check the answers as a class and ask students to justify their answers.

Answers

1E 2G 3A 4C 5D

Teaching Tip

You could round off this section by asking students if they have ever met any celebrities – either local or international. If so, ask them to tell the others about it. Encourage them to give details about the situation, how they reacted and if they had a conversation with the person.

Extra Class Activity

Ask students to write an extract similar to the ones they heard in E based on the picture at the bottom of the page. Remind them the main topic should be about meeting a celebrity. You could also ask them to write it in such a way that this extract could match up with one of the sentences that they didn't need to use in E.

Speaking

A

- Ask students to read the two questions and answer any queries they may have about them.
- Ask students to work in pairs to take turns to ask and answer the questions about themselves.
- Go round the class monitoring students to make sure they are carrying out the task properly. Don't correct any mistakes at this stage, but make a note of any problems in structure and pronunciation.
- Ask each pair to ask and answer one of the questions and repeat until each student has had a turn.
- Write any structural mistakes that students made on the board without saying who made them, and ask them to correct them. Deal with any problems in pronunciation that came up.

B

- Ask students to read the instructions and check that they know what they have to do.
- Ask students to look at the four photos. Ask students to briefly tell you what they think is happening in each one.
- Ask students to work with a partner to make a list of words connected to the photos. Remind them to look back at the examples they have already been given.
- Allow students five minutes to think of as many words as they can. Invite a pair to write their words on the board and other pairs to add to the list.

C

- Ask students to read the information in the *Exam Close-up*.
- Stress that students should compare the photos and not describe them. Remind them that they should talk about the similarities and differences between the two pictures and remember to keep their answer to the question fairly short, but clearly answer the question.
- Read the *Useful Expressions* to the students and encourage them to use these expressions when talking about the photos. Point out that they will be used by both students in turn when comparing their photos.
- Ask students to work in pairs and to decide who will be Student A and who will be Student B.
- Ask students to read the instructions again and look at the *Exam Task*. Explain anything students are still not sure about.
- Go round the class monitoring students to make sure they are carrying out the task properly and that they both compare their photos and answer the question. Don't correct any mistakes at this stage, but make a note of any problems in structure and pronunciation.
- Ask students to compare two of the photos for the class and repeat until each student has had a turn.
- Write any structural mistakes that students made on the board without saying who made them, and ask them to correct them. Deal with any problems in pronunciation that came up.

Ideas Focus

- Ask students to read the questions quickly and deal with any queries they may have.
- Ask students to work in pairs to take turns to answer the questions.
- Go round the class monitoring students to make sure they are carrying out the task properly. Don't correct any mistakes at this stage, but make a note of any problems in structure and pronunciation.
- Ask a student from each pair to answer one of the questions until each pair has had a turn. Ask other students if they agree or if they have something else to add.
- Write any structural mistakes that students made on the board without saying who made them, and ask them to correct them. Deal with any problems in pronunciation that came up.

Answers

Students' own answers

Grammar

A

- Write *Amelia Earhart* on the board and ask students if they know who she was. Tell them that the picture should give them a clue. Ask them if they know what happened to her and why she is famous today.
- Ask students to read sentences 1 and 2 to find out information about her. Ask one student to summarise in his or her own words what the sentences tell us about Earhart.
- Ask students to do the task in pairs to encourage discussion, but check as a class.

Answers

1 In *1*, *had been flying* happened first and *vanished* happened later. In *2*, *had happened* happened first and *was able to find out* happened later.
2 Past Simple

Now read the Grammar Reference on page 164 (3.3) with your students.

B

- Ask students to read the instructions and check that they understand what they have to do.
- Encourage students to read the whole sentence before circling any answers to look for clues to the right answer. Remind students to decide which action took place first to help them decide which option is correct.
- Remind students to read back through the sentences once they have finished to check their answers.
- Ask students to do the task individually, but check as a class.

Answers

1	saw	4 arrived
2	had already taken off	5 had been painting
3	had broken	6 phoned

C

- Ask students to read the instructions and check that they understand what they have to do.
- Encourage students to read the whole sentence before choosing any answers to look for clues to the right answer. Remind students that the options are time expressions and adverbs of time so they should pay particular attention to the tenses used in the sentences, especially in the clauses the options are found in.
- Remind students to read back through the sentences once they have finished to check their answers.
- Ask students to do the task individually, but check as a class.

Answers

1a 2b 3c 4a 5b 6c

D

- Ask students to read the instructions and check that they understand what they have to do. Point out that they have to use the verbs in brackets after each sentence in the order they appear in.
- Ask students to read through the sentences without filling in any answers at this stage, to work out which action happened first and which action happened second in each one.
- Remind students to read back through the sentences once they have finished to check the answers.
- Ask students to do the task individually, but check as a class.

Answers

1 was, had been following
2 Had … interviewed, wrote
3 realised, had removed
4 had been thinking, chickened out
5 was, had ever seen
6 had been talking, walked
7 had just introduced, went out
8 hadn't believed, began

Use your English

A

- Read the phrasal verbs in the yellow box to the students and ask them to repeat them. Correct their pronunciation where necessary.
- Remind students that they have to consider the meaning of the verb and the particle together and not just focus on the verb.
- Ask them to read the sentences on their own to work out the meaning of the missing phrasal verb. Also encourage them to underline the subject of each sentence so that they write the verbs in their correct form.
- Ask students to do the task individually, but check as a class.
- Encourage students to copy the phrasal verbs and their meanings into their notebooks.

Answers

1 go around
2 look down on
3 catches on
4 live up to
5 start out
6 comes in for

B

- Ask students to read the instructions and check that they understand what they have to do. Stress that they have to use the phrasal verbs from A in the correct form.
- Ask students to read the sentences first for gist to work out which phrasal verb might be missing from each one. Remind them to pay attention to the subject and also other tenses used in the sentences to help them write the verbs in the correct form.
- Ask students to do the task individually, but check as a class.

Answers

1 looks down on
2 live up to
3 catch on
4 started out
5 came in for
6 going around

C

- Read the prepositions in the yellow box to the students and explain that they will use these to complete the sentences. Point out that they should use one of the prepositions twice.
- Ask students to read the sentences carefully and pay attention to the words before or after the gap and try to think of a preposition which follows or precedes the words without filling in any answers at this stage. Point out that some prepositions require a capital letter.
- Ask students to do the task individually, but check as a class.

Answers

1 in, in
2 under
3 at
4 on
5 To
6 By
7 behind
8 Without

D

- Ask students to look at the *Exam Close-up* and explain anything they don't understand.
- Ask students to read the instructions and check that they understand what they have to do.
- Emphasise how important it is to read the text all the way through first so that they know what it is about and what tenses have been used. They should also look carefully at the words before and after the gap.
- Ask students to read the *Exam Task* and decide what type of word goes in each gap.
- Ask students to complete the task individually, read the text through again and then compare their answers with a partner. They should discuss any differences.
- Check answers as a class.

Answers

1 had
2 my
3 been
4 waving
5 when
6 kept
7 persuaded
8 stars

Writing: a story (1)

- Ask students to read the *Learning Focus* on thinking about the details when they write a story and answer any queries they might have.
- Ask students what the narrative tenses are (*Past Simple, Past Continuous, Past Perfect Simple and Past Perfect Continuous*). Elicit that we use the past perfect tenses to talk about actions or events that took place before the time of the narrative. Point out that we tend not to use the present tenses in stories unless we use direct speech.

A

- Ask students to read the instructions and check that they understand what they have to do.
- Remind students that the sentence given must fit in naturally with the rest of the story, so it's important to make sure that the sentence that follows on from it provides a good link between the prompt given and what comes next.
- Ask students to read item 1 and decide which is the best sentence. Discuss their answers as a class and ask students to justify their choice before moving on to the rest of the task.
- Ask students to do the task in pairs to encourage discussion, but check as a class.

Answers

1b *(a could be more dramatic and it's unlikely that Catherine would be shocked by what she saw.)*
2a *(b is a bit dull and wouldn't encourage the reader to read on.)*
3a *(b doesn't keep up the sense of drama and excitement that the first sentence has.)*

B

- Ask students to read the instructions and check that they understand what they have to do.
- Ask students to write their own sentences, making sure that they link properly to the sentence given and give the reader a reason to keep reading by creating a sense of drama, excitement or suspense.
- Ask students to write their sentences and then ask them to read them out to the class.

C

- Ask students to read the instructions and check that they understand what they have to do.
- Ask students to underline the key words in the task and in the sentence given.
- Explain that students should answer the questions as if they were planning to write this story. Point out that they should ask themselves questions like these when they are asked to write a story so that they can work out the basic plot of their story before they start writing.
- Ask students to do the task individually and then to discuss their answers with a partner to compare how they would develop this story.
- As a class, ask several students to read their answers and ask the other students to comment on their ideas.

D

- Ask students to read the instructions and check that they understand what they have to do.
- Tell students that you are going to time the fifteen minutes so that they get used to writing against the clock.
- Remind them that they actually have to write the sentence given at the beginning of their paragraph and not to change it in any way. Encourage students to use their ideas from C in order to write their opening paragraph.

- Ask some students to read out their paragraphs to the rest of the class. Preferably choose students who didn't read out their answers in C to read their paragraphs here. You could hang all paragraphs on the wall and ask students to read each others' paragraphs when they have time.

E

- Explain to students that they are now going to read an example story for the task in C.
- Ask them to read the first paragraph and ask them how it compares to their own.
- Ask them to read the rest of the story and discuss with them what makes it a successful story.

F

- Ask students to read the instructions and check that they understand what they have to do.
- Read the words in the yellow box to the students and ask them to repeat them. Correct their pronunciation where necessary.
- Ask students to scan the story to find the underlined words and read the story through again before they replace any of the word with those in the yellow box.
- Remind students to read the story all the way through when they have replaced the words.
- Ask students to do the task individually, but check as a class.

Answers

suddenly - out of the blue
A little later - Not long afterwards
Finally - At last
As if that wasn't enough - To make matters worse

Useful Expressions

- Read the *Useful Expressions* to the students and ask them to repeat them. Correct their pronunciation where necessary.
- If time allows, ask students to use one or two expressions from each category to write their own sentences. Point out that they can use expressions like these in their own stories.

G

- Ask students to read the paragraph plan and the information in the *Exam Close-up* and explain anything they don't understand.
- Explain to students that they should use the information in the *Exam Close-up* as a checklist when writing their own stories. Encourage them to read back through their stories before handing them in to check that they have included all of these features.
- Then ask students to read the *Exam Task* and ask them which two things they should use to help them write their stories *(the paragraph plan and the Useful Expressions)*.
- Ask students to read the sentence that they have to use and brainstorm for ideas about why the main character might be feeling so nervous.

- Ask students to answer the questions in C for this particular sentence. If time is short, remind them to do this at home before they begin writing their stories.
- Encourage students to use the Writing Reference and checklist for stories on page 181.

Suggested Answer

I had never felt so nervous before in my life. I couldn't believe my ears when my editor told me that I'd be interviewing Gary Baker, one of Hollywood's biggest stars!

And now here I was, sitting in a hotel room waiting for the star to appear. My heart was beating wildly at the thought that this great actor was about to walk in the door at any minute. It was the chance of a lifetime, but I was petrified that I would mess the whole interview up.

Just then, the door swung slowly open. 'Hi, you must be Ricky. It's a pleasure,' said Gary as he held out his hand for me to shake. At that moment, all my nervousness disappeared into thin air. Gary's friendliness and broad smile immediately put me at ease.

When it was all over, I laughed at how apprehensive I had been. Now all I had to do was to make the interview into the first-class article that my editor had asked me to write.

3 Confucianism in China

General Note

The National Geographic videos can be used as an interesting way to introduce your students to other cultures. They are authentic National Geographic videos, and it is not necessary for students to understand everything they hear to benefit from them. The videos have the option to play English subtitles so that students can read on screen exactly what is said in the documentary. This feature may help students with some of the tasks in the worksheets. The videos are also a good way to encourage your students to watch TV programmes and films in English so that they can get used to the sound of the language. The more students are exposed to English, the easier it will be for them to pick up the language.

Background Information

Confucius, who lived between 551 and 479 BC, was the founder of the Ru School of Chinese thought. His ideas focused on the education and behaviour of the ideal man. This included suggestions as to how the ideal man should live and interact with others. He believed that all men are responsible for their actions and how they treat other people.

Before you watch

A

- Explain to students that in this lesson they are going to watch a video about Confucius. Ask them to look at the globe to see where Confucius was from. Elicit what they know about him.
- Ask students to read the instructions and elicit that they will discuss some of the things that Confucius said.
- Give students time to read the quotations and explain anything they don't understand.
- Ask students to discuss the quotations in pairs and then as a class. Ask each pair to explain one of the quotations and to say whether they agree with it or not.

Suggested Answers

1 If you love what you do for a living, it won't feel like an obligation, but an enjoyable hobby.
2 Nobody knows everything, and if someone claims they do, they haven't realised the extent of knowledge that there is around us.
3 All books have something to teach us.
4 It is better to ask a question than forever not to know the answer.
5 It is better to show someone how to solve their problems so they can become independent in future than to provide them with a ready solution which is only temporary.

While you watch

B

- Explain to students that they are now going to watch the video. Ask them to read sentences 1-6 and explain anything they don't understand.

- Ask them to think about which answers might be true and which ones might be false before watching.
- Ask students to do the task individually, but check as a class.

Answers

1	F (famous philosopher)	(00.24)
2	T	(01.15)
3	T	(01.39)
4	F (The respect young people show towards elder family members is still an important aspect of Chinese society today.)	(02.00)
5	F (Confucius felt learning should be a pleasant experience …)	(02.33)
6	T	(03.47)

After you watch

C

- Explain to students that this is a summary of the information they heard on the video.
- Read the words in the yellow box to the students and ask them to repeat them. Correct their pronunciation where necessary. Ask students to write N, Adj, Adv or V beside each of the words depending on whether it is a noun, adjective, adverb or verb.
- Explain to students that they should read the whole summary before writing any answers first to work out what part of speech is missing.
- Tell students to read back through the text once they have finished to check their answers.
- Ask students to do the task individually, but check the answers as a class.

Answers

1 philosophers	5 adopted
2 moral	6 influences
3 dynasty	7 hard
4 retired	8 foundations

Ideas Focus

- Ask students to read the instructions and make sure they understand what they have to do. Then ask them to read the two questions and answer any queries they might have.
- Ask students to work in pairs and explain that they should both give their opinions on both questions.
- Go round the class monitoring students. Don't correct any mistakes at this stage, but make a note of any problems in structure and pronunciation.
- Ask each pair to answer one of the questions.
- Write the philosophers students mention on the board and ask them what they know about them and their philosophies.

Answers

Students' own answers

4 City Living

Reading:	multiple-matching, skimming and scanning for specific information
Vocabulary:	city living-related words
Grammar:	future forms, countable & uncountable nouns, quantifiers
Listening:	multiple-choice questions, preparing to listen
Speaking:	talking about living in urban & rural areas, decision making, expressing opinions, agreeing, disagreeing and partly agreeing
Use your English:	phrasal verbs, collocations & expressions, multiple-choice, choosing the correct word
Writing:	article, examples, engaging your reader, keeping your reader interested, direct & indirect questions, talking about the future

Unit opener

- Ask students to look at the title of the unit and to explain what aspect of city living is shown in the picture. Ask them to look at the people in the picture and ask them how they seem to feel about this fountain.
- Ask students why this kind of feature might be popular in a large city and how they think people in their country would react if something similar was built where they live.
- If students seem interested, give them more information using the Background Information box below.

Background Information

The Crown Fountain is found in Chicago's Millennium Park. It was opened in July 2004, and water pours from the fountain from May to October. The fountain has been constructed using glass bricks onto which digital videos of people's faces are displayed. The faces, which change every fifteen minutes, are of local people. Many locals visit the fountain not only for entertainment, but also to see if their face will be projected.

Reading

A

- Ask students to read the instructions and check that they understand what they have to do.
- Give students time to read the six bullet points and then ask them to discuss them with a partner.
- Allow students time to discuss all the points. Then ask pairs to tell the class what they think are the advantages and disadvantages of living in a big city.
- Encourage other students to add their opinions. Ask them to also consider other points as well, such as hospitals, education and social life.

B

- Ask students to read the instructions and ask them to look quickly at the article and give you the names of the four cities (Sao Paulo, Sydney, New York, Athens). Ask students to work with a partner and discuss what they think it would be like to live in these cities.
- Invite pairs to tell their ideas to the class and encourage other students to add their ideas.

- Then ask students to skim read the text to find out if any of their ideas were correct. Remind them that they don't have to read in detail as they will have another opportunity to read the text.
- Ask students to do the task individually, but discuss as a class what it is like to live in these cities.

Suggested answers

- **A:** small, simple homes; community spirit; residents are warm and friendly and live well together; middle-class look down on the people from the favela, so suffer from discrimination
- **B:** great lifestyle as city is on the water and near mountains; can go surfing, but sharks are a problem; good mix of ethnic group and cultures; opportunities for everyone; resources for immigrants and disadvantaged people
- **C:** some neighborhoods can make people feel insecure; have to be careful where you go and when you go there; have to use common sense about where to go; buzz and energy of the city; feel part of something special; feels like the most exciting city on Earth
- **D:** has ancient history; some ugly modern buildings; gritty side to the city; city of contrasts; pedestrian only areas; outside places to eat and drink; people break the law; not enough police; people spend a lot of time in cafes with friends drinking coffee

Word Focus

- Ask students to look at the words in red in the text and to re-read the sentences they are found in. Remind students that when they don't know the meaning of a word, they should look carefully at the sentence it is found in to work out its meaning. Ask students to work in pairs to decide what each of the words mean.
- Ask students to read the Word Focus box to compare their answers with the definitions given. Explain anything they don't understand.

C

- Ask students to read the information in the *Exam Close-up* and ask them to tell you what it says in their own words.
- Ask students to read the *Exam Task* and then underline the key words in the questions.
- Remind students that skimming a text means to read it quickly for a general understanding of it and scanning is when reading more carefully for specific information.

D

- Ask students to read the instructions and explain anything they don't understand.
- Explain to students that for this task they need to scan the text, looking for specific information.
- Ask students to read the questions again before reading the text to find the answers. Explain to students that they should make sure they choose the options that best express the key words they have underlined in the questions, and remind them that they will need to choose each option more than once.
- Ask students to do the task individually, but check as a class.

Answers

```
 1  D
 2  A
 3  C
 4  B
 5  C
 6  A
 7  D
 8  D ✗ B
 9  D
10  C
```

E

- Read the words in the yellow box to the students and ask them to repeat them. Correct their pronunciation where necessary.
- Ask students to scan the text again to find and underline these words. The paragraph where each one can be found is given. Remind them that they should always try to work out the meaning of the word from its context and ask them to read the sentences each word is in.
- Ask students to explain the meaning of each word to the class using their own words.
- Ask students to read all the sentences through before filling in any answers.
- Ask students to do the task individually, but check as a class.

Answers

1	resident	4	pedestrian
2	district	5	community
3	metropolis	6	alley

Ideas Focus

- Ask students to read the two questions and deal with any queries they may have.
- Ask students to work in pairs to ask and answer the questions.
- Go round the class monitoring students to make sure they are carrying out the task properly. Don't correct any mistakes at this stage, but make a note of any problems in structure and pronunciation.
- As a class, ask students at random to answer both of the questions and ask the others if they have anything else to add.
- Write any structural mistakes that students made on the board without saying who made them, and ask them to correct them. Deal with any problems in pronunciation that came up.

Answers

Students' own answers

Vocabulary

A

- Ask students to read the instructions and check that they understand what they have to do.
- Read the words in the yellow box to the students and ask them to repeat them. Correct their pronunciation where necessary. Elicit that they are all nouns and that they refer to kinds of people and are all related in someway to living in a place.
- Ask students to read the definitions and explain anything they don't understand.
- Ask students to do the task individually, but check as a class.
- Ask students to write sentences of their own using each of these words.

Answers

1D 2A, F 3E 4C 5A,F 6A, F 7B 8A

B

- Ask students to read the instructions and check that they understand what they have to do.
- Read the words in the yellow box to the students and ask them to repeat them. Correct their pronunciation where necessary. Ask students to write *Adj* or *N* next to each word depending on whether they are adjectives or nouns. Elicit that they are related to areas/places in some way.
- Ask students to read through the sentences, without filling in any answers at this stage, in order to work out which part of speech is missing in each one and for general meaning.
- Ask students to do the task individually, but check as a class.

Answers

1	outskirts	5	inner
2	urban	6	suburb
3	residential	7	district
4	commercial	8	industrial

C

- Ask students to read the instructions and check that they understand what they have to do. Explain that they have to decide which order each of the words comes in each sentence.
- Read the words in red to the students and ask them to repeat them. Correct their pronunciation where necessary. Elicit that they are all nouns and are related to streets and roads in some way.
- Encourage students to read the whole sentence before circling any answers.
- Ask students to do the task individually, but check as a class.

Answers

1. avenue, alley
2. pavement, parking meter
3. junction, traffic light
4. street sign, speed bump
5. zebra crossing, pedestrian area
6. speed limit, speed cameras

D

- Ask students to read the instructions and check that they understand what they have to do.
- Read the street names to the students and ask them to repeat them. Correct their pronunciation where necessary.
- Ask students to work in pairs to discuss each of the street names. If students can access the Internet fairly easily at school, you could ask them to research any streets they haven't heard of or aren't sure of.
- As a class, ask students at random to talk about each of the streets and ask the others if they think they are right.

Answers

Oxford Street is London's busiest shopping district.
Wall Street is where the New York Stock Exchange is.
Elm Street is the name of a fictional street in a famous horror film called *Nightmare on Elm Street*.
42nd Street is in New York and is where many cinemas and theatres are found.
Sesame Street is a fictional street from the American TV programme for young children which goes by this name.
Downing Street is in London and is where the Prime Minister's residence is found (at No 10).

Teaching Tip

If you are short of time in class, don't be tempted to skip this task. Although at first glance it may not seem as important as other vocabulary tasks, it is actually extremely useful to language learners. Tasks like this introduce them to the culture of English-speaking countries and this kind of knowledge is often just as important as having a vast vocabulary in English. It also gives them a good opportunity to practise their spoken English. You could extend the task by asking students if they know of any other famous streets like these either in English-speaking countries, their own country or in other foreign countries that they know about.

Grammar

- Ask students to work in pairs to discuss what their hometown will be like 50 years from now. Ask them to discuss which things will stay the same and which will change. Ask them to think about transportation, housing, shops, office buildings and schools.
- Elicit their ideas and write them on the board, eg *Students will be studying from home via the Internet. People will drive electric cars. People will be working from home.*
- Ask students to tell you which tenses are used to talk about the future (*Future Simple* and *Future Continuous*).
- Revise the affirmative, negative, question forms and short answers of these two tenses with the class. Then elicit the adverbs of frequency and time expressions that are used with each tense. Explain to students that in this lesson they will concentrate on these tenses as well as other future forms.

A

- Ask students to read sentences a-k quickly and focus on the words in bold. Ask them which future tenses and forms are used (*be going to, Future Perfect Simple, Future Perfect Continuous, shall*).
- Ask students to read the uses 1-11 and point out that some tenses and forms have more than one function.
- Ask students to do the task in pairs to encourage discussion, but check as a class.

Answers

1d 2k 3b 4i 5h 6a 7f 8c 9e 10j 11g

Extra Class Activity

You could extend this task by asking students to write one sentence of their own for each of the future tenses and forms covering all the uses mentioned in A.

Now read the Grammar Reference on pages 164 to 165 (4.1 to 4.5) with your students.

B

- Ask students to read the instructions and check that they understand what they have to do.
- Encourage students to read the whole sentence and to underline time expressions and adverbs of time before circling any answers.
- Ask students to do the task individually, but check as a class.
- While checking the answers, ask students to say which of the uses in A is found in each sentence.

Answers

1 will get
2 will have been working
3 won't have eaten
4 will have finished
5 will be watching
6 lands

C

- Ask students to read the instructions and check that they understand what they have to do. Explain that they mustn't change the word in bold in any way in the second sentence.
- Ask students to read the two sentences in item 1. Then ask them to underline the part in the first sentence that is missing from the second sentence. Explain to students that in order to complete the second sentence they will have to make a structural change.
- Ask students to complete the first item and correct it before they move on to the rest of the task.
- Ask students to do the task individually, but check as a class.

Answers

1 When I go
2 are having a meeting
3 will have left
4 until the traffic light changes
5 is going to
6 will have been building

Listening

A

- Read the words and phrases in red to the students and ask them to repeat them. Correct their pronunciation where necessary and make sure they understand the meaning of all the options.
- Explain that they will hear the correct options in a listening task a little later.
- Ask students to do the task individually, but check as a class.

Answers

1 city-dweller
2 pollution
3 rural
4 controls it
5 often
6 design towns and cities

B

- Ask students to read the instructions and check that they understand what they have to do.
- Ask students to read the three questions and to underline the key words.
- Play the recording once all the way through and ask students to write their answers. Ask students to compare their answers with a partner and to justify any answers they have that are different.
- Play the recording again and ask students to check their answers and to complete any missing answers.
- Check the answers as a class and ask students to justify their answers.

Answers

1 It's a seaside town that has everything / all the facilities a city can offer.
2 They're too crowded and noisy.
3 friendly people from all walks of life

C

- Ask students to look at the options in C, which are possible answers to the questions in B, and to underline the key words found there.
- Explain to students that they are going to listen again to the recording for B, but this time to choose the best answers from the options in C.
- Ask students to read the questions and the options again and to think about what the correct answers might be before they listen. Explain that they will hear the recording only one more time.
- Play the recording again and ask students to mark their answers.
- Check the answers as a class and ask students to justify their answers.

Answers

1c 2b 3c

D

- Ask students to read the information in the *Exam Close-up* and ask a student to tell you what it says in his or her own words.
- Explain that reading the questions and options thoroughly before they listen will mean that they have a good idea of what they are going to hear before listening to the recording.
- Ask students to read the *Exam Task* and underline the key words in each item.

E

- Ask students to read the instructions and check that they understand what they have to do.
- Elicit that the topic of the interview is the effects of city living on health. Ask students to look at the picture at the bottom of the page and ask them what it tells us about city living. Elicit what people have to do in a city to keep fit when they might be limited by space or opportunity.
- Ask students to read questions 1-6 and their options carefully. Make sure they have underlined key words and phrases. Explain anything students don't understand.
- Play the recording once all the way through and ask students to mark their answers. Ask students to compare their answers with a partner and to justify any answers they have that are different.
- Play the recording again and ask students to check their answers and to complete any missing answers.
- Check the answers as a class and ask students to justify their answers.

Answers

1c 2a 3a 4b 5a 6b

Speaking

- Ask students to look at the picture in the top right-hand corner and ask them if this is a rural or urban area *(rural)*. Ask them what they think it would be like to live in such a place and how it would be different from living in the place shown in the picture at the top of page 52.

A

- Ask students to read the three questions and answer any queries they have about them.
- Ask students to take turns to ask and answer the questions about their hometown.
- Go round the class monitoring students to make sure they are carrying out the task properly. Don't correct any mistakes at this stage, but make a note of any problems in structure and pronunciation.
- Ask each pair to ask and answer one of the questions and repeat until each pair has had a turn.
- Write any structural mistakes that students made on the board without saying who made them, and ask them to correct them. Deal with any problems in pronunciation that came up.

B

- Ask students to read the instructions and check that they understand what they have to do. Elicit that they should only note down the positive features found in big cities.
- Give students exactly one minute to note down their ideas. Tell them when to start and stop writing.
- Ask students to work in pairs to compare their answers and to look at the pictures in C to see if their ideas are shown there.
- As a class, discuss the positive features of big cities and elicit which features are shown by the pictures. If students disagree with features mentioned by other students, ask them to explain why they feel these features aren't positive.

C

- Ask students to read the information in the *Exam Close-up* and ask a student to tell you what it says in his or her own words.
- Explain to students that in this kind of task, it's more important that they discuss the ideas in full and present logical arguments for their choices than to agree with each other. However, they should acknowledge each other's opinions and comment on them in a polite manner.
- Remind students that they should justify why they would choose certain options as well as explain why they feel the others aren't so good.
- Read the *Useful Expressions* to the students and explain that we use these structures in order to show the extent to which we agree or disagree with another person's ideas.
- Encourage students to practise using these structures when they are discussing the features in C.
- Ask students to read the instructions again and ask them which two things they must do *(talk about why these things benefit people and decide which two are the most important advantages of living in a city)*.
- Point out to students that when they are faced with this kind of task it's very important to study the pictures carefully to work out how they relate to the task as the pictures have a specific role to play in their discussion. Remind them of the positive features they talked about in B and elicit that these pictures show transportation, entertainment/recreational choices, health services, education facilities, cultural activities/shopping areas and technical/environmental projects.
- Ask students to do the task in pairs. Remind them to use the *Useful Expressions* to agree, disagree and partly agree with each other. Give each pair enough time to complete the task.
- Go round the class monitoring students to make sure they are carrying out the task properly. Don't correct any mistakes at this stage, but make a note of any problems in structure and pronunciation.
- Ask each pair to tell the rest of the class which two benefits they decided on and why. Also ask them why they didn't choose the other benefits.
- Write any structural mistakes that students made on the board without saying who made them, and ask them to correct them. Deal with any problems in pronunciation that came up.

Ideas Focus

- Ask students to read the questions quickly and deal with any queries they have.
- Ask students to work in pairs to take turns to answer the questions.
- Go round the class monitoring students to make sure they are carrying out the task properly. Don't correct any mistakes at this stage, but make a note of any problems in structure and pronunciation.
- Ask each pair to ask and answer one of the questions and repeat until each pair has had a turn.
- Write any structural mistakes that students made on the board without saying who made them, and ask them to correct them. Deal with any problems in pronunciation that came up.

Answers

Students' own answers

Grammar

A

- Ask students to look at the pictures on page 49 and ask again and make a list of as many nouns as possible that they can see in the pictures. Then write *Countable* and *Uncountable* on the board and ask students to write the nouns they came up with under the correct heading (eg Countable – building, bus, window, laptop, doctor; Uncountable – sky, glass, grass).
- Read the information on Countable and Uncountable Nouns to the class and explain anything students don't understand. Elicit that in the task they should pay attention to whether or not *a/an* is used before each noun and whether the nouns are singular or plural to help them decide on the correct answers.
- Ask students to do the task in pairs to encourage discussion, but check as a class. Point out to students that there are two boxes next to each sentence as there are two nouns in bold in each one. They should record the answer for the first word in the first box and for the second word in the second box.

Answers

1 U, U	4 U, U
2 U, C	5 U, C
3 C, U	6 C, U

B

- Write the sentences below on the board and ask a student to underline the nouns. Then ask them what they notice about them (*In sentence 1, chocolate is uncountable, but in sentence 2 it is countable.*).
  - You need lots of chocolate for this recipe.
  - Can I have a chocolate, please?
- Ask students if the meaning is the same here (*no*) and ask them how the words are different (*In sentence 1, chocolate is referred to as a substance, whereas in sentence 2 an individual chocolate sweet is being referred to.*).
- Ask students if they know any other words in English which can be either countable or uncountable, but whose meaning changes.
- Ask students to read the instructions and check that they understand what they have to do.
- Ask students to do the task in pairs to encourage discussion, but check as a class.

Answers

an event in your life / knowledge or skill
a fire that someone has lit to keep warm / fire as an element
a drinking glass / glass as a material
a single hair / all the hair on your head
an individual light / light in general as a concept
a distinct or specific sound / noise all around you
a piece of paper / paper as a material
a room in a house / space in general

Be careful!

- Read the information in *Be careful!* with students and explain anything they don't understand.
- Ask students to write a few sentences of their own using words from both categories here.

Now read the Grammar Reference on page 166 (4.6 to 4.8) with your students.

C

- Read the information on quantifiers to the class and explain anything students don't understand.
- Ask students to look back at the sentences in A and to underline the quantifiers used in those sentences.
- Ask students to do the task in pairs to encourage discussion, but check as a class.

Answers

1 many, few
2 much, little

D

- Ask students to read the instructions and check that they understand what they have to do.
- Ask students to read the first sentence and ask them to tell you which word is the noun and if it is countable or uncountable and then to say if it is correct or not. Ask them to justify their answer.
- Ask students to complete the rest of the task.
- Ask students to do the task individually, but check as a class.

Answers

1 I rubbish - uncountable
2 C news - uncountable
3 I *many* should be *much* - used with uncountable nouns
4 C police - plural noun
5 I equipment - uncountable
6 I advice - uncountable, so cannot be used with the indefinite article

E

- Ask students to read the instructions and check that they understand what they have to do.
- Read words in 1-6 to the students and ask them to repeat them. Correct their pronunciation where necessary. Explain that all these words are countable and we can use them in phrases with uncountable nouns in order to refer to them in multiples.
- Ask students to do the task individually, but check as a class.

Answers

1c 2e 3b 4f 5a 6d

F

- Write *Lisbon* on the board and elicit that it is the capital of Portugal. If any students have been there, ask them to tell the others what it is like. If not, ask students what they imagine it to be like.
- Ask students to read the text, without filling in any answers at this stage, to find out what the writer says about this city. Ask them what they learnt about Lisbon.
- Ask students to read the instructions and check that they understand what they have to do.
- Ask students to do the task individually, but check as a class.
- Ask students for their opinion on the way in which abandoned buildings in Lisbon have been dealt with and to justify their answers.

Answers

1	few	4	many
2	much	5	little
3	many	6	no

Use your English

A

- Read the phrasal verbs 1-5 and ask students to repeat them. Correct their pronunciation where necessary.
- Remind students that they have to consider the meaning of the verb and particle together and not just focus on the verb part. Ask them to read the definitions a-e on their own and explain anything they don't understand.
- Ask students to do the task individually, but check as a class.
- Encourage students to copy the phrasal verbs and their definitions into their notebooks before moving on to B.

Answers

1c 2d 3e 4b 5a

B

- Ask students to read the instructions and check that they understand what they have to do. Stress that they have to use the phrasal verbs from A in the correct form.
- Explain to students that they should read through all the sentences quickly before filling in any answers. Ask them to focus on the meanings of the phrasal verbs in A to choose the one that fits the meaning of each sentence best.

Answers

1	settle down	4	get away
2	moving out	5	moving into
3	hang out		

C

- Ask students to read the instructions and check that they understand what they have to do. Explain that if they know one of these phrases, then they should use the same word to complete the others.
- Ask students to read through all the incomplete phrases before deciding on the word.

- Correct their answers to the first part of the task before moving on to the sentence completion part.
- Ask students to do the second part of the task individually, but check as a class.

Answers

The missing word is *town*.
1 paint the town red
2 hometown
3 talk of the town
4 town hall
5 ghost town
6 night on the town

D

- Read the *Exam Close-up* and ask a student to explain what it says in his or her own words.
- Remind students they should always read the text all the way through first so not only do they know what it is about, but what tenses are used. They should also read it through again when they have completed the gaps.
- Ask students to look at the first two sentences of the text and ask them what they think they will read about (*city living*). Ask them what their opinion of city living is and encourage them to discuss the advantages and disadvantages of living in a big city.
- Ask students to read the instructions and check that they understand what they have to do.
- Ask students to read the text in the *Exam Task* and then answer the two questions.
- Students do the task individually, but check as a class.

Answers

1 stressed and suffering from anxiety
2 apartment buildings

E

- Ask students to read the text again and decide which of the words a-d completes the sentences. Tell them to pay attention to the words before and after each gap. Point out that this task tests collocations so the correct answers will depend on how naturally each option goes with the following word or phrase.
- When they have finished, tell them to read back through the text to make sure the sentences make sense and to check they haven't chosen the wrong word, especially when the answer choices are similar in meaning.
- Ask students to do the task individually, but check as a class.

Answers

1b 2c 3a 4d 5c 6a 7c 8a

Ideas Focus

- Ask students to read the questions quickly and deal with any queries they may have.
- Ask students to work in pairs to take turns to answer the questions.
- Go round the class monitoring students to make sure they are carrying out the task properly. Don't correct any mistakes at this stage, but make a note of any problems in structure and pronunciation.

- Ask a student from each pair to answer one of the questions until each pair has had a turn. Ask other students if they agree or if they have something else to add.
- Write any structural mistakes that students made on the board without saying who made them, and ask them to correct them. Deal with any problems in pronunciation that came up.

Writing: an article

- Ask students to read the *Learning Focus* on engaging your reader, and to underline the techniques mentioned for making an article more interesting *(using direct and indirect questions, question forms, varying grammatical structures – passive voice, conditional sentences, comparisons, etc)*. Then ask them what they should do once they have finished their article *(proofread to find and correct errors)*.

A

- Ask students to read the instructions and check that they understand what they have to do.
- Explain to students that they should always spend time analysing writing tasks like this so that they know exactly what they have to write.
- Ask students to read the task carefully and to underline key words and phrases.
- Ask students to answer the questions individually, but check as a class.

Answers

1 two, what will be the biggest challenge for cities in the future; will we be able to deal with it. In answer to the first part, students will have to provide description and examples, but in the second part they will have to give an opinion.
2 Students' own answers

B

- Ask students to read the instructions and check that they understand what they have to do.
- Explain that the two introductions are possible ways of starting the article in the writing task in A.
- Give students time to read the introductions and then ask them to work in pairs to discuss them and answer the questions in the instructions.
- Explain to students that they should bear in mind the advice on writing articles above in order to assess each introduction.
- As a class, ask students to discuss which introduction is best and why.

Answers

Paragraph 1 is better because it engages the reader by asking questions to involve them personally. Also, there are examples to support the writer's opinion. Paragraph 2 could be improved by involving the reader and by including examples instead of just speaking generally.

C

- Ask students to look at the picture at the side of the example article and the article's title. Ask them what aspects of city life in the future they think will be covered in it.
- Ask students to read the instructions and check that they understand what they have to do. Explain that they should write one or two sentences for each paragraph containing only the writer's basic ideas and that they don't have to include examples.
- Give students time to read the article and explain anything they don't understand before they write their summaries.
- As a class, ask individual students to read out their summary of one paragraph and ask the others if they have anything else to add.

Suggested answers

Paragraph 1:	Traffic and pollution are huge problems in cities and many people think they will become worse, but they might not be the biggest problems.
Paragraph 2:	We rely on fossil fuels for power, but they are running out so this creates uncertainty about what cities will be like in future.
Paragraph 3:	Solar and wind power could produce the electricity we need in cities.
Paragraph 4:	Clean energy forms are the way forward for our cities and our planet.

D

- Ask students to read the instructions and check that they understand what they have to do.
- As a class, brainstorm with students about the possible challenges that large cities will face in the future. Make a list of their ideas on the board.
- Ask students to choose one main idea and then to make notes on how they would develop this idea in each paragraph. Encourage them to follow the structure used in the example article. Tell them they will have three minutes to do this and time them.
- As a class, ask students to read out their ideas.

E

- Explain to students that they are now going to analyse the example article in more depth.
- Ask them to read the questions and explain anything they don't understand.
- Ask students to do the task individually, but check as a class. Explain to students that you will deal with their paragraphs shortly.

Answers

1 yes
2 yes
3 Students' own answers

- Remind students that when they have finished a piece of writing they should always proofread it to check for mistakes.
- Ask students to swap books and give them a few minutes to read and underline any mistakes they find in their partner's paragraph. Explain that they don't have to correct them.
- Ask students to hand back their paragraphs and to correct any mistakes their partner has noted.
- As a class, ask several students to read out their paragraphs.

F

- Ask students to read the instructions and check that they understand what they have to do.
- Ask students to read the first item and ask for ideas as to how it can be changed into a question. Write the first question you are given on the board and elicit ideas to improve or change it to make it more attractive to the reader and make them want to read on.
- Ask students to work with a partner and complete the rest of the task.
- Ask pairs to tell the class their question and ask if anyone else has exactly the same question or something different.
- Write all their questions on the board and have a quick class vote at the end for which is the best for items 1-3 and would make them want to read the rest of the article.

Useful Expressions

- Read the *Useful Expressions* to students and explain anything they don't understand. Point out that when we talk about the future, we use future tenses and forms. Encourage students to revise the grammar section of this unit before writing their articles.
- As a class, ask each student to choose one of the structures here and to complete it to say something about cities of the future.
- Remind students that they can use these expressions when writing their own article.

G

- Ask students to read the information in the *Exam Close-up*. Remind students that these features will help to keep the reader's attention.
- Ask students to look back at the model article to underline the writer's opinion (*Cities need energy to survive. But one day, fossil fuels will run out.*, *Fortunately, we already have the technology to deal with this challenge. The problem is that we are not using it.*) examples to support these opinions (*We won't have electricity or heating and cooling systems ... will cease to function.*, *For example, all city buildings ... public transport could become electric.*) and questions (*But, what if the biggest challenge for cities is something else?*, *Have you ever wondered what city life will be like when they do?*).
- Ask students to read the instructions and the *Exam Task* and to underline the two things they have to do in the task (*Describe what cities of the future will be like and say how they will be different and how they will be similar to today's cities.*).

- Ask students to read the paragraph plan and ask them to note down ideas that they could use in each paragraph. If time allows, ask students to write the introduction to their article in class, and give them any help they may need with it.

H

- Ask students to write or complete their article at home.
- Remind students to give their article a title, and include the features found in the information on writing articles at the top of the page and the *Useful Expressions*.
- Advise students to use the Writing Reference and checklist for articles on page 182 when writing their article.

Suggested answer

The future face of urban areas
Have you ever wondered what our cities will be like in the future? Most people imagine they will look futuristic like cityscapes found in science-fiction films and video games. The reality may, however, be a long way from this image.

I wonder what cities will be like after a decade or two of economic recession. In the not too distant future, more and more people will leave large cities to go to rural areas. This will mean the population of many cities will be greatly reduced.

In **50** years' time, life in large cities will continue to be as stressful as it is today. More than ever, it will be survival of the fittest and those who choose to remain in the city will face even more competition for employment and housing. If businesses continue to close at the rate they are closing today, then jobs will become very scarce.

Without a doubt, cities of the future will be different to what they are today. The chances are, though, that they won't resemble the futuristic sci-fi cities that we may imagine them to be, but bleak urban jungles.

General Note

The National Geographic videos can be used as an interesting way to introduce your students to other cultures. They are authentic National Geographic videos, and it is not necessary for students to understand everything they hear to benefit from them. The videos have the option to play English subtitles so that students can read on screen exactly what is said in the documentary. This feature may help students with some of the tasks in the worksheets. The videos are also a good way to encourage your students to watch TV programmes and films in English so that they can get used to the sound of the language. The more students are exposed to English, the easier it will be for them to pick up the language.

Background Information

Urban art differs from other art forms as it is on display or takes place in public places. Examples of urban art forms are graffiti on walls, abandoned buildings, trains, buses, etc as well as music, dance and theatrical performances that take place on the street. Graffiti artists were once thought of as vandals who defaced the urban landscape. Today, however, their talents are more recognised and many people feel their works improve run-down areas. Some graffiti artists, like Banksy, have become household names all over the world for their innovative designs which comment on social problems.

Before you watch

A

- Explain to students that in this lesson they are going to watch a video about Urban Art. Ask them to look at the globe to see which city in particular they will concentrate on. Elicit what they know about Washington DC, and what they imagine urban art to be.
- Ask students to read the instructions and the three questions and explain anything they don't understand.
- Ask students to work in pairs to ask and answer the questions.
- Go round the class monitoring students to make sure they are carrying out the task properly. Don't correct any mistakes at this stage, but make a note of any problems in structure and pronunciation.
- As a class, ask students at random to answer each of the questions and ask the others if they agree or have something to add.
- Write any structural mistakes that students made on the board without saying who made them, and ask them to correct them. Deal with any problems in pronunciation that came up.

While you watch

B

- Explain to students that they are now going to watch the video. Ask them to read sentences 1-6 and explain anything they don't understand.
- Read the words in red to the students and ask them to repeat them. Correct their pronunciation where necessary.

- Ask them to think about which answers might be correct before watching.
- Ask students to do the task individually, but check as a class.

Answers

1 art (00.42)	**4** appreciate (02.05)
2 understand (01.14)	**5** clubs (03.08)
3 whole (01.38)	**6** exploration (03.52)

After you watch

C

- Explain to students that this is a summary of the information they heard on the video.
- Read the words in the yellow box to the students and ask them to repeat them. Correct their pronunciation where necessary. Ask students to write *N*, *V* or *Adj* beside each of the words depending on whether it is a noun, verb or adjective.
- Explain to students that they should read the whole summary before writing any answers first to work out what part of speech is missing.
- Tell students to read back through the text once they have finished to check their answers.
- Ask students to do the task individually, but check the answers as a class.

Answers

1 innovative	**5** works
2 graffiti	**6** generation
3 discovered	**7** company
4 respect	**8** nearby

Ideas Focus

- Ask students to read the instructions and make sure they understand what they have to do. Then ask them to read the two questions and answer any queries they might have.
- Ask students to work in pairs and explain that they should each give their opinions on both questions.
- Go round the class monitoring students to make sure they are carrying out the task properly. Don't correct any mistakes at this stage, but make a note of any problems in structure and pronunciation.
- Ask each pair to answer one of the questions and repeat until each pair has had a turn.

Answers

Students' own answers

Objectives

- To revise vocabulary and grammar from Units 3 and 4
- To practise exam-type tasks

Revision

- Explain to students that Review 2 revises the material they saw in Units 3 and 4.
- Remind students that they can ask you for help with the exercises or look back at the units if they're not sure about an answer, and stress that the review is not a test.
- Decide how you will carry out the review. You could ask students to do one task at a time and then correct it immediately, or ask students to do all the tasks and correct them together at the end. If you do all the tasks together, let students know every now and again how much time they have got left to finish the tasks.
- Ask students not to leave any answers blank and to try to find any answers they aren't sure about in the units.
- When checking students' answers to the review tasks, make a note of any problem areas in vocabulary and grammar that they still have. Try to do extra work on these areas so that your students will progress well.

Vocabulary Revision

- Ask students to write down as many nouns referring to people who stay in a place as possible. Then ask them to write sentences of their own which show the difference in meaning between the words. Make sure they revise *dweller, inhabitant* and *resident*.

- Write the verbs *catch, cater, come, go, live, look, nose* and *start* on the board and ask students to match them with the following particles to form the phrasal verbs they learnt in Unit 3: *about, around, down on, in for, on, out, to.* Then ask students to write sentences of their own with these phrasal verbs.

- Write the verbs *include, create* and *attract* on the board and ask students to write down the adjectives and nouns that can be formed from these verbs.

- Ask the questions below at random round the class and make sure all students answer at least one question.
  - What is your house/school/town surrounded by?
  - In what situations do you feel under pressure?
  - Are you interested in what goes on behind the scenes in celebrities' lives? Why/Why not?
  - What is more important to you: being happy or making money?
  - In which city/country would you like to settle down?
  - Do you buy magazines depending on how attractive their front page is? Why/Why not?

- Ask students to write sentences with the words *agent, cultural, majority, privacy* and *traditional*.

Grammar Revision

- Write the sentences below on the board and ask students to say which tense they are in and whether they are in the affirmative, negative or question form. Then revise all forms of these tenses as well as the time expressions used with them.
  - They had never seen a celebrity in person until now. *(Past Perfect Simple, negative)*
  - Had they been filming for long? *(Past Perfect Continuous, question)*
  - They soon cultivated the land around the river. *(Past Simple, affirmative)*

- Revise the future tenses and forms students learnt in Unit 4 by asking the questions below at random round the class. Make sure each student answers at least one question and revise any forms they have problems with.
  - What are you going to do this weekend?
  - Where will you go on holiday this year?
  - How many foreign countries will you have visited by this time next year?
  - Where do you think you will be living in the year 2030?

- Write the beginnings of sentences below on the board and ask students to complete them in their own words. Make sure they remember that future tenses cannot be used with the temporals in the sentences.
  - Let's go for a walk when ____.
  - We should stay indoors until ____.
  - Tell Jane about meeting Rihanna the moment ____.
  - Fasten your seat belt as soon as ____.
  - Why don't we go for a bite to eat after ____.

- Write the headings *Countable* and *Uncountable* on the board and ask students to make a list of as many nouns as possible under each heading. Give them one minute to do this and then make a list together on the board. Then ask students to write sentences of their own using some of these words and *few, many, much, little, a few, lots of* and *a lot of.*

Part 1

- Ask students to read the instructions and check that they understand what they have to do.
- Ask students to read the title of the text and ask them what they think the text will deal with. Then ask them to skim read the text, without circling any answers at this stage, to find out what manufacturing fame refers to *(the role the press plays in creating celebrities).* Ask students if people in their own country are obsessed with the lives of the rich and famous.
- Point out to students that they should read all four options for each item before deciding which word best fits each gap. Remind them to pay attention to the whole sentence each gap is in as the general context will help them understand what word is missing.
- Remind students to read back through the text once they have finished to check their answers.

1A 2D 3B 4A 5B 6A 7D 8B

Part 2

- Ask students to read the instructions and check that they understand what they have to do.
- Ask students what they know about the world's oldest cities and where they are/were located. Ask them which cities in their own countries are the oldest and if they know when they date from.
- Ask students to skim read the text, without filling in any answers at this stage, to find out what allowed people to settle in Mesopotamia (being able to control the river flood waters as this enabled them to cultivate the land and have a steady supply of food).
- Encourage students to pay particular attention to the words immediately before and after each gap to work out what part of speech is missing. However, remind them that they have to take into consideration the general context of the sentence so that they understand which structure is being used.
- Remind students to read back through the text once they have finished to check their answers.

Answers

9	has	13	was
10	were	14	by
11	down	15	like
12	had	16	under

Part 3

- Ask students to read the instructions and check that they understand what they have to do.
- Ask students to read the title of the text and ask them where Cappadocia is (Turkey). Ask them to skim read the text, without filling in any answers at this stage, to find out what is special about Cappadocia and why tourists flock to the area (It is an area of great interest due to the unique architecture of buildings that have been carved into rocks which are shaped like pinnacles.). Ask students if they would like to visit Cappadocia and to say why/why not.
- Read the words at the side of the text to the students and ask them to repeat them. Correct their pronunciation where necessary.
- Ask students to read back through the text and to decide which part of speech is missing from each gap, and to complete the gaps using the correct form of the words given.
- Remind students to read back through the text once they have finished to check their answers.

Answers

17	including	21	inhabitants
18	creation(s)	22	commercial
19	dwellers	23	majority
20	residents	24	traditional

Part 4

- Ask students to read the instructions and check that they understand what they have to do.
- Ask students to read both sentences in each item and to underline the information in the first sentence that is missing from the second sentence. Then ask them to look at the word given to decide how the missing information could be inserted into the second sentence using this word. Remind students that they will have to use a different structure in order to keep the meaning the same.
- Remind students that they mustn't change the word given in any way.
- Encourage students to read back through the completed sentences once they have finished to check their answers.

Answers

25	he is going to be/become
26	is there any good accommodation
27	was the first time
28	on my behalf
29	had not finished
30	as soon as Carol gets

5 Tied to Technology

Reading:	multiple-choice, spotting words in the text and questions
Vocabulary:	technology-related words
Grammar:	modals & semi-modals, perfect modals
Listening:	multiple-choice (pictures), choosing from pictures
Speaking:	talking about modern technology, giving your opinion and interacting, involving your partner, keeping the conversation going
Use your English:	phrasal verbs, word formation, filling the gaps, gapped text
Writing:	essay (I), deciding what language to use in an essay, supporting your points, expressing contrast & results, giving examples, adding points, expressing another person's opinions, presenting opposing views

Unit opener

- Ask students to look at the title of the unit and ask them what they think it might mean *(We are reliant on technology in our everyday lives.)*.
- Ask students to look at the picture and its accompanying caption and ask them in what way the bionic hand shown is *tied to technology*. Elicit other ways in which we rely on technology every day.
- If students seem interested, give them further information using the Background Information box below.

Background Information

Modern, hi-tech prosthetic hands and arms can be controlled naturally. They can also provide sensation and offers much greater movement than conventional prosthetic limbs. The hand or arm functions by using electrical signals from the wearer's chest muscles.

Reading

A

- Ask students to read the instructions and check that they understand what they have to do.
- Read the adjectives in the yellow box to the students and ask them to repeat them. Correct their pronunciation where necessary.
- Ask students to work in pairs to discuss which adjectives they associate with these forms of exploration. Ask them to justify their answers.
- As a class, ask each pair to report to the class how they see sea and space exploration. Ask the others if they agree or if they have anything else to add.

B

- Ask students to look at the picture next to the text and the title of the article. Elicit what they know about the Hubble Space Telescope. Then do the same for the second text on sonar mapping.
- Ask students to read the instructions and check that they understand what they have to do.

- Ask students to skim read the text to find relevant information. Explain that there are no right or wrong answers here as they should express their own opinion based on what they read. Explain that they don't have to read in detail as they will have another opportunity to read the text.
- Discuss students' choices of adjectives to describe the telescope and sonar mapping as a class and encourage them to justify their views.

Word Focus

- Ask students to look at the words in red in the text and to re-read the sentences they are found in. Remind students that when they don't know the meaning of a word, they should look carefully at the sentence it is found in to work out its meaning. Ask students to work in pairs to decide what each of the words mean.
- Ask students to read the *Word Focus* box to compare their answers with the definitions given.

C

- Ask students to read the information in the *Exam Close-up* and ask a student to tell you what it means in his or her own words. Explain that a scientific text should not put them off. It will often discuss a process or outline the history of an invention or discovery, but it won't test their scientific knowledge in any way.
- Ask students to look again at the text and the options a-d in the *Exam Task*. Explain anything the students don't understand.
- Ask students to find words in the texts that are similar to those used in the a-d options. Point out that in question 1, two examples are underlined.
- Students complete the task individually and then compare their words with a partner.
- Check answers as a class.

D

- Ask students to read the instructions and items 1-8 with their options. Explain anything the students don't understand.
- Ask students to identify the parts of the text that refer to each of the items. Point out that the information in the items follows the same order as the text.
- Ask students to do the task individually, but check as a class.
- If students are interested, give them more information about the Hubble Space Telescope and Sonar mapping using the Background Information box below.

Answers

1d (... *it has beamed hundreds of thousands of images back to Earth and has revolutionised ... about deep space and the universe.*)

2c (*Thanks to Hubble, we now know that the universe is about 13 to 14 billion years old.*)

3b (... *the Earth's atmosphere distorts light coming from the stars ...*)

4c (*Its successor, the James Webb Space Telescope, has already been developed.*)

5b (*These animals emit a sharp noise ... comes back as an echo.*)

6c (*By knowing the speed of sound in water and the time it takes the echo to return, the distance to the reflecting object can be calculated.*)

7c (... *it records the depth at every place it goes, and eventually a 3D map ... is created.*)

8b (... *making a map of the ocean floor is much more difficult as sound reflects back from many directions and geological features on the ocean floor.*)

Background Information

The Hubble Space Telescope, which was launched on April 24 1990, has been responsible for many important discoveries about our universe. It was able to give a more accurate estimate of the age of our universe than we previously had. In the past, the age was thought to be 10-20 billion years old. Hubble has also showed that the expansion of the universe is accelerating, probably due to a force called Dark Energy which scientists still know little about. Hubble has also proved that black holes are common at the centres of all galaxies.

Sonar is an acronym for Sound Navigation Ranging. Sonar mapping is the process of studying shapes, sizes and distances on the ocean floor. By mapping the ocean floor, ships' voyages become safer, however there are some negative effects of this mapping. As dolphins and whales emit similar sounds in order to catch their prey, the sounds given off by sonar mapping can confuse them. This can lead to the animals not feeding themselves or mating.

E

- Ask students to read the instructions and check that they understand what they have to do.
- Ask students to look back at the texts and find the phrasal verbs and underline them.
- Ask students to do the task individually, but check as a class.

Answers

1	put forward	4	spreads out
2	pointed out	5	bounces off
3	took off	6	worked out

F

- Ask students to write all six of the phrasal verbs in their notebook.
- Explain to students that they should choose three of the phrasal verbs and write a sentence using each one. Monitor and help if necessary.
- Ask students to read their sentences to the class. If time allows, ask students to write two or three more sentences, but this time leaving a gap for the phrasal verb.
- Then they should swap their book with another student who completes each sentence with the correct phrasal verb.

Ideas Focus

- Ask students to read the question and deal with any queries they may have.
- Ask students to work in pairs to ask and answer the question.
- Go round the class monitoring students to make sure they are carrying out the task properly. Don't correct any mistakes at this stage, but make a note of any problems in structure and pronunciation.
- As a class, ask students at random to answer the question and ask the others if they have anything else to add.
- Write any structural mistakes that students made on the board without saying who made them, and ask them to correct them. Deal with any problems in pronunciation that came up.

Answers

Students' own answers

Vocabulary

A

- Explain to students that in this task they will deal with words that are easily confused.
- Read the words in red to the students and ask them to repeat them. Correct their pronunciation where necessary.
- Encourage students to read the sentences through before circling any answers and to re-read them once they have finished to check their answers.
- Ask students to do the task individually, but check as a class.

Answers

1	proof	4	interactive
2	exhibition	5	potential
3	lecture	6	generate

Extra Class Activity

If time allows, ask students to write sentences of their own using the wrong words in each of the sentences.

B

- Write the word *machine* on the board and ask students to come up with as many different kinds of machines as possible. Ask them to explain what each machine does and what we normally use it for.
- Ask students to first read the sentences a-f. Read the words in bold to them and ask them to repeat them. Correct their pronunciation where necessary.
- Ask students to read sentences 1-6 and elicit that these sentences are linked to instances when you would use each machine.
- Ask students to do the task individually, but check as a class.

Answers

1f 2d 3a 4e 5c 6b

C

- Ask students to read the instructions and check that they understand what they have to do.
- Read the words in the yellow boxes to the students and ask them to repeat them. Correct their pronunciation where necessary.
- Encourage students to read through both sentences in each pair before filling in any answers.
- Ask students to do the task individually, but check as a class.

Answers

1	measure	4	lose
2	count	5	price
3	miss	6	cost

D

- Ask students to look at the title of the text and ask them if they think there can be too much technology. Elicit the forms of technology that young people use every day and ask them what they think the results of overusing them might be.
- Ask students to read the text quickly, without filling in any answers at this stage, to find out what too much technology can do to young people. Ask them for their reaction to these findings.
- Ask students to read the instructions and check that they understand what they have to do. Explain that they must use a different part of speech of the words given at the end of each line.
- Encourage students to underline the words immediately before and after the gaps and to think about what part of speech they are as this will give them a clue to what part of speech is missing from the gap.
- Ask students to do the task individually, but check as a class.

Answers

1	Technological	5	addiction
2	improvement	6	exposure
3	researchers	7	stimulation
4	harmful	8	evidence

Ideas Focus

- Ask students to read the question quickly and deal with any queries they may have.
- Ask students to work in pairs to take turns to answer the question.
- Go round the class monitoring students to make sure they are carrying out the task properly. Don't correct any mistakes at this stage, but make a note of any problems in structure and pronunciation.
- Ask each pair to ask and answer the questions and repeat until each pair has had a turn.
- Write any structural mistakes that students made on the board without saying who made them, and ask them to correct them. Deal with any problems in pronunciation that came up.

Answers

Students' own answers

Grammar

- Before students open their books, ask the questions below at random round the class, making sure all students answer at least one question.
  - Could you use a computer when you were six?
  - Do you need to take a laptop to school every day?
  - Are you able to fix electronic equipment if it breaks down?
  - What should you do to protect your computer from viruses?
  - How much time should you spend playing computer games per day?
  - Do you have to ask permission to use a computer at your school?
- Elicit from students that all these questions used modals or semi-modals. Elicit that these verb forms are followed by the bare infinitive form of a verb and that, with the exception of *be able to* and *have to*, we use the same form for all persons. Stress that we don't use *to* after affirmative or negative forms of *can, could, should, must, may* or *might*.

A

- Remind students that modals and semi-modals all have various uses and explain that they will deal with these uses in this lesson.
- Ask students to read the instructions and check that they understand what they have to do.
- Ask students to read the sentences 1-11 and point out that in sentences where more than one modal or semi-modal appears that these verbs have the same function in the sentence.
- Ask students to read the sentences again and underline the modal and semi-modal verbs.
- Ask students to do the task in pairs to encourage discussion, but check as a class.

Answers

1 must/have to	7 must
2 can't	8 can't/couldn't/won't
3 should/ought to	be able to
4 can/may	9 Can/could
5 don't have to/	10 mustn't/can't
needn't	11 could/may/might
6 can/could/will be	
able to	

B

- Ask students to read the instructions and check they understand what they have to do. Explain anything they don't understand.
- Read the *Be careful!* and ask students to give you examples using *ought* to for advice.
- Ask students to do the task in pairs to encourage discussion, but check as a class.

Answers

a can, could, will be able to	e could, may, might
b can't, couldn't, won't be able to	f mustn't, can't
	g mustn't
c can, could, may	h don't have to, needn't
d should, ought to, shouldn't	i must
	j can't

Now read the Grammar Reference on pages 166 to 167 (5.1 to 5.9) with your students.

C

- Ask students to read the instructions and check that they understand what they have to do.
- Ask students to read the two sentences in item 1 and then to underline the information in the first sentence that is missing from the second sentence. Ask them to rephrase this information in the second sentence using the word in bold. Remind them not to change the word given in any way. Check the answer to item 1 before moving on to the rest of the task.
- Ask students to do the task individually, but check as a class.

Answers

1 we have to bring	5 can't be
2 must be	6 ought to check
3 have to have	7 should recharge
4 you are not able to	8 might/may not work

D

- Ask students to read the instructions and check that they understand what they have to do. Elicit that they only have to write one word in each sentence.
- Encourage students to read the whole sentence before filling in any answers. Remind students to read back through the sentences once they have finished to check their answers.

- Ask students to do the task individually, but check as a class.

Answers

1 have	5 must
2 able	6 had
3 to	7 should
4 ought	8 may/might

Listening

A

- Ask students to read the instructions and check that they understand what they have to do.
- Explain to students that although they are guessing before they listen, they should get into the habit of doing this each time they do this type of listening task.
- Check answer as a class and ask students to justify their guess.

B

- Ask students to read the instructions and check that they understand what they have to do.
- Play the recording once for students to mark their answer.
- Check the answers as a class.

Answers

They are going to the computer fair on Sunday.

C

- Ask students to read the information in the Exam *Close-up* and ask a student to tell you what it says in his or her own words.
- Remind students that in this kind of task they won't know what the question is until after they have heard the conversation and that they will hear the conversation only once, so it's very important to have studied the pictures beforehand to prepare for the question.
- Explain to students that they should think of the name of specific objects as well as adjectives which could describe them or people that are depicted.
- Ask students to read the *Exam Task* and look at the pictures.
- Elicit guesses as to what each conversation will be about. Encourage everyone to have a guess.

D

- Ask students to read the instructions and check that they understand what they have to do.
- Ask students to look at the first set of items and elicit their names (*washing machine, vending machine, fridge*) and ask what they have in common (*They are all modern appliances.*).
- Play the recording, stopping after the first conversation and asking students to write down their answer. Check the answer to item 1 before moving on to the rest of the task.
- Give students time to analyse the rest of the pictures and to decide what they show, how they are similar or different and how they are related.

- Play the rest of the recording all the way through without stopping and ask students to write their answers. Ask students to compare their answers with a partner and to justify any differences.
- Check as a class. While checking the answers, ask students if any of their guesses in C were correct.

Answers

1c 2a 3a̶ 4a 5c 6b 7a 8c

Teaching Tip

If students ran into problems with the listening, play the recording again once you have checked their answers. Stop after each conversation and ask students what question was asked and to summarise the conversation in their own words.

Speaking

A

- Ask students to read the instructions and answer any queries they may have about them.
- Ask students to read the four statements and tell them to pay attention to the words in italics.
- Point out that they will hear instructions given by an examiner, as they would in a real examination.
- Play the recording through once and if necessary a second time for students to circle any answers they missed the first time.
- Check answers as a class. Ask students to work in pairs to take turns to ask and answer the questions.

Answers

| 1 | everybody's lives | 3 | technology |
| 2 | good and bad points | 4 | better |

B

- Ask students to work in pairs to make a list of different types of technology they discussed in A.
- Remind them to think of the different types of machines and electrical equipment they have in their home and at school.
- Go round the class monitoring students to make sure they are carrying out the task properly. Don't correct any mistakes at this stage, but make a note of any problems in structure and pronunciation.
- Write any structural mistakes that students made on the board without saying who made them and ask them to correct them. Deal with any problems in pronunciation that came up.

C

- Ask students to read the questions in the *Exam Task* and point out that these are the type of questions an examiner would ask them.
- Ask students to read the questions again and mark P for personal questions and G for general questions.
- Ask students to do the task individually and then compare their ideas with a partner.
- Check answers as a class and ask students to justify their answers.

Answers

1 P 2 G 3 P 4 P 5 P 6 G 7 G 8 P

Useful Expressions

- Read the *Useful Expressions* to the students and explain that we use these structures in order to include our partner and keep the conversation going. Point out that structures like these will help them to make sure they have a two-way conversation with their partner rather than a one-sided talk.
- If time allows, ask students to complete these structures with their own words.

D

- Ask students to read the *Exam Close-up* and check that they understand what they have to do.
- Ask students to work with a partner to take turns asking and answering the questions in the *Exam Task*.
- Remind students that this task is not a discussion but a conversation. They should use some of the *Useful Expressions* to keep the conversation going and to include and involve their partner.
- Go round the class monitoring students to make sure they are carrying out the task properly. Don't correct any mistakes at this stage, but make a note of any problems in structure and pronunciation.
- As a class, ask students at random to answer the questions and ask the others if they agree or have anything else to add.
- Write any structural mistakes that students made on the board without saying who made them, and ask them to correct them. Deal with any problems in pronunciation that came up.

Answers

Students' own answers

Ideas Focus

- Ask students to read the question quickly and deal with any queries they may have.
- Ask students to work in pairs to take turns to answer the question.
- Go round the class monitoring students to make sure they are carrying out the task properly. Don't correct any mistakes at this stage, but make a note of any problems in structure and pronunciation.
- Ask each pair to ask and answer the question and repeat until each pair has had a turn.
- Write any structural mistakes that students made on the board without saying who made them, and ask them to correct them. Deal with any problems in pronunciation that came up.

Answers

Students' own answers

Grammar

- Write the sentences below on the board and ask students when they refer to.
  - Jack can hook up the computer in no time. (present/ general)
  - They must put in the solar panels tomorrow. (future)
  - You mustn't put your finger in the socket! (present)
  - We have to pay for the excursion by Friday. (present/ future)
- Elicit from students that in order to talk about the past using modal verbs, we must use perfect modals.

A

- Read the instructions to the students and check that they understand what they have to do.
- Ask students to read item 1 and to explain what it means in their own words. Point out that the modal verb *should* here are followed by the perfect infinitive *have phoned* and that this tells us we're dealing with the past.
- Ask students to read the sentences and underline the perfect modal in each one.
- Ask students to do the task individually, but check as a class.

Answers

1 should have phoned
2 shouldn't have tried to
3 may/might/could have missed
4 could have become
5 can't have cooked
6 must have been
7 would have bought
8 needn't have told

B

- Ask students to read the instructions and check that they understand what they have to do.
- Ask students to read the explanations a-h and to reread the sentences in A.
- Ask them to work in pairs to encourage discussion while they match the explanations with the sentences in A.
- Check answers as a class.

Answers

1b 2h 3d 4a 5g 6c 7e 8f

Now read the Grammar Reference on pages 167 to 168 (5.10 to 5.16) with your students.

C

- Read the modal verbs in red to the students and ask them to repeat them. Correct their pronunciation where necessary.
- Ask students to do the task individually, but check as a class.

Answers

1 should	5 could	
2 may	6 must	
3 could	7 shouldn't	
4 needn't	8 would	

D

- Ask students to read the instructions and check that they understand what they have to do.
- Ask students to read the two sentences in item 1 and then to underline the information in the first sentence that is missing from the second sentence. Ask them to rephrase this information in the second sentence using the word in bold. Remind them not to change the word given in any way. Check the answer to item 1 before moving on to the rest of the task.
- Ask students to do the task individually, but check as a class.

Answers

1 must have been
2 may/might have missed
3 would have shown/told
4 ought to have updated
5 can't have been
6 shouldn't have given
7 needn't have got
8 should have finished

Use your English

A

- Read the phrasal verbs 1-6 and ask students to repeat them. Correct their pronunciation where necessary.
- Remind students that they have to consider the meaning of the verb + particle together and not just focus on the verb part.
- Ask them to read the definitions a-f on their own and explain anything they don't understand.
- Ask students to do the task individually, but check as a class.
- Encourage students to copy the phrasal verbs from A into their notebooks with their meanings before moving on to B.

Answers

1c 2b 3f 4a 5e 6d

B

- Ask students to read the instructions and check that they understand what they have to do. Stress that they have to use the phrasal verbs from A in the correct form.
- Explain to students that they should read through all six sentences quickly before marking any answers. Ask them to focus on the meanings of the phrasal verbs in A to choose the one that fits the meaning of each sentence best.

- Ask students to do the task individually, but check as a class.

1 shut down
2 hook up … to/hook … up to
3 set off
4 switch on
5 hacked into
6 plug … in

C

- Ask students if they have ever seen any films about the negative effects of technology, eg *Cyberbully*. Invite students to tell you if they have seen the film and their opinion of it. Encourage them to talk about any other films they have seen.
- Ask students to read the text, without filling in any answers at this stage. Ask them what they learned about the film, *Her*.
- Ask students to read the *Exam Close-up* and then read the instructions in the *Exam Task*. Check that they understand what they have to do.
- Ask students to do the task individually, but check as a class.

Answers

1 should   5 have
2 up   6 be
3 their   7 an
4 at   8 seem

Ideas Focus

- Ask students to read the two questions and deal with any queries they may have.
- Ask students to work in pairs to ask and answer the questions.
- Go round the class monitoring students to make sure they are carrying out the task properly. Don't correct any mistakes at this stage, but make a note of any problems in structure and pronunciation.
- As a class, ask students at random to answer both of the questions and ask the others if they have anything else to add.
- Write any structural mistakes that students made on the board without saying who made them, and ask them to correct them. Deal with any problems in
- pronunciation that came up.

Answers

Students' own answers

Writing: an essay (1)

- Ask students to read the information on writing essays in the *Learning Focus*.
- Remind students that a well-developed essay should have an introduction, two main paragraphs and a conclusion and that the paragraphs should follow on logically from one another. Also remind them that each paragraph should have one main idea which is introduced by the topic sentence and then supported by details and examples.

- When proofreading their essays, students should look out not only for spelling, grammatical and lexical errors, but also check that they have written in the appropriate register and stayed on topic.

A

- Ask students to read the instructions and check that they understand what they have to do.
- Ask students to read the things you should do in an essay 1-5 and explain anything they don't understand. Then ask them to read the topics a-e all the way through before writing any answers. Point out that they should write the corresponding letter for each reason in the boxes provided.
- Ask students to do the task individually, but check as a class.

Answers

1e 2a 3d 4b 5c

B

- Ask students to read the instructions and check that they understand what they have to do.
- Ask students to read the writing task carefully and underline the key words. Elicit the two questions they need to answer (*How has the most important modern invention affected our lives?*, *Has it had any negative effects?*).
- Ask students to read the questions 1-6 and deal with any queries they have.
- Ask students to do the task in pairs to encourage discussion, but check as a class.

Answers

1 Discuss what I think is the most important modern invention.
2 Two aspects – how it has affected our lives and the negative effects of the invention.
3 Students' own answers
4 Students' own answers
5 Students' own answers
6 Students' own answers

C

- Ask students to do the task individually, but check as a class.
- Ask students to look at the picture at the top of the page. Ask them what these people seem to be doing and what effects this activity may have on their lives.
- As a class, brainstorm the various modern inventions that affect our lives and make a list of them on the board. Ask students to say how these things affect us and what negative effects they may bring us.
- Ask students to decide on one particular invention and to write an introduction for the writing task in B, focusing on this invention.
- Once students have written their introductions, ask several students to read out their paragraphs.

D

- Ask students to read the instructions and check that they understand what they have to do.
- Ask students to read the example essay from start to finish and elicit which modern invention it focuses on (the television). Then ask them to work in pairs to discuss how their paragraphs compare to the introduction here. Encourage them to focus on content, length and register.
- As a class, ask students to comment on the introduction and compare it to their own.

E

- Ask students to read the instructions and check that they understand what they have to do.
- Ask students to read the question and items 1-4 and elicit an example of each type of linking word and phrase before they go back to look at the example essay again, to ensure that they understand the different functions.
- Ask students to do the task in pairs to encourage discussion, but check as a class.
- Once the answers have been checked, write the categories of linking words on the board and ask students to add other examples they can think of.

Answers

1 even so, However, despite, in spite of
2 consequently
3 for instance
4 What's more, In addition

F

- Ask students to read the instructions and check that they understand what they have to do.
- Elicit that the first main paragraph is the one that follows immediately after the introduction.
- Ask students to work in pairs to answer the questions and to justify their answers. Encourage them to underline any information in the paragraph which relates to their answers.
- Check as a class.

Answers

yes to all

Useful Expressions

- Read the Useful Expressions to students and explain anything they don't understand. Point out that these words and phrases link one idea to another and help the reader to follow the line of argument in the essay.

G

- Ask students to read the instructions and check that they understand what they have to do.
- Encourage students to write their paragraph directly below the introduction they wrote earlier so that it flows on directly from it. Remind them to focus on the invention they chose earlier.

- Give students no more than ten minutes to write their paragraphs and go round the class offering help where necessary and checking students' paragraphs as they write. Remind them to use appropriate linking words and phrases from the Useful Expressions.
- Ask several students to read their paragraphs out to the class.

H

- Ask students to read the information in the Exam Close-up and explain to students that they should use this list as a checklist when writing their own essays.
- Ask students to underline all the supporting examples the writer has used in the example essay (We depend on television for … current affairs; we enjoy it in the comfort of our own homes; the development of large screens … even more enjoyable; Some people spend too much time watching it; they spend less time … socialising with friends). Remind them to use examples like these to support their topic sentences in their main paragraphs.
- Ask students to read the Exam Task and check that they understand what they have to do.
- As a class, ask students to describe and discuss the picture at the bottom of the page. Ask them for their views on the subject and encourage them to touch on the advantages and disadvantages of children using computers.
- Ask students to write their essay plan. Allow them five minutes to do this and then ask students to tell you what they have included. Write their ideas on the board and as a class, agree on the essay plan.
- Ask students to read the Useful Expressions again before they start writing their essays.
- Encourage students to refer to the Writing Reference and checklist for formal essays on page 185 to help them with their essays.

Suggested answer

Computers have become an important part of our lives, and as a result parents often allow their children to use them from an early age. However, concerns have been raised that children have too much access to computers.

Computers have many negative effects on young users. For example, staring at a computer screen for long periods can harm a child's eyesight. Moreover, computers can be highly addictive so young people want to use them more and more instead of doing more active pastimes.

On the other hand, many people believe that computers can be beneficial to children. They claim that they will be better equipped for life if they learn to handle computers early on. As computers are necessary in today's world, they will be at an advantage over others who have poor computer skills.

In conclusion, although computers may have some benefits for children, I believe these benefits are superficial. Young people need to learn to engage with the real world around them and understand how it works before being exposed to the virtual world of computers.

5 Bionic Mountaineer

General Note

The National Geographic videos can be used as an interesting way to introduce your students to other cultures. They are authentic National Geographic videos, and it is not necessary for students to understand everything they hear to benefit from them. The videos have the option to play English subtitles so that students can read on screen exactly what is said in the documentary. This feature may help students with some of the tasks in the worksheets. The videos are also a good way to encourage your students to watch TV programmes and films in English so that they can get used to the sound of the language. The more students are exposed to English, the easier it will be for them to pick up the language.

Background Information

By the age of 17, Hugh Herr was recognised at one of the US's most accomplished climbers. During the accident in 1982 which resulted in him losing both his legs from the knee down, his climbing partner Jeff Batzer lost his lower left leg, the toes on his right foot and the fingers on his right hand. In the rescue mission to save these men, Albert Dow – rescue worker – was killed in an avalanche. Herr works in prosthetics at Harvard-MIT in the Division of Health Sciences and Technology.

Before you watch

A

- Explain to students that in this lesson they are going to watch a video about a bionic mountaineer. Ask them to look at the globe to see where this person comes from and ask them what they imagine a bionic mountaineer is.
- Ask students to read the instructions and the two questions and explain anything they don't understand.
- Ask students to work in pairs to ask and answer the questions.
- Go round the class monitoring students to make sure they are carrying out the task properly. Don't correct any mistakes at this stage, but make a note of any problems in structure and pronunciation.
- As a class, ask students at random to answer each of the questions and ask the others if they agree or have something to add.
- Write any structural mistakes that students made on the board without saying who made them, and ask them to correct them. Deal with any problems in pronunciation that came up.

While you watch

B

- Explain to students that they are now going to watch the video. Ask them to read sentences 1-6 and explain anything they don't understand.
- Ask them to think about which answers might be true and which might be false before watching.
- Ask students to do the task individually, but check as a class.

Answers

1 T		(00.14)
2 T		(01.24)
3 F	(… the legs that were given to me were designed for the horizontal world)	(01.38)
4 F	(music to my ears)	(02.05)
5 T		(02.55)
~~6 T~~ F		(04.25)

After you watch

C

- Explain to students that this is a summary of the information they heard on the video.
- Read the words in the yellow box to the students and ask them to repeat them. Correct their pronunciation where necessary. Ask students to write N, V or Adj beside each of the words depending on whether it is a noun, verb or adjective.
- Explain to students that they should read the whole summary before writing any answers first to work out what part of speech is missing.
- Tell students to read back through the text once they have finished to check their answers.
- Ask students to do the task individually, but check the answers as a class.

Answers

1 wandered	5 attempted
2 suffering	6 passion
3 save	7 control
4 occured	8 revolutionary

Ideas Focus

- Ask students to read the instructions and make sure they understand what they have to do. Then ask them to read the two questions and answer any questions they might have.
- Ask students to work in pairs and explain that they should both give their opinions on both questions.
- Go round the class monitoring students to make sure they are carrying out the task properly. Don't correct any mistakes at this stage, but make a note of any problems in structure and pronunciation.
- Ask each pair to answer one of the questions and repeat until each pair has had a turn.

Answers

Students' own answers

6 Fun, Fun, Fun!

Reading: multiple-choice, identifying the purpose of a text
Vocabulary: free-time- and sports-related vocabulary
Grammar: gerunds & infinitives, indirect questions, question tags, negative questions
Listening: sentence completion, predicting the answer
Speaking: talking about hobbies and free-time activities, decision making, giving opinions with reasons and examples, justifying choices
Use your English: phrasal verbs, collocations & expressions, sentence transformation
Writing: report, organising paragraphs, writing an effective report, introduction, reporting results, recommending

Unit opener

- Write the title of the unit on the board and as a class, brainstorm for as many ways as possible of having fun. Ask students which of these activities they do regularly, occasionally or have never done and to say why they do or have never done these things.
- Ask students to look at the picture and its accompanying caption on page 69 and ask them how it relates to the theme of the unit. Ask them if this is their idea of fun or not and to justify their answer. Discuss with students why people choose to do pastimes such as the one shown, and why others like to watch them.

Reading

A

- Ask students to read the instructions and check that they understand what they have to do. Explain that there are no right or wrong answers here, but that they should record their opinion on which activities are more popular based on what kind of things the young people they know like to do.
- Ask students to read the activities and explain anything they don't understand.
- Ask students to rate their activities on their own, but then to compare their answers with a partner. Encourage each pair to discuss any differences they have.
- As a class, discuss students' answers and allow them to justify their answers to the others.

B

- Ask students to read the instructions and check that they understand what they have to do. Point out that they don't have to read them in depth at this stage as they will have another chance to read the texts.
- Ask students to do the task individually, but check as a class.

Answer

They are all about what teens can do or do in their free time and they all mention either volunteering at / raising money for an animal shelter.

Word Focus

- Ask students to look at the words in red in the text and to re-read the sentences they are found in. Remind students that when they don't know the meaning of a word, they should look carefully at the sentence it is found in to work out its meaning. Ask students to work in pairs to decide what each of the words mean.
- Ask students to read the *Word Focus* box to compare their answers with the definitions given. Explain anything they don't understand.

Teaching Tip

Point out to students that in tasks like this one, they will be presented with several tasks which all have a different purpose, for example they could be a mixture of emails, notices, adverts, newspaper articles, reviews, etc. However, all the texts will have something in common. Explain that in order to do this task successfully, they need to develop their skimming and scanning skills in order to locate specific information.

C

- Ask students to read the information in the *Exam Close-up*.
- Encourage them to make notes about the purpose of each text, including text type, who wrote it and who will read it.
- Ask students to read the the *Exam Task* and check that they understand what they have to do.
- Encourage students to underline the key words in each question and point out that they should only look for the correct answer in the specific texts each time. Remind them to look back at the notes they made about purpose to help them answer correctly.
- Ask students to do the task individually, but check as a class.

Answers

1c 2d 3a 4c 5d 6b 7c

D

- Ask students to read the instructions and check that they understand what they have to do. Point out that the text letter is given at the end of each of the definitions. Ask students to read through all the definitions before they start looking in the texts for the words that mean the same.
- Ask students to do the task individually, but check as a class.

Answers

1	restless	4	attraction
2	out and about	5	socialise
3	worthwhile	6	book

E

- Ask students to read the instructions and check that they understand what they have to do. Explain that they have to use the words from D to complete each sentence.
- Ask students to read all the sentences before they write their answers.
- Ask students to do the task individually, but check as a class.

Answers

1	worthwhile	4	attraction
2	restless	5	out and about
3	book	6	socialise

Ideas Focus

- Ask students to read the questions quickly and deal with any queries they may have.
- Ask students to work in pairs and to take turns to ask and answer the questions.
- Go round the class monitoring students to make sure they are carrying out the task properly. Don't correct any mistakes at this stage, but make a note of any problems in structure and pronunciation.
- Ask each pair to ask and answer one of the questions and repeat until each pair has had a turn.
- Write any structural mistakes that students made on the board without saying who made them, and ask them to correct them. Deal with any problems in pronunciation that came up.

Answers

Students' own answers

Vocabulary

A

- Ask students to read the instructions and check that they understand what they have to do.
- Read the words in the yellow box to the students and ask them to repeat them. Correct their pronunciation where necessary. Elicit that they are all nouns that refer to places where sports are played.
- Ask students to read through the list of sports 1-10 and explain any that students don't know.
- Do item 1 together as a class and check the answer before moving on to the rest of the task.

- Ask students to do the task in pairs to encourage discussion, but check as a class.

Answers

1	track	6	pitch
2	pitch/field	7	course
3	alley	8	rink
4	ring	9	circuit
5	board	10	court

B

- Ask students to read the instructions and check that they understand what they have to do.
- Ask students to look at the words in capitals on the right before they read the sentences.
- Remind students to read each sentence carefully before they write their answer.
- Ask students to also read each sentence once they have written an answer to check that it makes sense.
- Ask students to do the task individually, but check as a class.

Answers

1	beaten
2	hosted
3	seating
4	awarded
5	came
6	crossed

C

- Ask students to read the instructions and check that they understand what they have to do. Explain that this is not a circling task! Instead, they should cross out the wrong word so that only the two words that can complete each sentence remain.
- Encourage students to read through the whole sentence before crossing out any words and to re-read the sentences once they have finished to check their answers.
- Ask students to do the task individually, but check as a class.

Answers

1	collection	5	look
2	wander	6	doing
3	share	7	path
4	fancy	8	medal

D

- Ask students to look at the picture and ask them to guess what the person might be doing. Ask them to read the accompanying caption and the title of the text and ask them if they have ever heard of geocaching. If so, ask them what they can tell you about it.
- Ask students to read the text quickly, without filling in any answers at this stage, to find out about geocaching. Ask them for their opinion on this pastime and whether it is something they are/would be interested in taking part in.
- Ask students to read the instructions and check that they understand what they have to do.

- Read the words in the yellow box to the students and ask them to repeat them. Correct their pronunciation where necessary. Elicit that some words are adjectives and some are nouns.
- Remind students to read back through the text once they have finished to check their answers.
- Ask students to do the task individually, but check as a class.

Answers

1	outdoor	5	gear
2	participants	6	outing
3	portable	7	beginners
4	active	8	trekkers

Grammar

- Ask students to look at the picture and the accompanying caption in the bottom right-hand corner. Ask students to rewrite the information in the caption, beginning with the word *Holding*. (*Holding the Olympic torch, Sir Steve Redgrave at the London 2012 Olympic opening ceremony.*)
- Ask students what type of word *Holding* is and elicit that it is a gerund and acts as the subject of the sentence. Ask students what the bare infinitive and the full infinitive would be (*hold/to hold*).

A

- Ask students to read the information and instructions and check that they understand what they have to do. Elicit that they have to underline the gerunds, bare infinitives and full infinitives in the sentences.
- As you check the verbs underlined, ask students to say what form they are.
- Ask students to do the task in pairs to encourage discussion, but check as a class.

Answers

1 encourage, to take up
2 going out
3 to get
4 Training
5 to see
6 watching
7 to beat

B

- Ask students to read the instructions and check that they understand what they have to do.
- Ask students to read the sentences in A again and then at the items in B. They can then decide which form follows each item and write their answer to each one.
- Ask students to do the task individually, but check as a class.

Answers

a F b G c F d G e B f F g G

C

- Ask students to read the instructions and check that they understand what they have to do.
- Ask students to read through the sentences, without filling in any answers at this stage, to underline the verbs and phrases immediately before the gaps. Point out that they should bear these in mind when deciding the correct form of the verbs in brackets.
- Ask students to do the task individually, but check as a class.

Answers

1	go	4	train
2	to buy	5	travelling
3	paying		

D

- Read the information in D to the students and explain anything they don't understand.
- Explain to students that in the task they should read each pair of sentences and write the letter which corresponds to the meaning of the sentence in each box.
- Ask students to do the task in pairs to encourage discussion, but check as a class.

Answers

1b 2a 3a 4b

Now read the Grammar Reference on pages 168 & 169 (6.1 to 6.5) with your students.

E

- Ask students to read the instructions and check that they understand what they have to do.
- Explain that they have to decide which is the correct verb form, gerund or infinitive, to complete each sentence.
- Encourage students to read the whole sentence before circling their answers.
- Ask students to do the task individually, but check as a class.

Answers

1 talking
2 to have escaped
3 to take
4 get
5 knowing

F

- Ask students what they know about the history of the Olympic Torch. Ask them if they have ever seen it in real life. Explain that they are going to read a text about its history.
- Ask them to skim read the text, without filling in any answers at this stage to find out when the Olympic Torch Relay began (*1936*). Ask students which facts they weren't aware of until they read the text.

- Ask students to re-read the text to underline verbs and phrases immediately before the gaps and remind them that these words should help them decide which form of the verbs in brackets to use.
- Ask students to do the task individually, but check as a class.

Answers

1 to create	5 to connect
2 burning	6 Using
3 lighting	7 become
4 starting	8 to see

Listening

A

- Ask students to read the instructions and check that they understand what they have to do.
- Elicit from students some other examples of information based on numbers and write two or three of their ideas on the board (ages, dates, years, times, platforms at stations, phone numbers).
- Ask students to work with a partner, write down the ideas on the board and add any others of their own. Invite students to tell you their ideas and add them to the list on the board.
- Ask the pairs to complete the sentences by predicting what might go in each gap.
- Check answers as a class.

Answers

1 year, age
2 temperature
3 flight number
4 phone number
5 time
6 address

B

- Explain to students that in this task they will have the opportunity again to predict what completes a gap in sentences.
- Ask students to read the instructions and check that they understand what they have to do.
- Ask students to read the six sentences and explain anything they don't understand. Remind students that they should always read through the sentences before listening so that they have an idea of what they are going to listen to and it will help them predict what will complete any gaps.
- Ask students to read the sentences again and make a note in the margin of their books about what kind of information they think might complete each sentence.
- Play the recording once all the way through and ask students to listen to see if their predictions were correct. Then ask students to compare their answers with a partner and to justify any answers that are different.

Answers

1 number of albums	4 month
2 name of album	5 date
3 number	6 number

C

- Explain to students that they will listen again and complete the sentences in B exactly with what they hear on the recording. Play the recording again and ask students to complete their answers.
- Check the answers as a class.

Answers

1 six albums	4 July
2 Basically Zero	5 May 28th
3 150,000	6 50

D

- Ask students to read the instructions and check that they understand what they have to do.
- Ask students to read the Exam Close-up and explain anything they don't understand.
- Ask students to read the Exam Task and try to predict what words or phrases might complete each gap.
- Ask them to compare their answers with a partner and to justify any different answers.

E

- Ask students to read the instructions and check that they understand what they have to do.
- Ask students to read through the Exam Task again and explain anything they don't understand.
- Play the recording once all the way through and ask students to write their answers. Then ask students to compare their answers with a partner.

F

- Play the recording again and ask students to check their answers and complete any missing answers.
- Check the answers as a class.

Answers

1 athletics stadium	6 from Africa
2 ten days and nights	7 local schools
3 kick-off	8 throughout the city
4 too many	9 fifteen dollars
5 dates and times	10 festival pass

Speaking

A

- Ask students to read the three questions and answer any queries they may have about them.
- Ask students to work in pairs and to take turns to ask and answer the questions about themselves.
- Go round the class monitoring students to make sure they are carrying out the task properly. Don't correct any mistakes at this stage, but make a note of any problems in structure and pronunciation.
- Ask each pair to ask and answer one of the questions and repeat until each pair has had a turn.
- Write any structural mistakes that students made on the board without saying who made them, and ask them to correct them. Deal with any problems in pronunciation that came up.

B

- Ask students to cover up the instructions and the yellow box and ask them to just look at the pictures. Ask them what they all have in common (*They are all kinds of parks.*). Then ask them what differences there are between them and why you would go to each of them.
- Read the words in the yellow box to students and ask them to repeat them. Correct their pronunciation where necessary.
- Ask students to do the task individually, but check as a class.

Answers

1	theme park	4	safari park
2	amusement park	5	public park
3	water park		

C

- Ask students to read the information in the *Exam Close-up*. Explain that they will take part in a decision-making task in this lesson.
- Ask students to read the *Exam Task* and ask them what kind of decision they will have to make (*which changes an amusement park should make*).
- Ask students to think of the pros and cons of each of the suggested changes.
- Explain to students that they will learn various structures for justifying their choices in *Useful Expressions* to help them explain to their partner why they choose certain options.

Useful Expressions

- Read the *Useful Expressions* to students and explain that we use these structures in order to justify our choices.
- Ask students to practice using these structures when they are trying to make a decision about which aspects of the amusement park should change in the *Exam Task*.

D

- Ask students to read the instructions again and ask them how many things they have to do here (*two*) and what they are (*talk about how popular suggestions shown might be and decide which two changes should be made*).
- Explain to students that in decision-making tasks like this, they should base their decision on the specific situation and not on their own personal preferences.
- As a class, elicit what potential change is shown in each of the pictures and encourage students to think about the advantages of each one.
- Ask students to do the task in pairs and to use the structures in *Useful Expressions* to justify their answers.
- Ask each pair to tell the rest of the class which suggestions they chose and to say why.
- Write any structural mistakes that students made on the board without saying who made them, and ask them to correct them. Deal with any problems in pronunciation that came up.

Ideas Focus

- Ask students to read the questions quickly and deal with any queries they may have.
- Ask students to work in pairs and to take turns to ask and answer the questions.
- Go round the class monitoring students to make sure they are carrying out the task properly. Don't correct any mistakes at this stage, but make a note of any problems in structure and pronunciation.
- Ask each pair to ask and answer one of the questions and repeat until each pair has had a turn.
- Write any structural mistakes that students made on the board without saying who made them, and ask them to correct them. Deal with any problems in pronunciation that came up.

Answers

Students' own answers

Grammar

- Write the questions below on the board and ask students what the difference between them is (*The first question is an indirect question and is more polite than the second, which is a direct question.*).
  - Could you show me how this vending machine works?
  - How does this vending machine work?

A

- Read the information to the students and explain anything they don't understand. Encourage them to underline subjects, auxiliary verbs, main verbs and question words in each question.
- Ask students to do the task in pairs to encourage discussion, but check as a class.

Answer

The direct question uses the normal word order of a question while the indirect questions use the word order of a statement and a phrase to introduce the question.

B

- Ask students to read the instructions and check that they understand what they have to do.
- Encourage students to actually say these questions to one another to help them decide why they are unusual.
- Ask students to do the task in pairs to encourage discussion, but check as a class.

Answers

They don't make use of a question mark as they are phrased as statements.

Teaching Tip

These structures will make more sense to students and sound more natural if they are given the opportunity to use them. Create cards with the situations below on them to give to each student. Then ask students to stand up and wander around the class as if they were walking in the street. They should then stop a 'passer-by' and ask him or her an indirect question using one of the structures in A and B based on the situation on their card.

Situations
- You want to know what time it is.
- You need to find the nearest bank.
- You can't carry all your shopping to your car.
- You don't know which bus you need to take to get to another neighbourhood.
- You don't know how the parking meter works.
- You're hungry and want to find a good place to have lunch.

C

- Read the information on question tags to the students and explain anything they don't understand. Remind students that the verb tense and subject used in the statement part of the question should be used in the question tag.
- Ask students to read the two questions and to underline the subjects and verbs. Encourage them to think about which tense the verbs are in and whether they are positive or negative.
- Ask students to do the task individually, but check as a class.

Answers

1 isn't it
2 did they

Be careful!

- Read the information in *Be careful!* to students and ask them why this question tag is irregular (*because the verb form used in the question tag isn't otherwise used with the first person*).
- Write the question below on the board and ask students which question tag can complete it (*shall we*).
  - Let's have a pizza tonight, ____?

D

- Write the questions below on the board and ask students what they notice about them (*They all use a negative verb form.*). Explain that these are called negative questions.
  - Weren't you training for the Olympics at some point?
  - Isn't he that famous golf player?
  - Haven't they applied for gym membership yet?
- Ask students to do the task individually, but check as a class.

Answers

1 Didn't
2 Hasn't
3 Isn't
4 weren't

Now read the Grammar Reference on page 169 (6.6 to 6.8) with your students.

E

- Ask students to read the instructions and check that they understand what they have to do.
- Encourage students to read the whole sentence first before filling in any answers. Remind them to read back through the sentences once they have finished to check their answers.
- Encourage students to look back at A and B when filling in their answers.
- Ask students to do the task individually, but check as a class.
- You could expand on this task once the answers have been checked by asking students to work in pairs to take turns asking and answering these questions with a partner.

Answers

1 Would
2 like
3 if
4 when
5 wonder

F

- Ask students to read the instructions and check that they understand what they have to do.
- Remind students to underline subjects and verbs in the statement part of the question and to note if the verb is positive or negative.
- Remind students to read back through their sentences once they have finished to check their answers.
- Ask students to do the task individually, but check as a class.

Answers

1 aren't they
2 will you
3 shall we
4 hadn't they
5 won't you
6 isn't it
7 weren't there
8 aren't I

G

- Ask students to read the instructions and check that they understand what they have to do.
- Point out that they have to pay attention to the word order in each question to work out which one is correct.
- It might help to ask students to work in pairs to actually ask each other these questions so that they can hear which one sounds more natural.
- Check as a class.

Answers

Students should tick the following:
1 Weren't they late for training yesterday?
2 Wasn't the race great?
3 Haven't they bought camping equipment?
4 Why haven't you gone to the match?

Use your English

A

- Ask students to read the instructions and check that they understand what they have to do.
- Read the phrasal verbs in the yellow box to the students and ask them to repeat them. Correct their pronunciation where necessary. Ask students if they know what any of the verbs mean.
- Encourage students to read through all the sentences for meaning before they fill in any answers.
- Remind students to re-read the sentences once they have finished to check their answers.
- Ask students to do the task individually, but check as a class.
- Ask students to copy the phrasal verbs and definitions into their notebooks before moving on to B.

Answers

1 show up	5 sleep in
2 run into	6 sit back
3 turn down	7 sit around
4 feel up to	8 get together

B

- Ask students to read the instructions and check that they understand what they have to do.
- Ask students to read the text, without filling in any answers at this stage, to see how it is related to the theme of the unit (*It talks about how the writer spends his or her free time.*).
- Ask students to do the task individually, but check as a class.

Answers

1 sleep in	5 get together
2 sit around	6 run into
3 sit back	7 show up
4 feel up to	8 turn down

C

- Write the verbs *do*, *go* and *play* on the board and ask students to come up with at least two collocations for each verb. Explain that learners of English often confuse these verbs in common collocations, as similar expressions in their own language may use only one verb.
- Ask students to read the instructions and check that they understand what they have to do. Make sure they realise they should fill in the correct form of each verb.
- Ask students to read through the sentences, without filling in any answers at this stage, to underline the nouns that appear immediately after the gaps. Explain to students that they should decide which of the three verbs each word can collocate with.
- Ask students to do the task individually, but check as a class.

Answers

1 went	5 goes
2 doing	6 plays
3 is playing	7 does
4 do	8 go

D

- Ask students to read the instructions and check that they understand what they have to do.
- Explain that they mustn't change the word in bold in any way in the second sentence.
- Ask students to read the two sentences in item 1. Then ask them to underline the part in the first sentence that is missing from the second sentence. Explain to students that in order to complete the second sentence they will have to make a structural change. Remind them to also count the number of words they have written. They should have between two and five words.
- Ask students to complete the first item and correct it before they move on to the rest of the task.
- Ask students to do the task individually, but check as a class.

Answers

1 tell me whether there are	3 suppose *there is*
2 when the train arrives	4 stand too close to
	5 turned down
	6 with reference to

Writing: a report

- Read the information in the *Learning Focus* on writing a report to the students and explain anything they don't understand.
- Point out that normally reports are written following a specific request from someone wanting information about a place, services, etc. Elicit from students that in order to maintain a neutral and impersonal tone, they should avoid using the first person singular when presenting opinions/findings. Using the passive voice is a good way to achieve the correct tone and level of formality.
- Explain to students that reports are different from other kinds of writing that they have done up till now as they are split into distinct sections. These sections don't have to flow into each other the way paragraphs do in essays, stories, articles, etc.

A

- Ask students to read the instructions and check that they understand what they have to do.
- Ask students to work in pairs to encourage discussion and encourage them to make lists in their notebooks.
- As a class, discuss the points raised by each pair and make a list on the board of suitable ideas.

Suggested answers

Factual information: opening hours, efficiency of staff, location of cinema, size of auditoriums, acoustics, cleanliness, temperature, ticket prices, snacks available
Films: variety, appropriateness for certain age groups, kind of audience they appeal to, length of films

B

- Ask students to read the instructions and check that they understand what they have to do.
- Ask students to read the writing task and to underline key words and phrases.
- Ask students to answer the questions in pairs to encourage discussion, but check as a class.

Answers

1 the manager
2 at least three (screening times, tickets, food/drinks must all be discussed; add anything else if you want to)
3 to suggest ways in which the management can attract more young people to the cinema

C

- Ask students to read the instructions and check that they understand what they have to do. Elicit which group of people the manager wishes to attract (young people) and what three things they should make notes on (screening times, cost of tickets, food and drink).
- Ask students to do the task individually, but check as a class.
- You might want to put the three headings on the board and note down relevant ideas from each student so that you have comprehensive lists with the points that could be made in a report.

Suggested answers

1 Screening times: more films should be screened at the weekend; during the week, there should be more screenings in the afternoon and not at night
2 Cost of tickets: should be more affordable for students/young people; give student discounts; free drink with every ticket sold
3 Food and drinks: provide a greater variety of snacks that are popular with young people, e.g. hot dogs, nachos; provide tables at snack bar so people can eat before they watch the film

D

- Ask students to look at the example report without reading in detail yet. Ask them to talk about how the writer has laid it out.
- Ask students to read the report to see which, if any, of the points they mentioned in C have been included in the example report.

Answers

Formal report layout is used, starting with To:, From:, Subject:, and continuing with distinct paragraphs with clear headings

E

- Explain to students that they are going to look back at the example report to analyse the language used and its content.
- Ask students to read the questions and explain anything they don't understand.
- Ask students to do the task in pairs to encourage discussion, but check as a class.

Answers

1 The aim of this report is to …, Most people feel that …, Almost everyone agrees that …, Regarding …, the majority of people …, I would therefore recommend that …
Interchangeable: Most people feel that …, Almost everyone agrees that …, Regarding …, the majority of people …,
Not interchangeable: The aim of this report is to …, I would therefore recommend that …
2 Two sentences per paragraph; they are enough – any more than that and the word limit would be exceeded

F

- Ask students to read the instructions and check that they understand what they have to do.
- Give students five minutes to write their paragraphs and go round reading them and giving them any help they might need.
- As a class, ask students to read out their paragraphs.

G

- Ask students to read the information in the *Exam Close-up*. Remind students that they should use the points here when writing their own report.
- Ask students to look at the *Exam Task* and explain they have to make a paragraph plan for their report, following the structure of the plan on the page.
- Monitor to see students are completing the task correctly.
- Ask two or three students to read their paragraph plan to the class.

Useful Expressions

- Read the *Useful Expressions* to the students and ask them to repeat them. Correct their pronunciation where necessary.
- If time allows, ask students to use several of these expressions to write sentences of their own.

H

- Ask students to read the instructions and check that they understand what they have to do.
- Ask students to read the writing task and underline the key words and phrases. Then ask them the questions below.
  - Who will read your report? (your supervisor)
  - How many paragraphs should it include and what should they be about? (three – exhibits on display, entrance fee, souvenir shop)
  - What is the purpose of your report? (to suggest ways the museum could attract more visitors)
- Remind students to use the *Useful Expressions* when writing their reports, for introducing the topic, reporting results and making recommendations.

- Ask students to write their reports at home.
- Encourage students to use the Writing Reference and checklist for reports on page 184.

Suggested answer

To: Carol Flynn
From: Tim Beam
Subject: Report on Maritime Museum

Introduction

This report is intended to suggest ways of attracting a larger number of visitors to the museum. I spoke with recent visitors and these are my findings.

Exhibits on display

The majority of people felt that the museum needed to invest in some new exhibits. It was suggested that examples of state-of-the-art warships would appeal to potential visitors.

Entrance fee

Some people felt that the entrance fee is still too high, despite last year's reduction. In particular, visitors expressed the need for a special-priced family ticket.

Souvenir shop

Almost everyone agreed that the range of souvenirs on sale in the museum shop is rather poor. Customers would like to be able to purchase replicas of exhibits and books relevant to the exhibits.

Conclusion

On the basis of the points mentioned above, I believe the museum should increase its range of exhibits, introduce a family ticket and include a wider range of souvenirs in the shop.

6 Canyaking Adventure

General Note

The National Geographic videos can be used as an interesting way to introduce your students to other cultures. They are authentic National Geographic videos, and it is not necessary for students to understand everything they hear to benefit from them. The videos have the option to play English subtitles so that students can read on screen exactly what is said in the documentary. This feature may help students with some of the tasks in the worksheets. The videos are also a good way to encourage your students to watch TV programmes and films in English so that they can get used to the sound of the language. The more students are exposed to English, the easier it will be for them to pick up the language.

Background Information

Canyaking is a relatively new sport. It is a tough outdoor activity that combines canyoneering (travelling down canyons by a variety of means) and kayaking (paddling across water), and requires the co-operation of all team members.

Before you watch

A

- Explain to students that in this lesson they are going to watch a video about canyaking. Ask them to look at the globe to see where the documentary is set (*Reunion Island, Indian Ocean*) and ask them what they think canyaking might be.
- Ask students to read the instructions and check that they understand what they have to do.
- Read the words 1-4 to the students and ask them to repeat them. Correct their pronunciation where necessary.
- Ask students to read the meanings a-d and explain anything they don't understand.
- Ask students to do the task individually, but check as a class.

Answers

1b 2a 3d 4c

While you watch

B

- Explain to students that they are now going to watch the video. Ask them to read sentences 1-6 and explain anything they don't understand.
- Read the words in red to the students and ask them to repeat them. Correct their pronunciation where necessary.
- Ask them to think about which answers might be correct before watching.
- Ask students to do the task individually, but check as a class.

Answers

1	challenge	(00.25)	4	first-hand	(05.33)
2	lives	(02.08)	5	paid off	(06.56)
3	aware	(03.45)	6	certainly	(07.22)

After you watch

C

- Explain to students that this is a summary of the information they heard on the video.
- Read the words in the yellow box to the students and ask them to repeat them. Correct their pronunciation where necessary. Ask students to write *N*, *V* or *Adj* beside each of the words depending on whether it is a noun, verb or adjective.
- Explain to students that they should read the whole summary before writing any answers first to work out what part of speech is missing.
- Tell students to read back through the text once they have finished to check their answers.
- Ask students to do the task individually, but check the answers as a class.

Answers

1	outdoor	5	hike
2	train	6	highest
3	descent	7	serious
4	vertical	8	introduces

Ideas Focus

- Ask students to read the instructions and make sure they understand what they have to do. Then ask them to read the three questions and answer any questions they might have.
- Ask students to work in pairs and explain that they should both give their opinions on all three questions.
- Go round the class monitoring students to make sure they are carrying out the task properly. Don't correct any mistakes at this stage, but make a note of any problems in structure and pronunciation.
- Ask each pair to answer one of the questions and repeat until each pair has had a turn.
- Write kinds of extreme sports students mention on the board and ask them where they could take part in these sports.

Answers

Students' own answers

Objectives

- To revise vocabulary and grammar from Units 5 and 6
- To practise exam-type tasks

Revision

- Explain to students that Review 3 revises the material they saw in Units 5 and 6.
- Remind students that they can ask you for help with the exercises or look back at the units if they're not sure about an answer, and stress that the review is not a test.
- Decide how you will carry out the review. You could ask students to do one task at a time and then correct it immediately, or ask students to do all the tasks and correct them together at the end. If you do all the tasks together, let students know every now and again how much time they have got left to finish the tasks.
- Ask students not to leave any answers blank and to try to find any answers they aren't sure about in the units.
- When checking students' answers to the review tasks, make a note of any problem areas in vocabulary and grammar that they still have. Try to do extra work on these areas so that your students will progress well.

Vocabulary Revision

- Write these words on the board and ask students what part of speech they are: *appeal (v), cost (v, n), enjoy (v), evaluate (v), exhibit (v, n), invent (v), inform (v), succeed (v)* and *total (v)*. Ask students to write down any other parts of speech of these words that they know. Make sure they revise the parts that they will need to complete Part 3.
- Play a word association game with words from Unit 6. Say one word related to sport and ask each student in turn to say another word which they associate with the previous word, for example, *bowling – alley – pitch – football.*
- Ask students to explain the difference between the following pairs of words and phrases: *beat/win, lose/ miss, spend money/make money, department store/ supermarket.* Tell them to either give a definition or a sentence that shows the meaning of each word or phrase.
- Write the verbs *get, feel, run, show, sit, sleep* and *turn* on the board and elicit the phrasal verbs students learnt in Unit 6 with these verbs. Ask them to write a sentence for each phrasal verb.
- Write the following words on the board and ask students to use them in sentences with the verbs *do, go* or *play: athletics, aerobics, basketball, cricket, running, shopping.*

Grammar Revision

- Write the following on the board and elicit that they are the uses of modal and semi-modal verbs: *ability, inability, permission & requests, advice & suggestions, necessity & obligation, prohibition, lack of necessity or obligation, certainty, possibility, impossibility.* Ask students which modals and semi-modals can be used with each use and ask them to write sentences to demonstrate their use. Encourage students to write some sentences using modals with a present or future meaning and others with modals perfect.
- Write the following on the board.
  - I'm playing in the match tonight, ____? *(aren't I)*
  - Let's go bungee jumping, ____? *(shall we)*
  - You're an inventor, ____? *(aren't you)*
  - They haven't been here before, ____? *(have they)*
  Ask students to complete the question tags and revise the forms.
- Write the following question on the board: *How much is this CD player?*. Then ask students to rewrite the question in various ways beginning:
  - Do ____? *(you know how much this CD player costs)*
  - Could ____? *(you tell me how much this CD player costs)*
  - Would ____? *(you mind telling me how much this CD player costs)*
  - I wonder ____. *(if you know how much this CD player costs)*
  - I'd like ____. *(to know how much this CD player costs)*
  - I would like ____. *(to ask you how much this CD player costs)*
  - I don't suppose ____. *(you know how much this CD player costs)*
- Ask the following questions at random round the class, making sure each student answers at least one question, then revise the forms of negative questions.
  - Didn't you use to play tennis when you were younger?
  - Isn't *Close-Up* an exciting book?
  - Haven't you just arrived?
  - Why aren't you wearing a coat?
  - Hasn't it been very cold/hot/mild lately?
  - Which places haven't you visited in this country?
- Write the sentences below on the board and ask students to complete them using the gerund, bare infinitive or full infinitive form of the verbs in brackets.
  - Clark doesn't enjoy ____ *(play)* cards. *(playing)*
  - Is Marc good enough ____ *(be)* in the national team? *(to be)*
  - It's not worth ____ *(try)* to sell your invention. *(trying)*
  - You didn't remember ____ *(bring)* your kit so you can't play. *(to bring)*
  - I don't feel like ____ *(read)* this article on prosthetics. *(reading)*
  - Let's ask the coach ____ *(help)* us out. *(to help)*

Part 1

- Ask students to read the instructions and check that they understand what they have to do.
- Ask students to read the title of the text and ask them what they think the text will deal with. Then ask them to skim read the text, without circling any answers at this stage, to find out who is aiming for the top and in which profession (*Gary Beville wants to be a top-class footballer.*). Ask students which career they think they will choose and if they personally want to aim for the top in this profession.
- Point out to students that they should read all four options for each item before deciding which word best fits each gap. Remind them to pay attention to the whole sentence each gap is in as the general context will help them understand what word is missing.
- Remind students to read back through the text once they have finished to check their answers.

Answers

1D 2C 3A 4B 5A 6D 7B 8C 9A 10D 11C 12B

Part 2

- Ask students to read the instructions and check that they understand what they have to do.
- Ask students if they like to go shopping and what their favourite stores are.
- Ask students to skim read the text, without filling in any answers at this stage, to find out how shoppers can be encouraged to spend more money (*by having to spend more time in the shop in order to get to the goods that they want, eg if they have to pass other products to get to the ones they want or to get to the changing rooms or escalators to go to another floor*).
- Encourage students to pay particular attention to the words immediately before and after each gap to work out what part of speech is missing. However, remind them that they have to take into consideration the general context of the sentence so that they understand which structure is being used.
- Remind students to read back through the text once they have finished to check their answers.

Answers

13	gone	19	This
14	spends/invests	20	order
15	make	21	stores
16	to	22	have/need
17	them	23	missing
18	like	24	can/could

Part 3

- Ask students to read the instructions and check that they understand what they have to do.
- Ask students to read the title of the text and ask them why it might be hard work being an inventor. Ask them to skim read the text, without filling in any answers at this stage, to find out how many steps there are in the process of inventing and what they are (*There are three steps: getting a patent for your invention, evaluating the product and developing and marketing the product.*).
- Read the words at the side of the text to the students and ask them to repeat them. Correct their pronunciation where necessary.
- Ask students to read back through the text and to decide which part of speech is missing from each gap, and to complete the gaps using the correct form of the words given.
- Remind students to read back through the text once they have finished to check their answers.

Answers

25	enjoyable	30	appealing
26	invention	31	satisfied
27	information	32	costly
28	evaluation	33	exhibitions
29	totally	34	successful

Part 4

- Ask students to read the instructions and check that they understand what they have to do.
- Ask students to read both sentences in each item and to underline the information in the first sentence that is missing from the second sentence. Then ask them to look at the word given to decide how the missing information could be inserted into sentence 2 using this word. Remind students that they will have to use a different structure in order to keep the meaning the same.
- Remind students that they mustn't change the word given in any way.
- Encourage students to read back through the completed sentences once they have finished to check their answers.

Answers

35	you mind telling me when
36	must have been
37	were made to work
38	Didn't you win
39	not tall enough to play
40	not worth spending
41	feel up to working
42	can't have sent

7 Right or Wrong?

Reading:	multiple-choice, dealing with distractors
Vocabulary:	crime-related vocabulary
Grammar:	passive voice: tenses, passive voice: gerunds, infinitives & modal verbs, causative
Listening:	multiple-choice, expressing feelings through words
Speaking:	talking about crime, comparing photographs, answering the second question: student B, linking ideas
Use your English:	phrasal verbs, prepositions, sentence transformation
Writing:	formal letter, analysing the question, thinking about style, greetings, introductory comments, agreeing, disagreeing, explaining your views, clarifying, signing off

Unit opener

- Ask students to look at the title of the unit and ask them what they think it will be about (*justice, law and order, crime*).
- Tell students you are going to give them a minute to write down as many words as they can think of related to these topics. When they have finished writing, make a note of all the words students came up with on the board. Check their spelling and pronunciation and ask students what part of speech each word is.
- Ask students to work in pairs to discuss the picture and its accompanying caption. Encourage them to discuss how this picture may be related to the theme of the unit (*It brings up questions about whether it is right or wrong to protest in public.*).

Reading

A

- Ask students to cover up the instructions and the words in the yellow box. Then ask them to work in pairs to discuss what the pictures show and how they are related to the theme of the unit.
- Ask students to read the instructions and make sure they understand what they have to do.
- Read the words in the yellow box to the students and ask them to repeat them. Correct their pronunciation where necessary.
- Ask students to do the task individually, but check as a class.
- Once the answers have been checked, ask students to discuss the question in pairs or small groups. Then have a class discussion about which punishments fit these crimes. Encourage students to justify their answers.

Answers

1	burglary	5	pickpocketing
2	illegal parking	6	robbery
3	vandalism	7	arson
4	kidnapping	8	computer hacking

B

- Ask students to look at the picture in the top right-hand corner of the page and ask them which aspect of law and order it is linked to (*justice, courts*). Then ask them to look at the title of the text and its accompanying picture and ask them what they think *Teen courts* might be.
- Ask students to read the instructions and make sure they understand what they have to do.
- Remind students that they don't have to read in detail as they will have another opportunity to read the text.
- Ask students to do the task on their own and then to compare their answers with a partner.
- Check the answers as a class.

Answer

misdemeanours – anything from theft to non-violent offences

Word Focus

- Ask students to read the words in red and to re-read the sentences they are found in. Remind students that when they don't know the meaning of a word, they should look carefully at the sentence it is found in to work out its meaning. Ask students to work in pairs to decide what each of the words mean.
- Ask students to read the *Word Focus* box to compare their answers with the definitions given. Explain anything they don't understand.

C

- Ask students to read the information in the *Exam Close-up*.
- Remind students that when they read the options for each question, they should underline key words and ideas and compare these to the information in the text where they think the answer comes from.
- Ask students to read the *Exam Task* and make sure they understand what they have to do.
- Ask students to underline the key words and phrases in the sentence stems and distractors. Encourage them to scan the text for the information that relates to each question, underline it and compare it carefully to each of the options.

- Ask students to bear in mind the kind of distractors common in multiple-choice tasks that they looked at in the *Exam Close-up*.
- Ask students to do the task individually, but check as a class.
- If students seem interested give them further information using the Background Information box below.

D

- Ask students to read the *Exam Task* again and look at the words they have underlined.
- Ask them to read the text again and then complete the *Exam Task*.
- Ask students to do the task individually and compare their answers with a partner. Ask them to justify their answers if there are any differences.
- Check answers as a class.

Answers

1b *(As teen courts …, they have proved to be popular and successful.)*
2b *(Teen courts operate on a voluntary basis. They are open to first-time offenders …)*
3d *(They must be given permission to attend a teen court by their parent or guardian, …)*
4d *(The sentences are designed to make the offender think about the crime and give something back to the community.)*
5b *(The defendants are always sentenced to community service …)*
6b *(… once their sentence has been carried out, offenders are free to walk away with a clean record.)*

Background Information

One of the earliest youth courts began in Naperville, Illinois in June 1972, although there are reports that a youth court operated in Horseheads, NY as early as 1968. Teens who volunteer for youth court have to complete around ten hours' training on average. Over half of the youth courts in operation require defendants to do jury duty as part of their sentence. In addition to community service, defendants may also be given other punishments such as apologising to victims, writing essays on their crimes, attending educational workshops, tutoring and counselling.

E

- Ask students to do the task individually, but check as a class. Point out that the paragraph each word is found in is noted in brackets at the end of each sentence.
- Encourage students to scan the paragraphs to find and underline the words and to check their meaning in the context of the sentence they are found in before completing the questions.
- Ask students to do the task individually, but check as a class.

Answers

1	peer	**4**	misdemeanour
2	fine	**5**	authority
3	sentence	**6**	record

Ideas Focus

- Ask students to read the instructions and make sure they understand what they have to do.
- Read the five words in the yellow box to students and ask them to repeat them. Correct their pronunciation where necessary.
- Ask students to work in pairs to encourage discussion.
- Go round the class monitoring students to make sure they are carrying out the task properly. Don't correct any mistakes at this stage, but make a note of any problems in structure or pronunciation.
- As a class, discuss who each person is and the role they play in court.
- Write any structural mistakes students made on the board without saying who made them, and ask them to correct them. Deal with any problems in pronunciation that came up.

Answers

lawyer: represents people in court and presents their case
judge: listens to evidence given and passes sentence
clerk: keeps a record of what is said in court
defendant: is the person being tried
witness: gives evidence about a crime

Vocabulary

A

- Ask students to read the instructions and make sure they understand what they have to do.
- Read the words in the yellow boxes to the students and ask them to repeat them. Correct their pronunciation where necessary.
- Encourage students to read through the whole sentence to decide which word should come first and to pay attention to the subject of the verb and any time references in order to use the correct form of the verbs.
- Ask students to do the task individually, but check as a class.

Answers

1	broken, taken	**5**	pleaded, taking
2	pay, found	**6**	made, set
3	committing, received	**7**	held, confessed
4	tried, reach	**8**	dismiss, accused

B

- Read the words in red to the students and ask them to repeat them. Correct their pronunciation where necessary.
- Ask students to read through the sentences and to underline the nouns which follow the options. Explain that the correct answers are those that collocate naturally with these nouns.
- Remind students to read through the sentences once they have completed them to check their answers.
- Ask students to do the task individually, but check as a class.

Answers

1	stolen	5	hardened
2	main	6	masked
3	plain	7	armed
4	criminal	8	deadly

C

- Ask students to read the instructions and make sure they understand what they have to do.
- Read the words in capital letters to the students and ask them to repeat them. Correct their pronunciation where necessary.
- Ask students to read the sentences before they complete any answers They should also reread each sentence carefully as they complete them to check they have the correct form of the word to make sense in the sentence.
- Ask students to do the task in pairs to encourage discussion, but check as a class.

Answers

1	criminal	4	offence
2	deadly	5	unbreakable
3	terrorism	6	professional

D

- Ask students to read the instructions and make sure they understand what they have to do.
- Encourage students to read through the prompts to decide which word is the subject of the sentence, which word is the verb, and which is the object of the sentence.
- Complete the first sentence together. Ask students at random to supply the subject, verb and object of the sentence. Check that everyone has written it correctly in their book.
- Ask students to do the rest of the task individually, but check as a class.

Answers

1. I can't believe you were robbed last night.
2. My bike was stolen from outside my house.
3. Are we allowed to park here or is it illegal?
4. He was planning to rob the bank in the high street.
5. The police won't let anyone enter the street.
6. How much money did they steal from the old lady?

Grammar

- Write the sentence below on the board and ask students if we know who did the action.
  - Our house was broken into last night. *(We don't know who it was, but we can assume it was done by a burglar.)*
  Ask a student to come up to the board to underline the verb form in the sentence *(was broken into)* and elicit that the verb is in the passive voice. Elicit that the passive voice has been used here as the action is more important than who did it.
- Ask students to write the sentence in the active voice *(Someone/A burglar broke into our house last night.)* and elicit that the Past Simple tense is used because this action took place at a definite time in the past. Ask students what the object of this sentence is *(our house)* and point out that this became the subject of the passive sentence. Remind students that only verbs that have objects can be used in the passive voice.
- Elicit that in order to form the passive voice we put the auxiliary verb *be* in the same tense as the main verb in the active sentence and in the same person as the object of the active sentence, then put the main verb into the past participle.
- Write the two sentences below on the board and ask students who or what did the action.
  - He was punched by a football hooligan. *(a football hooligan)*
  - She was hit with a baseball bat. *(a baseball bat)*
- Ask students what is different in these two sentences *(the prepositions that introduce who or what did the action – by is used for a person, with is used for a thing).*

A

- Ask students to read the sentences 1-5 and to underline the passive verbs. Elicit which tenses have been used in each *(1 – Present Continuous, 2 – Past Simple, 3 – Present Perfect Simple, 4 – Past Simple, 5 – modal + passive infinitive).*
- Then ask students to underline the actions being completed.
- Ask students to do the task individually and compare their answers with a partner. Check answers as a class.

Answers

1. demolished
2. filmed
3. arrested
4. destroyed
5. sprayed

B

- Read through the rules with the students, without circling any answers at this stage, and explain anything they don't understand. Explain to students that they should refer back to sentences 1-5 when choosing their answers and try to work out why the passive has been used in each one.
- Ask students to do the task in pairs to encourage discussion, but check as a class.

- Once the answers have been checked, ask students to write the sentences 1-5 from A in the active voice.

Answers

don't know
more
unclear
by
with

C

- Ask students to read the sentences 1-3 and to underline the passive structures. Ask them what they notice about them (*They are in the full or bare infinitive or gerund.*).
- Ask students to circle the verb form or structure that comes before the passive (*objected, is … going, must*) and explain that these are three types of verbs that require either a gerund or infinitive.

Answers

1 being told
2 is … going to be tried
3 must be obeyed

D

- Read the rules to the students, without filling in any answers at this stage, and explain anything they don't understand.
- Encourage students to look back at sentences 1-3 in C when choosing their answers.
- Ask students to do the task in pairs to encourage discussion, but check as a class.
- Once the answers have been checked, ask students to look back at the Reading text to underline any examples of the passive voice they can find (*Paragraph 1 – was born, was needed, has been repeated, Paragraph 2 – should be made, are judged and sentenced, being tried, being given, Paragraph 3 – are referred, must be given, is heard, been carefully trained, Paragraph 4 – are always sentenced, be given, may be ordered, are thought, are designed, Paragraph 5 – has been carried out, is reported*).

Answers

being
be
be

Now read the Grammar Reference on pages 169 & 170 (7.1 & 7.2) with your students.

E

- Ask students to read the instructions and check that they understand what they have to do.
- Ask students to read the two sentences in item 1 and ask them to underline the information in the first sentence that is missing from the second sentence. Ask them what structural change has taken place in the second sentence (*The object of the first sentence has become the subject of the second sentence.*) and what this tells us (*The passive voice is needed.*). Then ask them how the missing information could be expressed using the word given. Remind them that they mustn't change the word given in any way. Check the answer to item 1 before moving on to the rest of the task.
- Ask students to do the task individually, but check as a class.

Answers

1 should be installed
2 is he supposed to be
3 were questioned by
4 was hit with
5 It is believed (that)

F

- Ask students to read the instructions and check that they understand what they have to do.
- Ask students to read the text, without filling in any answers at this stage, and ask them to underline the subjects of the missing verbs and to think about what tense each verb should be in.
- Ask a student to tell you in his or her own words what the text is about.
- Remind students that they should read back through the text once they have completed it to check their answers.
- Ask students to do the task individually, but check as a class.

Answers

1 was being flown
2 was hijacked
3 was given
4 to be taken
5 is still being investigated
6 has never been discovered
7 is believed
8 could be flown
9 was uncovered
10 were found

Listening

A

- Ask students to read the instructions and check that they understand what they have to do. Explain that they will hear seven sentences by different people and that they should pay attention to how they speak as well as to what they say.
- Read the words in the yellow box to students and ask them to repeat them. Correct their pronunciation where necessary. Explain anything they don't understand.

- Play the recording, stopping after the first speaker and ask students as a class to decide how the person sounds. Ask students to justify their answers.
- Play the rest of the recording all the way through and ask students to write down their answers. Ask them to compare their answers with a partner and to justify any answers that are different.
- If necessary, play the recording again. Check as a class.

Answers

1 angry	5 anxious
2 indifferent	6 exhausted
3 sympathetic	7 disgusted
4 ecstatic	

B

Ask students to read the instructions and check that they understand what they have to do. Explain that they should only write a few words or a phrase.

Play the recording again, stopping after each speaker to give students plenty of time to write their answers. Ask students to compare their answers with a partner and to justify any different answers.

Check the answers as a class and ask students what else helped them decide how the people feel.

Answers

1 It's an absolute outrage
2 I couldn't care less
3 My heart goes out to
4 Guess what!
5 Oh my goodness … I hope Jenny isn't in trouble
6 Oh no, not another case!
7 Yuck! … absolutely filthy.

The speakers' tone of voice also helps.

C

- Ask students to read the information in the *Exam Close-up* and ask a student to tell you what it says in his or her own words.
- Point out to students that sometimes in multiple-choice questions they are asked to say how someone feels and are given a choice of adjectives as options. Explain that all three will be linked to the conversation in some way. For instance, the speaker may talk about someone else who or another situation where they were in a particular mood and use one or two of the specific adjectives in the options. However, they must answer the focus of the question and not be distracted by such options.
- Ask students to scan the *Exam Task* and ask them which item focuses on the speaker's feelings *(4)*. Ask them which feelings appear in the options and how they would expect someone to sound if they felt in these ways.
- Ask students to read the instructions again in the *Exam Task* and check that they understand what they have to do.
- Ask students to read the situations, questions and options and to underline the key words and phrases. Explain anything that they don't understand.

- Play the recording all the way through without stopping and ask students to mark their answers. Ask students to compare their answers with a partner and to justify any different answers.

D

- Play the recording again and ask students to check their answers and to complete any missing answers.
- Check as a class and ask students to justify their answers.

Answers

1b 2b 3b 4a 5c 6b 7c

Speaking

A

- Ask students to read the two questions and answer any queries they may have about them.
- Ask students to work in pairs to take turns to ask and answer the questions about themselves.
- Go round the class monitoring students to make sure they are carrying out the task properly. Don't correct any mistakes at this stage, but make a note of any problems in structure and pronunciation.
- Ask each pair to ask and answer one of the questions and repeat until each student has had a turn.
- Write any structural mistakes that students made on the board without saying who made them, and ask them to correct them. Deal with any problems in pronunciation that came up.

B

- Ask students to read the instructions and check that they understand what they have to do.
- Ask students to look at the pictures in the *Exam Task* and read the main question below each one. Explain anything they don't understand.
- Ask different students to tell you what the two crimes and the two jobs are. Invite students to say if these crimes are common in their country and tell you what they know about the two jobs.

C

- Ask students to read the instructions and check that they understand what they have to do.
- Ask student to read the sentences 1-5, paying attention to the underlined parts of them.
- Ask students to work individually to correct the mistakes. Remind them to read back through the sentences once they have finished to check their answers.
- Check as a class.

Answers

1 vandalism is quite common, broken
2 would, stressful
4 much, that

D

- Ask students to read the instructions and check that they understand what they have to do.
- Ask them to look at the two short answers 3 and 5 in C. Ask students for suggestions as to how they could be made longer to give more information. Give an example, eg *A police officer, yes, definitely, because I think I'd be helping people who are victims of crime and also to prevent crime.*
- Ask students to tell you their ideas and write their suggestions on the board. Point out that they should give longer responses like those in items 1, 2 and 4 in C when they are talking about the pictures and answering the question.

Useful Expressions

- Read the *Useful Expressions* to the students and ask them to repeat them. Correct their pronunciation and intonation where necessary.
- Ask students which expressions they should use to add information (*but, although, so, because, and*), which they should use to explain the reason for something (*For this reason ... This is why ...*), and which they should use to introduce examples (*For example ...*).
- Point out to students that they should use some of these expressions when they do the *Exam Task*.

E

- Ask students to read the information in the *Exam Close-up* about answering the second question (Student B).
- Ask students to read the instructions in E again and check that they understand what they have to do.
- Ask students to work in pairs and to decide who will be Student A and who will be Student B. Ask them to read the instructions for their role and to spend a few minutes looking at their own set of photos.
- Remind students that this kind of task isn't a discussion and that each student is expected to speak for about a minute on his or her photos and then respond briefly to the question about his or her partner's photos. Remind students to use the *Useful Expressions* to help them.
- Ask Student A to begin discussing photos in Task 1 and for Student B to answer their question once Student A has finished. Then ask them to reverse the process so that Student B talks about photos in Task 2 and Student A answers their question.
- Go round the class monitoring students to make sure they are carrying out the task properly. Don't correct any mistakes at this stage, but make a note of any problems in structure and pronunciation.
- Ask one pair of students to carry out the task in front of the class and ask the other students if they have anything to add.
- Write any structural mistakes that students made on the board without saying who made them, and ask them to correct them. Deal with any problems in pronunciation that came up.

Ideas Focus

- Ask students to read the questions quickly and deal with any queries they may have.
- Ask students to work in pairs and take turns to answer the questions.

- Go round the class monitoring students to make sure they are carrying out the task properly. Don't correct any mistakes at this stage, but make a note of any problems in structure and pronunciation.
- Ask a student from each pair to answer one of the questions until each pair has had a turn. Ask other students if they agree or if they have something else to add.
- Write any structural mistakes that students made on the board without saying who made them, and ask them to correct them. Deal with any problems in pronunciation that came up.

Answer

Students' own answers

Grammar

- Write the sentences below on the board and ask students to copy them into their notebooks and underline the verb forms. Then ask them what they notice about them (*They are in the causative form.*).
  - We've never had anything stolen.
  - They had their windows smashed last night.
  - Jan is having a security system put in next week.
- Elicit that the causative form is formed with *have* in the correct tense, followed by an object and the main verb in the past participle.

A

- Ask students to read the instructions and check that they understand what they have to do.
- Ask students to read the sentences 1-5 and to underline the causative forms they contain.
- Elicit which tenses have been used in each case and what this tells us about the time of the action.
- Ask students to do the task individually, but check as a class.

Answers

1 had a new burglar alarm installed
2 will have the man followed
3 is getting her locks changed
4 had their car stolen
5 had everyone vacate

B

- Read the rules to the students, without filling in any answers at this stage, and explain anything they don't understand.
- Ask students to do the task in pairs to encourage discussion, but check as a class.

Answers

have
by

Be careful!

- Write the sentence below on the board and ask students if it is in the causative form (yes) and ask them to explain how it is different from sentences 1-5 (It uses get instead of have and the full infinitive instead of the past participle.).
  - She got the police to investigate the disappearance of her cat.
- Ask students to read the information in *Be careful!* and explain anything they don't understand. Point out that we use *get* in the causative when we refer to an action that we asked someone to do for us.
- Ask students to rewrite the sentence on the board and the sentence in their books using *have* and discuss the change in structure (*She had the police investigate the disappearance of her cat. I had a technician install the alarm for me.*).

Now read the Grammar Reference on page 170 (7.3) with your students.

C

- Ask students to read the instructions and check that they understand what they have to do.
- Remind students to read through the whole sentence before circling their answer. Tell them to pay attention to where *have* and *get* are used and to the structures that follow them as well as to the time reference in the sentences.
- Encourage students to read back through the sentences once they have finished to check their answers.

Answers

1 had a tattoo done	5 have had
2 stolen	6 had him
3 had him killed	7 got
4 have	8 knocked

D

- Ask students to read the instructions and check that they understand what they have to do.
- Ask students to read the first sentence and elicit that it is in the passive voice. Remind students that as they have to turn it into the causative, they will have to use either *have* or *get* plus the appropriate structure as well as the word given. Ask students to write the new sentence and check their answers before moving on to the rest of the task.
- Ask students to do the task individually, but check as a class.

Answers

1 They are having the prisoners transferred today.
2 We have had our broken windows replaced.
3 We had our house burgled last night.
4 I am going to have my case investigated by the police./I am going to get the police to investigate my case.
5 Terry had his nose broken in a fight.
6 She will get an experienced lawyer to defend her in court.
7 Jim's manager is going to have Jim's criminal record checked.
8 The police had had information about the criminal sent to them.

Use your English

A

- Read the phrasal verbs 1-6 to students and ask them to repeat them. Correct their pronunciation where necessary. Elicit that they are all crime-related.
- Ask students to read the definitions a-f and explain anything they don't understand.
- Point out to students that they should write the correct letters a-f in the boxes provided.
- Ask students to do the task individually, but check as a class.
- Give students time to copy the phrasal verbs in A and their definitions into their notebooks and ask them to write a sentence for each phrasal verb. Either ask them to leave a gap for the phrasal verb and swap books with a partner to complete each other's sentences, or students write complete sentences and read them to the class.

Answers

1d 2e 3b 4f 5a 6c

B

- Elicit that the words in red are all prepositions and explain that they will either be part of prepositional phrases or follow certain verbs.
- Ask students to read the sentences, without circling any answers at this stage, to underline the phrases or verbs that determine what the correct answers should be.
- Remind students to read back through the sentences once they have finished to check their answers.
- Ask students to do the task individually, but check as a class.

Answers

1 against	5 from
2 of	6 of
3 under	7 from
4 in	8 to

C

- Ask students to read the instructions and check that they understand what they have to do.
- Explain that they mustn't change the word in bold in any way in the second sentence.
- Ask students to read the two sentences in item 1. Then ask them to underline the part in the first sentence that is missing from the second sentence. Explain to students that in order to complete the second sentence they will have to make a structural change. Remind them to also count the number of words they have written. They should have between two and five words.
- Ask students to complete the first item and correct it before they move on to the rest of the task.
- Ask students to do the task individually, but check as a class.

Answers

1 can't have been eaten	4 behind bars
2 can't stand being lied	5 put me off
	6 put you away
3 to do away with	7 in exchange for
	8 seen to

Writing: a formal letter

- As the students to read the information on writing formal letters in the *Learning Focus* and explain anything they don't understand.
- Elicit that by asking questions about the task they are helping themselves to think more carefully about the topic, as well as the style of writing they should use and the tone they need to use.

A

- Ask students to read the instructions and check that they understand what they have to do. Explain that this task requires them to answer questions about the task.
- Give students time to read the task and questions 1-10. Explain anything they don't understand. Ask students to read each question again carefully and look back at the text to answer them.
- Ask students to complete the task individually and then compare their answers with a partner. Check answers as a class.
- After checking the answers, ask students to tell you their opinion about the crimes and the punishments. Ask students why there might have been this increase and how severely they would punish these teenagers.

Answers

Analysing the stimulus

1 Teenage shoplifting and vandalism has increased over the past few months.
2 They are considering giving tougher punishments to these teenagers.
3 Sentenced to time in a young offenders's institution

Analysing the prompt

4 a letter
5 to give your opinion
6 readers of a newspaper
7 formal
8 Your opinion on different types of punishment and which would be most effective and most suitable for young people.

Forming your view

9 Students' own answers
10 Students' own answers

B

- Ask students to read the example letter and explain anything they don't understand.
- Ask students to look at the task and ask them how many parts there are to it (two) and elicit that the first is to say what the writer's opinion is and the second to say if it agrees or differs from their own opinion.
- Ask students to read the example letter carefully and to underline key words and phrases. Then ask them to answer the questions.
- Ask students to do the task in pairs to encourage discussion, but check as a class.

C

- Explain to students that in this task they are going to look back at the example letter in B and analyse it.
- Ask students to read questions 1-3 and answer any queries they may have about them.
- Ask students to do the task individually, but check as a class.

Answers

1 four
bringing together all of the ideas - 4
examining other forms of punishment and choosing one - 3
expressing an opinion on the proposal - 1
explaining why the usual punishment doesn't work - 2
2 b
3 formal phrases: Dear Mr Jones, Dear Madam, Best Regards, Respectfully

D

- Ask students to read the instructions and check that they understand what they have to do.
- Ask the class their opinion on the two questions in the rubric. Allow time for students to give their opinion and then ask them to read the five statements about the example letter carefully.
- Students answer individually, but check as a class and ask students to justify their answers.

Answers

Students should tick: 1, 3, 4 and 5

Useful Expressions

- Ask students to read the *Useful Expressions* and explain anything they don't understand.
- Ask students to practise using these expressions by writing sentences of their own with them.
- Point out that they can use some of these words and phrases in their own letter.

E

- Ask students to read the instructions and the *Useful Expressions* again, and explain anything they don't understand.
- They should then read through the text and complete the gaps using the *Useful Expressions* to help them.
- When they have completed the gaps, ask them to read the text again to see that what they have written makes sense.
- Ask students to complete the task individually, but check as a class.

Suggested Answers

1 agree with
2 therefore
3 other
4 strongly

F

- Ask students to read the information in the *Exam Close-up* and remind students that the writer of the example has done all these things and this is what makes the letter successful.
- Point out to students that they should use the points here as a checklist when they come to write their own letter.
- Ask students to read the instructions and ask them what three things they should refer to when writing their letter *(analysing the question, use a formal register and the Useful Expressions)*.
- Have students ask themselves questions like the ones in A. For example:
  About the stimulus
  - Why are Rivertown residents concerned? *(rising crime rate)*
  - What has happened as a result of rising crime? *(Police have asked locals to protect their homes and possessions.)*
  - What can residents do to protect their neighbourhoods? *(Students' own answers)*
  The questions in A for *Analysing the stimulus, Analysing the prompt and Forming your view* can apply to this task.
- Ask students to note down specific ideas that they will write about in their letters.
- Ask students to write their letters at home.
- Explain to students that they should use the Writing Reference and checklist for formal letters on page 179.

Suggested answer

Dear Editor,
I am a resident of Rivertown and I read your article about the increase in crime rate in our town and how residents can protect themselves. I believe that this is not only the responsibility of local residents, but also of the police force. Only if both work together, can crime be reduced.
I fully agree that crime must be reduced, however the police have an important role to play. To my mind, there should be more police patrols in our neighbourhoods and police should investigate anything suspicious they see. That way, potential criminals will be deterred from committing crimes. Residents also have their part to play. Valuable objects should be kept out of sight. Also, burglar alarms should be installed by all residents to protect their property.
In short, I believe that joint action is needed to reduce crime. In other words, both the police and local residents must act in order to deter criminals.
Yours faithfully,

7 Capoeira: The Fighting Dance

General Note

The National Geographic videos can be used as an interesting way to introduce your students to other cultures. They are authentic National Geographic videos, and it is not necessary for students to understand everything they hear to benefit from them. The videos have the option to play English subtitles so that students can read on screen exactly what is said in the documentary. This feature may help students with some of the tasks in the worksheets. The videos are also a good way to encourage your students to watch TV programmes and films in English so that they can get used to the sound of the language. The more students are exposed to English, the easier it will be for them to pick up the language.

Background Information

Capoeira originates from African slaves in Brazil. In recent years, it has become popular worldwide as a means of personal expression through a combination of dance and martial arts. Capoeira takes place in a circle and participants take turns to play instruments, sing and divide into pairs to dance with each other. The dances are an impressive mix of acrobatics, dance moves and martial arts punches and kicks. It takes a great deal of technique and strategy to perform capoeira. The circle represents the fights for freedom, dignity and peace that are played out in the circle of life.

Before you watch

A

- Explain to students that in this lesson they are going to watch a video about capoeira. Ask them to look at the globe and to tell you which part of the world it comes from (*Brazil*) and ask them what they know about it.
- Read the words 1-4 to the students and ask them to repeat them. Correct their pronunciation where necessary.
- Ask students to read the meanings a-d and explain anything they don't understand.
- Ask students to do the task individually, but check as a class.

Answers

1d 2a 3b 4c

While you watch

B

- Explain to students that they are now going to watch the video and do a task based on the information they hear.
- Ask students to read the statements 1-6 and ask them if the documentary will only focus on capoeira today (*No – it will talk about its history.*).
- Explain anything in the statements that the students don't understand. Then ask them to think about which ones may be true and which ones may be false before watching.

- Play the video all the way through without stopping and ask students to mark their answers. Ask students to compare their answers with a partner's and to justify any answers that are different. Play the video again so that they can check their answers.
- Ask students to do the task individually, but check as a class.

Answers

1T	(00.12)
2F (*The organisation uses capoeira to help street kids and others at risk.*)	(00.42)
3T	(01.55)
4T	(02.20)
5F (*After slavery was abolished in 1888, capoeira became popular for both amusement and sport.*)	(03.10)
6T	(03.36 and 03.56)

After you watch

C

- Explain to students that this is a summary of the information they heard on the video.
- Read the words in the yellow box to the students and ask them to repeat them. Correct their pronunciation where necessary. Ask students to write *N, V* or *Adj* beside each of the words depending on whether it is a noun, verb or adjective.
- Explain to students that they should read the whole summary before writing any answers first to work out what part of speech is missing.
- Tell students to read back through the text once they have finished to check their answers.
- Ask students to do the task individually, but check the answers as a class.

Answers

1	combination	5	respect
2	social	6	move
3	operates	7	education
4	body	8	owners

Ideas Focus

- Ask students to work in pairs and explain that they should both give their opinions on both questions.
- Go round the class monitoring students to make sure they are carrying out the task properly. Don't correct any mistakes at this stage, but make a note of any problems in structure and pronunciation.
- As a class, ask students to discuss their answers to the questions and encourage other students to add to the ideas raised by fellow students.
- Write the ideas that students came up with for helping street children in their country and ask them to comment on how effective they think each idea would be.

Answer

Students' own answers

Reading:	missing sentences, identifying linking words in a text
Vocabulary:	environment-related vocabulary
Grammar:	conditionals: zero, first, second & third, mixed conditionals, conditionals without *if*
Listening:	multiple matching, identifying the functions of speech
Speaking:	talking about the environment, environmental issues, decision making, reaching a decision, persuading & convincing
Use your English:	phrasal verbs, prepositions, gapped text
Writing:	essay(2), avoiding common mistakes, checking your work, comparing & contrasting, becoming more specific

Unit opener

- Ask students to read the title of the unit and ask them what they expect the unit to deal with.
- Ask them to look at the picture and the accompanying caption and ask them how this might be linked to the theme of the unit (*It shows wind turbines in the Mojave Desert. Wind turbines convert kinetic energy from the wind into electrical power. They are used in many countries as part of their strategy to reduce their reliance on fossil fuels.*).

Reading

A

- Ask students to look at the picture in the top right-hand corner and to describe what they see. Ask them which element is responsible for this natural phenomenon and what the result of it might be (*wind, destruction of anything in its path*). Elicit that this picture shows the negative effects of wind and explain that in this lesson they will learn about both the negative and positive effects of wind.
- Ask students to read the instructions and check that they understand what they have to do.
- Ask students to read the questions quickly and explain anything they don't understand. Then ask them to do the quiz and to compare their answers with a partner. Ask them to justify any answers that are different.
- As a class, discuss students' answers to the questions without providing the correct answers at this stage.

B

- Ask students to read the instructions and check that they understand what they have to do.
- Ask students to skim read the text to find relevant information. Explain that they don't have to read in detail now as they will have another opportunity to read the text later on. Encourage students to underline the information that relates to the four questions as they read.
- Ask separate students to answer each of the questions and to justify their answers with information from the text.
- Once you have discussed the answers, ask students which fact about wind surprised them the most.

Answers

1a 2a 3a 4b

Word Focus

- Ask students to look at the words in red in the text and to re-read the sentences they are found in. Remind students that when they don't know the meaning of a word, they should look carefully at the sentence it is found in to work out its meaning. Ask students to work in pairs to decide what each of the words mean.
- Ask students to read the *Word Focus* box to compare their answers with the definitions given.

C

- Ask students to read the information in the *Exam Close-up* and ask a student to tell you what it says in his or her own words.
- Point out to students that it's a good idea to underline the verbs in the sentences before and after the gap and in the missing sentence to check that the sequence of tenses is logical.
- Then ask students to look at the two pictures that accompany the text and ask them what they have in common and how they are different (*They are both connected to wind and can cause extreme damage on land, but the hurricane has much stronger winds.*).
- Ask students to read the instructions and check that they understand what they have to do.
- Ask students to read through the seven sentences A-G and explain anything they don't understand. Remind students to underline the verbs and make a note of which tenses they are in. They should also pay attention to subjects, pronouns and linking words that will help them to place the sentences in the right gaps. Remind students that the sentences should link both with the sentence before the gap and with the sentence after each gap.

D

- Ask students to read the article again to decide where each sentence goes. Tell them to pay attention to the words before and after each gap.
- When they have finished, tell them to read back through the text to make sure the sentences make sense and to check the sentence they haven't used doesn't fit in anywhere.

- Ask students to do the task individually, but check as a class.

Answers

1G 2D 3F 4A 5B 6C

E

- Ask students to read the instructions and check that they understand what they have to do.
- Read the words in the yellow box to the students and ask them to repeat them. Correct their pronunciation where necessary.
- Ask students to scan the text again to find the words. Remind them that they should always try to work out the meaning of a word from its context and ask them to read the sentences each word is in.
- Ask students to do the task individually, but check as a class.

Answers

1 tornado
2 surface
3 breeze
4 clouds
5 thunderstorm
6 sails
7 coast
8 landscape

Ideas Focus

- Ask students to read the questions quickly and deal with any queries they may have.
- Ask students to work in pairs and take turns to answer the questions.
- Go round the class monitoring students to make sure they are carrying out the task properly. Don't correct any mistakes at this stage, but make a note of any problems in structure and pronunciation.
- Ask a student from each pair to answer one of the questions until each pair has had a turn. Ask other students if they agree or if they have something else to add.
- Write any structural mistakes that students made on the board without saying who made them, and ask them to correct them. Deal with any problems in pronunciation that came up.

Answers

Students' own answers

Vocabulary

A

- Ask students to read the instructions and check that they understand what they have to do.
- Read the words in the yellow box to the students and ask them to repeat them. Correct their pronunciation where necessary. Ask students which words are nouns (*ecosystem, evaporation, moisture, rainfall*) and which are adjectives (*coastal, torrential*).

- Ask students to do the task individually, but check as a class. Remind students to read each sentence again to make sure the word they have chosen makes sense in the sentence.

Answers

1 coastal
2 torrential
3 ecosystem
4 evaporation
5 rainfall
6 moisture

B

- Ask students to read the instructions and check that they understand what they have to do.
- Read the words in the yellow box to the students and ask them to repeat them. Correct their pronunciation where necessary. Explain that these are the topic names for the paragraphs and ask them what they would expect to read about in paragraphs with these titles.
- Ask students to read the four paragraphs, without circling any words at this stage, to decide which title goes with each one. Ask students if the paragraphs contain information that they expected to find.
- Read the words in red to the students and ask them to repeat them. Correct their pronunciation where necessary.
- Remind students to read back through the paragraphs once they have finished to check their answers.
- Ask students to do the task individually, but check as a class.

Answers

1 Climate change: droughts, levels, forces
2 Global warming: emission, atmosphere, gases
3 Fossil fuels: natural, renewable, consumed
4 Natural resources: crude, solar, deforestation

Extra Class Activity

You could extend this task by asking students to choose an environmental topic that interests them, for instance recycling, renewable energy, organic agriculture, etc, and ask them to write a similar paragraph to those in B about their topic. Encourage them to use vocabulary relevant to the topic.

C

- Read the words in the yellow box to the students and ask them to repeat them. Correct their pronunciation where necessary.
- Ask students which words are linked to water in some way (*bank, current, delta, downpour*) and which is related to wind (*gust*).
- Ask students to read through all the sentences for meaning before they fill in any answers.
- Remind students to read back through the sentences once they have finished to check their answers.
- Ask students to do the task individually, but check as a class.

Answers

1	habitat	5	delta
2	downpour	6	gust
3	bank	7	flames
4	current	8	Agriculture

Grammar

- Write the sentences below on the board and ask students what kind of structures they are.
  - If we had cleaned up the beach, the birds wouldn't have died. *(Third Conditional)*
  - If they had a car, they wouldn't be so environmentally-friendly. *(Second Conditional)*
  - If it doesn't rain for months, the crops die. *(Zero Conditional)*
  - If the winds reach gale force, we'll have to stay indoors. *(First Conditional)*
- Elicit the verb tenses used in the *if* clauses and in the result clause of each conditional *(Zero: Present Simple, Present Simple; First: Present Simple, Future Simple; Second: Past Simple, would + bare infinitive; Third: Past Perfect Simple, would + have + past participle)*. Point out that conditionals can be formed with modal verbs instead of *will* or *would*.
- Explain that students are going to revise the use and forms of these conditionals in this lesson.

A

- Ask students to read the instructions and check that they understand what they have to do.
- As a class, ask different students to read out one of the sentences 1-4 and to say which verb forms are used in the *if* clause and in the result clause in each one.

Answers

1. Past Simple, *would* + bare infinitive
2. Present Simple, Present Simple
3. Past Perfect Simple, *would* + *have* + past participle
4. Present Simple, Future Simple

B

- Read the items a-d to the students and elicit that the questions focus on the use of each of the conditionals. Point out that they should write the correct sentence numbers (1-4) from A in the boxes provided.
- Ask students to do the task in pairs to encourage discussion, but check as a class.

- Once the answers have been checked, ask students to look back at the Reading text and the missing sentences on pages 96-97 to find conditional sentences. Ask them which conditional each one is *(Paragraph 1 – If you have ever tried windsurfing, you will know … – First; … you wouldn't get it airborne if it wasn't windy enough – Second; Paragraph 2 – When the sun warms land or water … it also becomes warmer – Zero; Paragraph 4 – If wind is harnessed using wind turbines, it can generate electricity – First; If more wind farms are built, more electricity will be generated – First; Paragraph 5 – If wind above the ground moves … the air in between creates a spinning tube – Zero; If the air rising inside a thunderstorm moves this tube upright, then a tornado is formed – Zero; Paragraph 6 – If tornadoes are frightening, hurricanes are even worse – Zero; If winds reach 119 kilometres per hour, the storm is known as a hurricane – Zero; If hurricanes hit land, they often do extreme damage – Zero; Sentence B – They form over tropical oceans when warm moist air rises … – Zero; Sentence G – If you wanted to go sailing, you wouldn't get far without a good breeze – Second)*.
- Ask students which sentences are slightly different from the ones they looked at in A *(When the sun warms land … and They form over tropical oceans when warm moist air rises …)*. Elicit that *when* has been used in these sentences instead of *if* and that they are still conditional sentences. Explain that the writer could have used *if* here without changing the meaning of the sentences.

Answers

a2 b4 c1 d3

Now read the Grammar Reference on pages 170 & 171 *(8.1 to 8.4)* with your students.

C

- Ask students to read the first sentence and underline the verb form in the result clause. Elicit which conditional we use this form with *(wouldn't + have + past participle, Third)*. Elicit what form we use in the *if* clause in Third Conditional sentences *(Past Perfect)* and ask them to circle the correct option in red. Explain that they should use the same process to work out the answers to items 2-8.
- Remind students to read back through the sentences to check their answers once they have finished.
- Ask students to do the task individually, but check as a class.

Answers

1	hadn't adapted	5	freezes
2	buy	6	lived
3	increases	7	had stayed
4	could lead	8	will improve

D

- Ask students to read the instructions and check that they understand what they have to do.
- Ask students to read the first sentence and elicit that the verbs are missing from both the *if* clause and the result clause. Ask students if the question at the beginning asks about something in the present, past or future *(past)* and elicit that it expresses regret about a past action. Ask the students what this tells us about the sentence that follows *(It will talk about a hypothetical situation in the past, so it needs a Third Conditional.)*. Ask students to fill in the answer and check it before moving on.
- Explain that they should analyse sentences 2-6 in this way to help them decide which verb forms should be used in each gap.
- Ask students to do the task individually, but check as a class.

Answers

1. would/could have helped, had booked into
2. would buy, had
3. recycle, can/will save
4. comes, causes
5. would/could go out, wasn't/weren't
6. will happen, run out

E

- Ask students to read the instructions and check that they understand what they have to do.
- Ask students to read the first sentence and ask them if it is a conditional sentence *(no)*. Ask them the following questions: *Did we see the sign? – No, Did we enter the restricted area? – Yes*. Elicit that both verb forms are Past Simple so this tells us that we are dealing with a past situation.
- Ask students to look at the beginning of the new sentence and elicit that it will talk about the situation in the first sentence in a hypothetical way so we need the Third Conditional. Ask students to fill in the answer before moving on to the rest of the task.
- Ask students to do the task individually, but check as a class.

Answers

1. have entered the restricted area if we had seen the sign
2. lend me your car, I will/can return it on Tuesday
3. become a billionaire if he invented a new form of fuel
4. Sam eats shellfish, he gets a nasty rash
5. I would do more to reduce traffic in the city centre

Listening

A

- Ask students to read the instructions and check that they understand what they have to do.
- Read the words in the yellow box to the students and ask them to repeat them. Correct their pronunciation if necessary. Elicit that they are all reasons why we say or write something and explain that in some listening tasks they have to recognise why the speaker says something.
- Ask students to work in pairs and take it in turns to read each of the statements 1-5. Encourage them to use the intonation the actual speaker might have used. Then together they should decide which two functions go with each statement. If necessary, do item 1 as a class before moving on to the rest of the task.
- Check as a class.

Answers

1. admitting, promising
2. complaining, suggesting
3. enquiring, seeking permission
4. informing, guessing
5. predicting, warning

Teaching Tip

In order to do more practice on these functions, you could ask students to choose two functions and write a statement on an environmental topic including the functions they choose. Then ask them to read their statements to the rest of the class and ask the other students to decide which functions appear in each statement.

B

- Ask students to read the information in the *Exam Close-up* and ask a student to tell you what it says in his or her own words. Point out to students that in this kind of listening task they should be listening out for the whole meaning rather than focusing on specific detail and individual words.
- Explain to students that they are now going to listen to five statements and have to decide what the function of each one is.
- Ask students to read the five sets of functions and discuss the kinds of structures and phrases that people may use to convey them.
- Play the recording stopping after the first statement and ask students to circle the function they think fits best. Check their answer before moving on to the rest of the task and make sure students realise that although the words *discourage* and *suggesting* are heard on the recording, they talk about the organisation the speaker wants to inform listeners about.
- Play the rest of the recording all the way through and ask students to circle their answers. Ask students to compare their answers with a partner and to justify any answers that are different.
- If necessary, play the recording again and ask students to check their answers or circle any missing answers.
- Check as a class and ask students to justify their answers.

Answers

1	informing	4	discouraging
2	prohibiting	5	admitting
3	predicting		

C

- Ask students to read the instructions and check that they understand what they have to do.
- Ask students to read the functions A-H and ask them how these functions are different to the ones they saw in A and B *(They refer to specific situations.)*. Explain to students that as they listen, they will have to pay attention to the function and the general situation in order to choose the correct answers.
- Point out to students that they should write the correct letter A-H in the boxes to the right of each speaker number and that there are three statements that they won't use.
- Ask students what kind of structures or phrases they might hear for each of the functions A-H.
- Play the recording once all the way through and ask students to mark their answers. Then ask students to compare their answers with a partner and to justify any that are different.

D

- Play the recording again and ask students to check their answers and to complete any answers they haven't already completed.
- Check the answers as a class and ask students to justify their answers.

Answers

Speaker 1:	F	Speaker 4:	C
Speaker 2:	D	Speaker 5:	B
Speaker 3:	A		

Speaking

A

- Ask students to read the three questions and answer any queries they may have about them.
- Ask students to work in pairs and take turns to ask and answer the questions about themselves.
- Go round the class monitoring students to make sure they are carrying out the task properly. Don't correct any mistakes at this stage, but make a note of any problems in structure and pronunciation.
- Ask each pair to ask and answer one of the questions and repeat until each student has had a turn.
- Write any structural mistakes that students made on the board without saying who made them, and ask them to correct them. Deal with any problems in pronunciation that came up.

B

- Ask students to read the instructions and check that they understand what they have to do.
- Ask students to look at the picture at the bottom of page 100 and ask them what it shows *(recycling bins)*. Ask students whether this is something that damages or helps the environment *(It helps it.)* and what would have the opposite effect *(putting all our rubbish in landfills)*. Ask students if their families recycle their rubbish. Those who do should write *recycling rubbish* in the green column of the table, and those who don't should write *throwing away all rubbish* in the red column.
- Ask students to fill in the rest of the table with the various ways their families damage or help the environment. Don't discuss their points at this stage.

C

- Ask students to read the instructions and check that they understand what they have to do.
- Allow enough time for each pair to discuss all the points in their tables and to discuss those that are similar.
- As a class, ask each student to tell you one of the points from both columns in his or her table. Use their answers as a basis for a class discussion on how environmentally-friendly their families are and in which ways they could improve.

Useful Expressions

- Read the *Useful Expressions* to the students and explain that we use these structures in order to talk about ourselves. Point out that linking expressions are used to add further information.

D

- Ask students to quickly read the instructions for the *Exam Task* and elicit that this is a decision-making task.
- Ask students to first read the information in the *Exam Close-up*. Explain that in this type of task if their partner doesn't agree with them, they will have to develop their arguments in order to persuade and convince them so that they can both come to a decision. Remind them that this is necessary in order to complete the task.
- Encourage students to use the *Useful Expressions* in the second part of the decision-making task if they disagree with something their partner has said or want to persuade their partner that another option is best.
- Ask students to underline the two parts to the task and elicit what they are *(Discuss the different things their family could do to be more environmentally-friendly and decide which two will have the biggest impact on the environment.)*.
- Ask students to look at the pictures 1-6 and elicit which aspects of helping the environment they show *(installing photovoltaic panels, cultivating their own crops, recycling materials, cycling instead of using cars, switching off electrical appliances when not in use, becoming an environmental activist)*. Encourage students to spend a minute to think about how effective these activities are in helping the environment and which ones could be more achievable by their families.
- Go round the class monitoring students to make sure they are carrying out the task properly. Don't correct any mistakes at this stage, but make a note of any problems in structure and pronunciation.

- Ask each pair to say which two activities they decided would have a greater impact on the environment and to justify their choices.
- Write any structural mistakes that students made on the board without saying who made them, and ask them to correct them. Deal with any problems in pronunciation that came up.

Ideas Focus

- Ask students to read the questions quickly and deal with any queries they may have.
- Ask students to work in pairs and take turns to answer the questions.
- Go round the class monitoring students to make sure they are carrying out the task properly. Don't correct any mistakes at this stage, but make a note of any problems in structure and pronunciation.
- Ask a student from each pair to answer one of the questions until each pair has had a turn. Ask other students if they agree or if they have something else to add.
- Write any structural mistakes that students made on the board without saying who made them, and ask them to correct them. Deal with any problems in pronunciation that came up.

Answers

Students' own answers

Grammar

A

- Ask students to look at the picture in the bottom right-hand corner and ask them what the children appear to be doing *(sorting out rubbish for recycling)* and why they are doing this *(to help reuse plastic/paper, etc in order to help the environment)*.
- Write the sentence below on the board and ask students what they notice about it *(The* if *clause uses the Third Conditional, but the result clause uses the Second Conditional.)*. Explain that this is a mixed conditional.
  - If they hadn't recycled their plastic bottles, we wouldn't be able to produce other goods from them.
- Ask students to read the instructions and check that they understand what they have to do.
- Ask a student to read out the sentence and elicit which conditionals have been used *(Third and Second)*. Then ask students to answer the questions.
- Ask students to do the task individually, but check as a class.

Answers

1 Yes
2 No
3 Yes

B

- Read the rule to students and explain anything they don't understand.
- Encourage students to look back at the sentence in A and the one you wrote on the board to help them fill in the blanks here.

- Ask students to do the task in pairs to encourage discussion, but check as a class.

Answers

past, present

C

- Read the sentences to the students and ask them to underline the verb forms in each one.
- Ask students to read the questions and elicit that the number of lines provided for them to write on will help them with their answers. Elicit that they have to write the words in bold on these lines.
- Ask students to do the task individually, but check as a class.

Answers

1 unless
2 provided/providing that/on condition that/as long as
3 supposing/suppose
4 otherwise

Now read the Grammar Reference on page 171 (8.5 & 8.6) with your students.

D

- Ask students to read the instructions and check that they understand what they have to do.
- Ask students to read the first sentence and ask them if the council provided recycling bins *(no)* and whether we can recycle *(no)*. Elicit that because the council didn't take action in the past, it has had an effect on the present.
- Ask students to read the gapped sentence in item 1 and elicit that in the *if* clause they will use the Third Conditional and in the result clause *would* + bare infinitive. Ask them to fill in the gaps and check their answers before moving on to the rest of the task.
- Ask students to do the task individually, but check as a class.

Answers

1 had provided, would be able to/could recycle
2 hadn't explained, wouldn't know
3 wouldn't be, hadn't been
4 hadn't put, would be working

E

- Ask students to read the instructions and check that they understand what they have to do.
- Ask students to read the two sentences in item 1 and ask them to underline the information in the first sentence that is missing in the second sentence. Then ask them how this could be rephrased using the word given. Remind students not to change this word in any way.
- Encourage students to look back at the sentences in D for help if necessary.
- Ask students to do the task individually, but check as a class.

Answers

1 suppose you were caught
2 Don't call me unless
3 as long as they
4 On condition (that) global warming stops
5 provided (that) we protect

Use your English

A

- Read the phrasal verbs in the yellow box to the students and ask them to repeat them. Correct their pronunciation where necessary. Explain that all these phrasal verbs can be used to talk about weather or natural disasters.
- Ask students to read the definitions in 1-6 and answer any queries they have about them. Remind students that they may have to change the form of the phrasal verbs so they should pay attention to the tense used in each sentence.
- Ask students to do the task individually, but check as a class.
- Ask students to copy the phrasal verbs and their definitions into their notebooks before moving on to B.

Answers

1 worn away	4 bursts into
2 wiped out	5 blows over
3 block ... out	6 freezes over

B

- Ask students to read the instructions and check that they understand what they have to do.
- Ask students to read through all the sentences for meaning and to pay attention to the tenses used so that they know which phrasal verb from A goes in each gap and which form it should go in.
- Remind students to read back through the sentences once they have finished to check their answers.
- Ask students to do the task individually, but check as a class.

Answers

1 burst into	4 froze over
2 wore away	5 wiped out
3 blocked out	6 blew over

C

- Ask students to look at the second paragraph of the text in D and find and underline the phrases *adapted to* and *prepared for*. Point out to students that the verb *adapt* is followed by the preposition *to* and then an object. Also, the adjective *prepared* is followed by the preposition *for* when it has an object. Explain that there are many nouns, verbs and adjectives that are followed by certain prepositions.

- Ask students to read the list of prepositions in the yellow box and explain that they will use them to complete prepositional phrases. Point out that they can use them more than once.
- Read the lists of nouns, verbs and adjectives to students and ask them to repeat them. Correct their pronunciation where necessary. Explain any words the students don't understand.
- Ask students to do the task individually, but check as a class.

Answers

1 from	10 on
2 on	11 in
3 for	12 for
4 to	13 of
5 of	14 to
6 in	15 about
7 with	16 from
8 from	17 with
9 to	18 on

D

- Ask students to read the instructions and check that they understand what they have to do. Point out that they should use just one word in each gap.
- Ask students to read the text, without filling in any answers at this stage, to work out whether a noun, verb or adjective is missing. Point out that they should pay attention to what part of speech the words immediately before the gaps are in order to work this out.
- Remind students to read back through the text once they have finished in order to check their answers.

Answers

1 away
2 with
3 all
4 in
5 where
6 up
7 as
8 its

Teaching Tip

Point out to students that dependent prepositions have to be learnt by heart. Encourage them to copy the list into their notebooks and to study them for homework. At the next lesson, give them a quick quiz based on the phrases found here. Also, encourage students to underline dependent prepositions in new phrases they come across when reading English and point out that they should always record nouns, verbs and adjectives with their prepositions in their notebooks.

Writing: an essay (2)

- Read the information on avoiding common mistakes in the *Learning Focus* to students and explain anything they don't understand.
- Explain to students that it is a good idea to keep a list of the mistakes they make all the time and use this as a checklist when they have finished any writing task.
- Remind students that they should always read through their writing again to look for mistakes in spelling, prefixes and suffixes, double 'l's at the end of words that end in 'l', subject-verb agreement, pronouns, tenses and punctuation.
- Remind students that their written work is a chance for them to show how good a command of the English language they have. Explain that when they proofread their essays they should check not only for errors, but whether or not they have varied their language enough.

A

- Ask students to read the instructions and check that they understand what they have to do.
- Ask students to read through all the sentences before correcting any mistakes. Point out that there is one mistake in each sentence.
- Ask students to do the task individually, and read each sentence through again to check that their answer is correct.
- Check answers as a class.

Answers

1 Generally
2 was raining
3 to buy
4 in spite of
5 it's

B

- Ask students to look at the pictures on pages 104 and 105 and ask them how they are related to the theme of the unit (*They show heavily polluted cities as a result of burning fossil fuels.*) and ask them if they live in a place that is similar to the places shown and to say how their hometown is similar or different.
- Ask students to read the instructions and check that they understand what they have to do.
- Give each pair enough time to discuss and note down the problems associated with both urban and rural areas.
- As a class, ask each pair to discuss the problems they came up with and use their ideas as the basis for a discussion on whether environmental problems are worse in the countryside or city. Ask students to justify their opinions.

Suggested answers

Cities
   noise pollution, air pollution, temperature rises due to number of cars, buildings, etc

Countryside
   soil erosion, water and land pollution due to chemical fertilisers and pesticides used in agriculture

C

- Ask students to read the instructions and explain anything they don't understand. Elicit that students have to answer the questions about the writing task.
- Ask students to read the writing task and notes and then the six questions. They should then answer the questions, referring back to the task.
- Ask students to complete the task individually and then compare their answers with a partner. Check answers as a class.

Answers

Students should tick items 1, 4, 5 and 6

D

- Ask students what their opinion would be of the statement in the writing task in C and ask them to justify their opinions.
- Ask students to read the instructions and check that they understand what they have to do.
- Ask students to read the example essay and then to discuss with a partner what the writer's opinion is and whether or not they agree with it.
- As a class, discuss the points the writer makes and ask students to comment on them.

Answers

The writer's main view is that there are problems in both cities and in the countryside, but on the whole there are more serious environmental problems in cities.

Students' own answers

E

- Ask students to read the instructions and check that they understand what they have to do.
- Explain that these words and phrases don't appear in the same order as their equivalents in the example essay.
- Ask students to read the first paragraph to find the answer to item 1 and make sure students understand that *better than* could be used instead of *preferable to* without any other changes being necessary, and that they should be able to do the same with the other words and phrases.
- Ask students to do the task individually, but check as a class.

Answers

1 preferable to
2 But
3 it is a sad fact that
4 as a result
5 Similarly
6 Of course
7 Firstly
8 Fortunately
9 To sum up
10 indeed

F

- Ask students to read the instructions and check that they understand what they have to do.
- Remind students that the last point in the information on writing essays mentions showing a good range of vocabulary and grammatical structures. Point out that more credit is given to essays that attempt more complex structures, even if slight errors are present, than to essays which only use very simple structures even though there are no structural mistakes.
- Read through the grammatical structures listed and ask students to give an example of their own of each.
- Ask students to work in pairs to find examples of these structures in the example essay. Encourage them to underline the sentences they are found in and to write at the side what kind of structure is found.
- Check as a class.

Answers

question forms: The question is, is it as bad as cities?
gerunds: … living in … preferable to living in …
passive voice: Not all countryside areas are polluted. In contrast, … that must be solved.
modal verbs: Today's cities can indeed be …, … they can get into rivers …, … that must be solved.
infinitives: … it used to be …, … become dangerous to eat …
conditionals: If farmers use …, they can get into …, If it did, the countryside would be …

Useful Expressions

- Read the words and phrases in *Useful Expressions* to students and ask them to repeat them. Correct their pronunciation where necessary.
- Ask them to circle words and phrases from this list that are used in the example essay (*indeed, similarly, in contrast*).
- Remind students that they can use these expressions in their own essays, but that they shouldn't overuse them.

G

- Ask students to read the information in the *Exam Close-up* and point out to them that the example essay contains all of these features.
- Remind students that they should use the information here as a checklist when they come to write their own essay.
- Ask students to read the instructions and check that they understand what they have to do.
- Ask students to read the *Exam Task* and to underline key words and phrases. Explain anything that students don't understand.
- Write the following questions on the board:
  - What can people do to help the environment?
  - Which of these things are young people interested in?
- Then ask students to work in small groups to answer these questions.
- As a class, write the main points discussed by each group on the board and ask students whether they agree or disagree with the statement in the writing task. Remind them to justify their opinions.

- Ask students to read the paragraph plan for the essay and explain anything they don't understand. If time allows, ask students to note down the ideas they will use to expand each paragraph.
- Encourage students to use the *Useful Expressions* in their essays for comparing and contrasting opinions and for focusing in on specific ideas.
- Encourage students to use the Writing Reference and checklist for essays on page 185.

Suggested answer

It is no secret that our environment is suffering and that young people, who are the future of the Earth, must become active in saving it. The question is, are they willing to get involved in protecting our natural environment?

It is often claimed that young people have no interest in environmental issues. While it is true that young people often have many obligations and little time to devote to saving the environment, many young people still find time to be active. Indeed, the number of environmental groups in our schools proves that young people are willing to get involved.

Many young people are interested in environmental issues both in their local area and on an international level. In fact, they often take part in activities such as cleaning up beaches, recycling materials and campaigning against those who pollute our environment.

To sum up, it is unfair to claim that all young people are not interested in helping the environment. Although they have other commitments, many young people make time to support and participate in environmental programmes.

8 Global Warming

General Note

The National Geographic videos can be used as an interesting way to introduce your students to other cultures. They are authentic National Geographic videos, and it is not necessary for students to understand everything they hear to benefit from them. The videos have the option to play English subtitles so that students can read on screen exactly what is said in the documentary. This feature may help students with some of the tasks in the worksheets. The videos are also a good way to encourage your students to watch TV programmes and films in English so that they can get used to the sound of the language. The more students are exposed to English, the easier it will be for them to pick up the language.

Background Information

Global warming is the increase in temperatures worldwide. Although the Earth's temperature has greatly fluctuated since its creation, temperatures have been increasing at an alarming rate since the late 19th century. Scientists attribute this increase to human activity. In particular, burning fossil fuels and deforestation are the main causes of this phenomenon. The results of global warming will be extreme weather conditions such as heatwaves, floods, droughts, etc and this will have a catastrophic effect on crop production. The high temperatures recorded in 1998 can be put down to the El Niño phenomenon which took place in that year.

Before you watch

A

- Explain to students that in this lesson they are going to watch a video about global warming. Ask them what they know about this phenomenon and how it is affecting the Earth.
- Read the compound nouns 1-5 to the students and ask them to repeat them. Correct their pronunciation where necessary.
- Ask students to read the meanings a-e and explain anything they don't understand.
- Ask students to do the task individually, but check as a class.

Answers

1b 2e 3a 4c 5d

While you watch

B

- Explain to students that they are now going to watch the video and do a task based on the information they hear.
- Ask students to read the statements 1-6 and ask them what they will learn about on the documentary *(how rising temperatures are affecting certain parts of the Earth)*.
- Explain anything in the statements that the students don't understand. Then ask them to think about which words might be correct before watching.

- Play the video all the way through without stopping and ask students to mark their answers. Ask students to compare their answers with a partner's and to justify any answers that are different. Play the video again so that they can check their answers.
- Ask students to do the task individually, but check as a class.

Answers

1	Scientists	(00.27)	4 shrinking	(01.52)
2	energy	(01.06)	5 patterns	(02.36)
3	Evidence	(01.30)	6 simple	(03.10)

After you watch

C

- Explain to students that this is a summary of the information they heard on the video.
- Read the words in the yellow box to the students and ask them to repeat them. Correct their pronunciation where necessary. Ask students to write *N*, *Adj* or *V* beside each of the words depending on whether it is a noun, adjective or verb.
- Explain to students that they should read the whole summary before writing any answers first to work out what part of speech is missing.
- Tell students to read back through the text once they have finished to check their answers.
- Ask students to do the task individually, but check the answers as a class.

Answers

1 cause	5 coastal
2 produce	6 adapt
3 atmosphere	7 emissions
4 rise	8 energy

Ideas Focus

- Ask students to read the instructions and make sure they understand what they have to do. Then ask them to read the three questions and answer any queries they might have.
- Ask students to work in pairs and explain that they should both give their opinions on all three questions.
- Go round the class monitoring students to make sure they are carrying out the task properly. Don't correct any mistakes at this stage, but make a note of any problems in structure and pronunciation.
- Ask each pair to answer one of the questions and repeat until each pair has had a turn.
- Write the ways students save energy on the board and ask them if they think they could do more and if so, what.

Answers

Students' own answers

Objectives

- To revise vocabulary and grammar from Units 7 and 8
- To practise exam-type tasks

Revision

- Explain to students that Review 4 revises the material they saw in Units 7 and 8.
- Remind students that they can ask you for help with the exercises or look back at the units if they're not sure about an answer, and stress that the review is not a test.
- Decide how you will carry out the review. You could ask students to do one task at a time and then correct it immediately, or ask students to do all the tasks and correct them together at the end. If you do all the tasks together, let students know every now and again how much time they have got left to finish the tasks.
- Ask students not to leave any answers blank and to try to find any answers they aren't sure about in the units.
- When checking students' answers to the review tasks, make a note of any problem areas in vocabulary and grammar that they still have. Try to do extra work on these areas so that your students will progress well.

Vocabulary Revision

- Write the nouns, verbs and adjectives below on the board and ask students to copy them into their notebooks along with the prepositions that usually follow them:
- - effect *(on)*, victim *(of)*, rise *(in)*, cope *(with)*, discourage *(from)*, rely *(on)*, exposed *(to)*, satisfied *(with)*, keen *(on)*
- Ask students which phrasal verbs they remember from Unit 7 which are related to crime using the following verbs:
- - do *(away with)*, get *(away with)*, give *(up)*, hold *(up)*, own *(up)*, put *(away)*, see *(through)*, take *(in)*
- Tell them to think of a sentence for each one and to write them down in their notebooks.
- Say and write the words below on the board and ask students what part of speech they are:
- - coast *(noun)*, end *(noun/verb)*, environment *(noun)*, important *(adjective)*, reuse *(verb)*, cycle *(noun/verb)*, solve *(verb)*, torrent *(noun)*
- Ask students to write down any other parts of speech of these words that students know. Make sure they revise the parts that they will need to complete Part 3.
- Write the words below in a box on the board and the sentences underneath the box. Ask students to copy the sentences into their notebooks completing them with the words from the box.
  accused   affected   crime   habitat   lives   penalty released   trees
  - He has lead a life of ____ for years now. *(crime)*
  - The defendant was shocked when he was given the death ____. *(penalty)**
  - Dangerous fumes were ____ into the atmosphere. *(released)*
  - When the earthquake struck, many people ran to save their ____. *(lives)*
  - The tiger's natural ____ is under threat. *(habitat)*
  - Which areas are ____ by El Niño? *(affected)*
  - Let's plant ____ where last year's forest fire took place. *(trees)*
  - The company has been ____ of smuggling. *(accused)*
  * Remind students that we say 'a death sentence', but 'the death penalty'.

Grammar Revision

- Write the sentences below on the board and ask students to rewrite them in the passive.
  - The hurricane blew off our roof. *(Our roof was blown off by the hurricane.)*
  - They ought to close down the swimming pool. *(The swimming pool ought to be closed down.)*
  - They should have warned us about the tornado. *(We should have been warned about the tornado.)*
  - A brick smashed the window during the storm. *(The window was smashed with a brick during the storm.)*
- Ask students the questions below at random round the class.
  - What would you do if you were accused of a crime you hadn't committed?
  - What happens if the atmosphere has too much moisture?
  - What would life be like if fossil fuels hadn't been discovered?
  - What activities would you get involved in if you were a member of an environmental group?
- Ask students to write conditional sentences of their own using the words: *otherwise, unless, provided, on condition that, suppose* and *as long as.*
- Ask students how we form the causative using the verbs *have* and *get* and ask them to write sentences of their own using these structures.

Part 1

- Ask students to read the instructions and check that they understand what they have to do.
- Ask students to read the title of the text and ask them why they think the rainforests are important. Then ask them to skim read the text, without circling any answers at this stage, to find out how rainforests are connected to global warming *(Global warming increases when rainforests disappear. Trees absorb the greenhouse gas carbon dioxide and produce oxygen so if they are cut down the Earth's atmosphere is negatively affected.).* Ask students if they do anything to protect the rainforests.
- Point out to students that they should read all four options for each item before deciding which word best fits each gap. Remind them to pay attention to the whole sentence each gap is in as the general context will help them understand what word is missing.
- Remind students to read back through the text once they have finished to check their answers.

1B 2A 3B 4D 5C 6A 7D 8A 9B 10A 11D 12B

Part 2

- Ask students to read the instructions and check that they understand what they have to do.
- Ask students to read the title of the text and ask them what they imagine the lost treasure consisted of.
- Ask students to skim read the text, without filling in any answers at this stage, to find out who Captain William Thompson was *(the person in charge of transporting the treasure by ship from Peru to Mexico who decided to steal it instead)*.
- Encourage students to pay particular attention to the words immediately before and after each gap to work out what part of speech is missing. However, remind them that they have to take into consideration the general context of the sentence so that they understand which structure is being used.
- Remind students to read back through the text once they have finished to check their answers.

13 there	19 until/till
14 would/could	20 of
15 was	21 penalty
16 crime	22 lives
17 away	23 When
18 where	24 never/not

Part 3

- Ask students to read the instructions and check that they understand what they have to do.
- Ask students to read the title of the text and ask them why plastic might be dangerous. Ask them to skim read the text, without filling in any answers at this stage, to find out why plastic bags are a danger to sea turtles *(because they mistake them for jellyfish, which is their favourite food, but may die as a result of trying to eat them)*.
- Read the words at the side of the text to the students and ask them to repeat them. Correct their pronunciation where necessary.
- Ask students to read back through the text and to decide which part of speech is missing from each gap, and to complete the gaps using the correct form of the words given.
- Remind students to read back through the text once they have finished to check their answers.

25 endless	30 environmentally
26 coastal	31 discouraged
27 torrential	32 reusable
28 endangered	33 importantly
29 solutions	34 recycle

Part 4

- Ask students to read the instructions and check that they understand what they have to do.
- Ask students to read both sentences in each item and to underline the information in the first sentence that is missing from the second sentence. Then ask them to look at the word given to decide how the missing information could be inserted into the second sentence using this word. Remind students that they will have to use a different structure in order to keep the meaning the same.
- Remind students that they mustn't change the word given in any way.
- Encourage students to read back through the completed sentences once they have finished to check their answers.

35 ought to be installed
36 if I had known
37 Provided/Providing that you complete
38 it would not look
39 should have been taken
40 Don't use this unless
41 if I were you
42 as long as there is

9 And What Do You Do?

Reading:	multiple-matching, reading for overall meaning
Vocabulary:	job-related vocabulary
Grammar:	relative clauses, participle clauses
Listening:	multiple-choice, using stem questions to find the answer
Speaking:	talking about employment, problem solving, giving advice, providing advice
Use your English:	phrasal verbs, collocations & expressions, word formation
Writing:	formal letter (2), presenting yourself in a positive light, explaining your skills and experience, greetings, reason for writing, highlighting skills & experience, ending the letter

Unit opener

- Ask students to look at the title of the unit and ask them in what situation they may hear this question and why people usually ask it (*when being introduced to someone, to find out what someone's job is*).
- Ask students to look at the picture and its accompanying caption and ask them how it is related to the title of the unit (*It shows people who earn their living or feed their family by fishing.*). Ask students what kind of skills and qualities these fishermen need (*patience, a good sense of balance, ability to use a fishing rod well, knowledge of best times, places to fish, etc*).
- Ask students if this occupation appeals to them and to say why/why not. If it doesn't appeal to them, ask them which occupation they are most interested in and why.

Reading

A

- Write *qualities* and *qualifications* on the board and ask students what the difference between them is. Encourage them to provide examples to discuss the difference.
- Ask students to read the instructions and check that they understand what to do.
- Read the words under *Jobs* and *Qualities* and ask the students to repeat them. Correct their pronunciation if necessary. Explain anything they don't understand.
- Ask students to work in pairs to encourage discussion and ask them to justify their answers.
- As a class, ask each pair to sum up the points they made during their discussion and to say which ones need academic qualifications.
- Once the answers have been checked, ask students to look at the picture to the right of the task and ask them what job the people depicted might do and which qualities from A they probably need to do it.

Answer

A manager and a writer would need academic qualifications.

B

- Ask students to read the instructions and check that they understand what to do.
- Ask students to work with a partner and discuss each of the jobs in A. They should say why or why not they would like to do them.
- Go round the class monitoring students to make sure they are carrying out the task properly. Don't correct any mistakes at this stage, but make a note of any problems in structure and pronunciation.
- As a class, ask each student to talk about one of the jobs and say whether they would like to do it or not and their reasons. Ask other students how they feel about that job.
- Continue until all the jobs have been discussed.
- Write any structural mistakes that students made on the board, without saying who made them, and ask them to correct them. Deal with any problems in pronunciation that came up.

C

- Ask students to read the instructions and check that they understand what they have to do.
- Ask students to skim read the four texts to find the relevant information to answer the question. Explain that they don't have to read in detail as they will have another opportunity to read the text. Encourage students to underline the information that relates to the question as they read.
- Ask separate students to answer the question and to justify their answer with information from the text.

Answer

communication

Word Focus

- Ask students to look at the words in red in the text and to re-read the sentences they are found in. Remind students that when they don't know the meaning of a word, they should look carefully at the sentence it is found in to work out its meaning. Ask students to work in pairs to decide what each of the words mean.
- Ask students to read the *Word Focus* box to compare their answers with the definitions given. Explain anything they don't understand.

D

- Ask students to read the information in the *Exam Close-up* and explain that understanding every word in a text is not necessary.
- Explain that it is more important to understand what the main purpose of each paragraph is rather than every word in it.
- Ask students to read the instructions and check that they understand what to do.
- Explain to students that they should pay attention to which paragraphs each question refers to and remind them to look only at that paragraph or paragraphs in order to find the answers.
- Ask students to read the questions and to underline key words and phrases. Then ask them to take each paragraph at a time in order to answer the relevant questions.
- Ask students to do the task individually, but check as a class.

Answers

1 D *(Feedback is an aspect of recruiting ... feedback from a company after an interview they have arranged.)*
2 A *(The recruiting company I work for has built a good reputation ... I've contributed to that.)*
3 C *(The most valuable skill that successful recruiters ... communication.)*
4 B *(... they tell me the vacancy they need ... talented staff to do the work.)*
5 A *(It doesn't sound like much of a workforce, ... I also socialise with my colleagues outside of work.)*
6 B *(I also have to be the bearer of bad news ... they chose another candidate.' Those conversations are tough.)*
7 C *(I pride myself on being a good communicator; ... in order to get a clear picture of who they are.)*
8 A *(There are four full-time staff – a receptionist, ... a secretary and two more recruiters.)*
9 B *('You don't have the right qualifications', 'You lack experience')*
10 D *(What was their impression of the candidate? What did they see ... believe the candidate needs to improve on?)*

E

- Ask students to read the instructions and check that they understand what to do.
- Ask students to scan the texts again to find and underline the words. Remind them that they should always try to work out the meaning of a word from its context and ask them to read the sentences each word is in.
- Point out that numbers 1-6 are the definitions and a-f are the sentences they will use the answers from 1-6 in.
- Ask students to do the task individually, but check as a class.

Answers

1	applicant	a	income
2	availability	b	amateur
3	income	c	applicant
4	workforce	d	feedback
5	amateur	e	workforce
6	feedback	f	availability

Ideas Focus

- Explain to students that they are going to answer some questions about jobs and employment.
- Ask them to read the questions and explain anything they don't understand.
- Ask students to work in pairs to answer the questions and encourage them to use their own experience to help them support their opinions.
- Go round the class monitoring students to make sure they are carrying out the task properly. Don't correct any mistakes at this stage, but make a note of any problems in structure and pronunciation.
- As a class, ask each student to answer one of the questions and ask the others if they agree or whether they have anything else to add.
- Write any structural mistakes that students made on the board, without saying who made them, and ask them to correct them. Deal with any problems in pronunciation that came up.

Answers

Students' own answers

Vocabulary

A

- Read the words in red to the students and ask them to repeat them. Correct their pronunciation if necessary.
- Encourage students to read the whole sentence before circling any answers.
- Remind students to read back through the sentences once they have finished to check their answers.
- Ask students to do the task individually, but check as a class.

Answers

1	involves	5	apply
2	fill	6	attend
3	suit	7	hire
4	ran	8	commute

B

- Ask students to read the instructions and check that they understand what they have to do.
- Read the words in the yellow box to students and ask them to repeat them. Correct their pronunciation where necessary.
- Ask students to read the sentences and to pay attention to the meaning of the words in bold. Then ask them to decide which word from the yellow box best replaces each one.

- Remind students to read back through the sentences once they have finished to check their answers.
- Ask students to do the task individually, but check as a class.
- Once the answers have been checked, ask students to write the new words from the yellow box and their synonyms in bold in their notebooks.

Answers

1 employees	5 client
2 candidate	6 insurance
3 supervisor	7 rise
4 opening	8 leave

C

- Ask students to read the instructions and check that they understand what they have to do.
- Explain to students that they should read the whole sentence and all three options before circling their answers.
- Remind students to read back through the sentences once they have finished to check their answers.
- Ask students to do the task individually, but check as a class.

Answers

1c 2a 3b 4b 5c 6c 7a 8c

Extra Class Activity

Ask students to look at the picture on page 112 and elicit the job it shows (construction worker). Ask them to write either a paragraph as if they were the person in the photo talking about his job or a dialogue between him and a co-worker where they talk about their job. They should include details like what the job involves, what the working conditions are like, what qualities and qualifications they need for their job, what they like/dislike about their job and any other information they feel is relevant. Encourage them to use as much vocabulary from this unit as possible.

D

- Ask students to read the instructions and check that they understand what they have to do.
- Read the words in the yellow box to the students and ask them to repeat them. Correct their pronunciation if necessary.
- Ask students to read all of the sentences without completing any of the gaps. Ask them to work out what part of speech is missing from each gap before they write their answers.
- Remind students to read each sentence again to check their answers.
- Ask students to do the task individually, but check as a class.

Answers

1 bearer of bad news	4 interact
2 bounce (our) ideas	5 possess
3 amateurs	6 workforce

Grammar

- Write the sentence *Yvonne was the one who interviewed the candidate* on the board. Ask students what kind of word *who* is in this sentence (a relative pronoun) and elicit other relative pronouns that they know (that, where, when, why, whose). Explain that in this lesson, they are going to revise relative clauses.

A

- Ask students to read the instructions and check that they understand what they have to do.
- Ask students to read the sentences and to underline the words that the missing relative pronouns refer to.
- Remind students to read back through the sentences once they have finished to check their answers.

Answers

1 when	4 whose
2 why	5 who/that
3 which/that	6 where

B

- Ask the students to read the instructions and to work in pairs to complete the task and encourage discussion.
- Check answers as a class.

Answers

who, that
which, that
whose
when
where
why

C

- Ask students to read the instructions and check that they understand what they have to do.
- Ask them to underline the relative clauses.
- Ask students to do the task in pairs to encourage discussion, but check as a class.

Answers

1 which pay a million euros a year
2 which are getting harder to find

D

- Ask students to read the instructions and check that they understand what they have to do.
- Ask students to read the questions and do the task in pairs to encourage discussion, but check as a class.

Answers

a1 b2 c1

E

- Read the information to the students and explain anything they don't understand.
- Ask students to read the two sentences and ask them to underline the object found in one of the sentences (*The pay rise*).
- Ask students to answer the question and to rewrite the sentence omitting the pronoun.

Answer

2

Now read the Grammar Reference on page 171 (9.1 to 9.3) with your students.

F

- Ask students to read the sentences and to underline the words which the relative pronouns refer to.
- Encourage them to think about what kind of word it is and to refer to the list of the uses of relative pronouns in A before circling their answers.
- Ask students to do the task individually, but check as a class.

Answers

1	which	4	where
2	when	5	who
3	who		

G

- Ask students to read the instructions and explain anything they don't understand.
- Then ask students to read the sentences and underline the pronouns. Ask them to read each one carefully and write 'Y' if they can omit the pronoun and 'N' if they cannot.
- Ask students to do the task individually, but check as a class. Ask students to justify their answers.

Answers

1	N	4	N
2	Y	5	N
3	Y		

H

- Ask students to read the title of the text and ask them if they know of any famous people who had an ordinary job before they became famous. If so, ask them which job they did.
- Ask students to read the text, without filling in any answers at this stage, to find out who Michael Dell is and what his first job was (*the founder of Dell Corporation, dishwasher at a Chinese restaurant*).
- Remind students to underline the words the relative pronouns or adverbs refer to before filling in their answers.

- Remind students to read back through the text once they have finished to check their answers.

Answers

1	who	6	when
2	whose	7	which/that
3	when	8	where
4	why	9	when
5	where	10	which

Listening

A

- Ask students to read the instructions and check that they understand what they have to do.
- Ask students to read the four options in each item to decide which options could answer *what (2), where (4), when (1)* and *why (3)*.
- Ask students to work on their own to write questions for 1-4, then ask them to compare their questions with a partner.
- As a class, ask students at random to read out one of their questions, making sure all items are covered.

Suggested answers

1 When did he start/leave his previous job?
2 What skills does the man have?/What skills did the man need/not need in his previous job?
3 Why did he leave his job?
4 Where was his previous job?/Where is his current job?

B

- Ask students to read the instructions and check that they understand what they have to do.
- Explain to students that they will hear the man speaking and then the four questions for the options in 1-4 in A.
- Point out that they should focus on the questions asked at this stage.
- Play the recording all the way through without stopping and then ask students to comment on how similar their questions are to the ones asked.

C

- Explain to students that they are going to hear the recording again, but this time they will answer the questions asked by circling the options in A.
- Ask students to read the options in A again before they listen.
- Play the recording all the way through and ask students to circle their answers. Then ask students to compare their answers with a partner and to justify any answers that are different.
- Check the answers as a class.

Answers

1b 2a 3c 4b

D

- Ask students to read the information in the *Exam Close-up*. Remind students that they should spend time before they listen reading the questions so that they know what information to concentrate on when they are listening. They should try to answer the question using their own words, but it must be based on what they hear and not their general knowledge of the topic.
- Ask students to answer the question individually, but check the answer as a class.

Answer

They will focus on the questions.

E

- Ask students to read the instructions and check that they understand what they have to do. Explain to students that they will hear the whole broadcast and then the questions and their options.
- Ask students to read the questions and their options to underline key words and phrases. Remind them to listen out for the main ideas they express on the recording and that they won't necessarily hear the exact same words.
- Play the recording all the way through and ask students to circle their answers. Then ask students to compare their answers with a partner and to justify any answers that are different.

F

- Play the recording again and ask students to check their answers and to complete any answers they haven't already completed.
- Check the answers as a class and ask students to justify their answers.

Answers

1a 2c 3a 4b 5a 6a

Speaking

A

- Ask students to read the four questions and answer any queries they may have about them.
- Ask students to work in pairs and take turns to ask and answer the questions about themselves.
- Go round the class monitoring students to make sure they are carrying out the task properly. Don't correct any mistakes at this stage, but make a note of any problems in structure and pronunciation.
- Ask each pair to ask and answer one of the questions and repeat until each student has had a turn.
- Write any structural mistakes that students made on the board without saying who made them, and ask them to correct them. Deal with any problems in pronunciation that came up.

B

- Ask students to read the instructions and check that they understand what they have to do.
- Elicit that students should include advantages and disadvantages such as working hours, pay, conditions/place of work, occupational hazards, etc.
- Give students five minutes to note down their ideas in their notebooks. Then ask them to compare their answers with a partner and to explain why they consider each aspect to be an advantage or disadvantage for each job.
- As a class, make a list on the board of as many advantages and disadvantages as possible for these jobs. Allow students to justify any differences of opinion they have.

Suggested answers

1 Advantages: relatively good working environment, contact with other people, easy job
Disadvantages: can be boring at times and very stressful at others, sedentary job, doesn't pay very well, long hours
2 Advantages: good working environment, can learn useful skills
Disadvantages: very responsible job, sedentary job, can be boring at times
3 Advantages: contact with other people
Disadvantages: difficult working conditions, not a job that everyone could do
4 Advantages: good working conditions, highly paid, creative job
Disadvantages: sedentary job, very responsible job
5 Advantages: good working environment in good weather, keeps you fit, work close to nature
Disadvantages: can be physically demanding at times, difficult working conditions in bad weather, poor pay
6 Advantages: creative and diverse job, contact with other people
Disadvantages: job insecurity, unsociable hours, can have negative effect on health (hearing, etc)

Useful Expressions

- Read the *Useful Expressions* to students and ask them to repeat them.
- Elicit that these expressions can be used in C by Student A once he or she has gathered all the information necessary to give advice to Student B.

C

- Ask students to quickly read the instructions in C and elicit that this is a problem-solving task.
- Ask students to read the information in the *Exam Close-up* and ask a student to tell you what it says in his or her own words.

- Explain to students that they should ask the questions in the order given as otherwise the conversation won't flow well. For example, if they ask the third question first, Student B will have to tell them the answers to questions 1 and 2 in order for their answers to question 3 to make sense.
- Ask students to work in pairs and to decide who will be Student A and who will be Student B.
- Ask students to read their problem and the three questions.
- Go round the class monitoring students to make sure they are carrying out the task properly. Don't correct any mistakes at this stage, but make a note of any problems in structure and pronunciation.
- Ask Students A to tell the rest of the class what advice they gave their partner and then ask Students B if they thought it was good advice or not.
- Write any structural mistakes that students made on the board without saying who made them, and ask them to correct them. Deal with any problems in pronunciation that came up.

Ideas Focus

- Ask students to read the questions quickly and deal with any queries they may have.
- Ask students to work in pairs and take turns to answer the questions.
- Go round the class monitoring students to make sure they are carrying out the task properly. Don't correct any mistakes at this stage, but make a note of any problems in structure and pronunciation.
- Ask a student from each pair to answer one of the questions until each pair has had a turn. Ask other students if they agree or if they have something else to add.
- Write any structural mistakes that students made on the board without saying who made them, and ask them to correct them. Deal with any problems in pronunciation that came up.

Answers

Students' own answers

Grammar

A

- Read the information on participle clauses to the students and explain anything they don't understand.
- Ask students to read the sentences and ask them to underline the present participle and the past participles in two of the sentences (*Holding, Asked*).
- Ask students to answer the questions individually, but check as a class.

Answers

a 2, 4   c 4
b 2   d Yes

B

- Read the rules to the students and explain anything they don't understand.
- Ask students to fill in the rules individually, but check as a class.

Answers

present, past

C

- Read the information to the students and explain anything they don't understand. Then ask them to look at the sentences and to underline the relative pronoun and verb.

Answers

a who applied
b which were advertised

D

- Ask students to read the instructions and explain anything they don't understand.
- Ask them to complete the task individually and then compare their answers with a partner.
- Check answers as a class.

Answers

a University graduates applying for jobs might be lucky.
b The positions advertised last month have been filled.

Now read the Grammar Reference on pages 171 (9.4) with your students.

E

- Ask students to read the instructions and check that they understand what they have to do.
- Encourage students to read through the sentences before they circle an answer. They should read the sentences again after making their choice to see it makes sense in the context of the sentence.
- Ask students to do the task individually, but check as a class.

Answers

1 Reading   4 advertised
2 Having spoken   5 Not being
3 wishing   6 woman dancing

F

- Ask students to read the instructions and check that they understand what they have to do. Point out that they may have to make other changes so that the new sentence makes sense.
- Ask students to read the first sentence and ask them if the words in bold will be replaced by a present or past participle (*present*). Then ask them what word in bold must appear somewhere else in the sentence to make it grammatically correct (*Lionel*). Ask students to complete this sentence and check the answer before moving on to the rest of the task.
- Ask students to do the task individually, but check as a class.

Answers

1 Gossiping about the manager, Lionel didn't hear her walk in.
2 Our manager spoke to the staff working at a different branch.
3 Being unable to provide references, Tom wasn't hired.
4 Having been chosen for the conference, the venue was cleaned.
5 Fired on the spot, the employee left immediately.
6 The person shouting in the shop was a customer.

Use your English

A

- Read the phrasal verbs 1-5 and ask students to repeat them. Correct their pronunciation where necessary.
- Explain that they have to consider the meaning of the verb + particle together and not just focus on the verb part. Ask them to read the definitions a-e on their own and explain anything they don't understand.
- Ask students to do the task individually, but check as a class.
- Encourage the students to copy the phrasal verbs and their definitions into their notebooks before moving on to B.

Answers

1c 2a 3e 4d 5b

B

- Ask students to read the instructions and check that they understand what they have to do. Point out that they may have to change the form of some verbs.
- Ask students to read through the sentences to work out the meaning of the missing verb and to decide what form the verb should be in.
- Remind students to read back through the sentences once they have finished to check their answers.
- Ask students to do the task individually, but check as a class.

Answers

1 hold down
2 move on
3 fill in
4 taking on
5 Keep up

C

- Ask students which collocations they learnt in Unit 6 related to sports and leisure with the verbs do (aerobics, athletics, gymnastics), go (windsurfing, jogging, sailing) and play (cards, basketball, football, volleyball). Explain that in this lesson they are going to learn work-related collocations with the verbs get, make and take. Ask them if they know any collocations with these verbs.

- Ask students to read the sentences and to underline the nouns or adjectives that immediately follow the gaps. Explain that the missing verb must collocate naturally with these words.
- Remind students to read back through the sentences once they have finished to check their answers.
- Ask students to do the task individually, but check as a class.

Answers

1 take	4 make
2 take	5 got
3 get	

D

- Ask students to read the title of the text and to look at the picture. Ask them how they think the person in the picture would answer this question and to justify their answer.
- Read the words in capitals to the students and ask them to repeat them. Correct their pronunciation if necessary. Ask students what part of speech each word is (verbs: satisfy, achieve, promote, produce, rely, depress; adjectives: suitable, satisfied) and which other parts of speech of these words they know.
- Ask students to read the text, without filling in any answers at this stage, to find out what the 'Sunday night blues' are and which kind of workers are most affected by them (A feeling of depression which people feel because they have to return to work on a Monday morning. Workers who are not satisfied with their job are more likely to suffer from this.).
- Ask students to work out what part of speech is missing from each gap before they write their answers.
- Remind students to read back through the text once they have finished to check their answers.
- Ask students to do the task individually, but check as a class.

Answers

1 satisfaction	5 dissatisfied
2 achievement	6 productive
3 suitably	7 reliable
4 promotion	8 depressed

Ideas Focus

- Explain to students that they are going to answer a question about why people should leave a job.
- Ask them to read the question and explain anything they don't understand.
- Ask students to work in pairs to answer the question and encourage them to use their own experience to help them support their opinions.
- Go round the class monitoring students to make sure they are carrying out the task properly. Don't correct any mistakes at this stage, but make a note of any problems in structure and pronunciation.
- As a class, ask each student to answer the question and ask the others if they agree or whether they have anything else to add.

- Write any structural mistakes that students made on the board, without saying who made them, and ask them to correct them. Deal with any problems in pronunciation that came up.

Writing: a formal letter (2)

- Read the information on writing a formal letter in the *Learning Focus* to the students and explain anything they don't understand. Elicit that a letter of application is usually written in reply to a job advert, which someone is interested in applying for. Ask students if they have ever written a letter of application before. If they have, ask them what the job was and whether they were successful in getting the job.
- Ask students to underline the three things they should provide in a letter of *application (information about qualifications, experience and your personality)*. Point out that although they should present themselves in a positive light, they shouldn't overdo it. Remind them that the letter should be written in a formal style.
- Ask students which tenses they should use when talking about previous experience *(Past Simple if they refer to the time period they worked in a certain position; Present Perfect Simple if they don't refer to a time period, but concentrate more on the experience gained; Present Perfect Continuous to talk about how long they have been working in their present position)*.

A

- Ask students to read the instructions and check that they understand what they have to do.
- Read the words in the yellow box and ask students to repeat them. Correct their pronunciation if necessary.
- Read the stem and the sentence ending in item 1 to the students and ask them which quality from the yellow box could replace the ending *(positive attitude)*. Ask students to write the answer on the line provided and make sure that they realise that the part after the arrow completes the answer.
- Ask students to do the task in pairs to encourage discussion, but check as a class.
- Once the answers have been checked, elicit that in a letter of application the second way of finishing the stem in each item would be more appropriate.

B

- Ask students to read the instructions and check that they understand what they have to do.
- Ask students to read the writing task and explain anything they don't understand.
- Ask students to do the task individually, but check as a class.

C

- Ask students to read the instructions and check that they understand what they have to do.
- Ask students to read the example letter and to underline information that relates to the main points in the writing task. Then ask them to compare the parts they underlined with a partner.
- As a class, ask students if every point has been dealt with and to quote the parts in the letter that deal with each point.

D

- Ask students to read the instructions and check that they understand what they have to do.
- Ask students to do the task individually, but check as a class.

E

- Ask students to read the instructions and check that they understand what they have to do.
- Remind students that we use these tenses when talking about past experience, but that we use them in different ways.
- Ask students to underline these tenses in the letter and then to discuss why they have been used with a partner.
- Check the answers as a class before students go on to write their own paragraphs.

Answers

I have been learning: Present Perfect Continuous for an action that started in the past, but continues until now

I have won: Present Perfect Simple for an action that happened at an indefinite time in the past

Last year, I worked: Past Simple for an action that happened at a definite time in the past

My job involved: Past Simple for an action that happened at a definite time in the past

Students' own answers

- After students have completed their paragraphs, ask them to swap with a partner so that they can edit each other's work. Give students five minutes to do this. When the paragraphs have been checked, ask some students to read out their own paragraphs.

Useful Expressions

- Read the *Useful Expressions* to the students and ask them to repeat them. Correct their pronunciation and intonation if necessary.
- Elicit in which part of their letter they can use each category of expressions and remind them to use them when writing their letter for F.

F

- Ask students to read the information in the *Exam Close-up* and point out that the writer of the example letter did these things.
- Remind students that they can use the information here as a checklist when writing their own letters.
- Ask students to read the instructions and the writing task and ask them to underline key words and phrases in the task. Explain anything they don't understand.
- Ask students to answer the questions in B about this writing task so that they know what they have to do.
- Ask students what the job advertised is (*festival organiser*) and whether this is a permanent or temporary position (*temporary – a two-week festival*).
- Ask students to read the paragraph plan and ask them to make notes for each paragraph if time allows. Ask students how they will begin and end their letters (*Dear Mr Luss, Yours sincerely,*).
- Encourage students to use the Writing Reference and checklist for formal letters on page 179.

Suggested answer

Dear Mr Luss,

I am writing regarding your advertisement for a festival organiser which I saw in a national newspaper. I am 22 years old and I have been learning English for fifteen years. I am currently studying for a degree in festival and conference management and I am a keen cinema-goer.

As part of my degree course, I gained relevant experience organising a European film festival at my college last year. My job involved helping to select appropriate films, contacting production companies for permission to show films, creating a film schedule and advertising the event.

I have very good interpersonal and communication skills and love working with people my own age. In addition, I am very hard working and enjoy team work. For these reasons, I believe I would be suitable for the position.

I look forward to hearing from you.

Yours sincerely,

Marion Streep

9 Dinosaur Builder

 Video

General Note

The National Geographic videos can be used as an interesting way to introduce your students to other cultures. They are authentic National Geographic videos, and it is not necessary for students to understand everything they hear to benefit from them. The videos have the option to play English subtitles so that students can read on screen exactly what is said in the documentary. This feature may help students with some of the tasks in the worksheets. The videos are also a good way to encourage your students to watch TV programmes and films in English so that they can get used to the sound of the language. The more students are exposed to English, the easier it will be for them to pick up the language.

Background Information

Peter May's company makes dinosaur skeletons for museums around the world. One of the company's most impressive projects to date has been for the Royal Ontario Museum in Canada. The team built over 42 life-sized dinosaur skeletons for the museum's Ultimate Dinosaur exhibition.

Before you watch

A

- Explain to students that in this lesson they are going to watch a video about a dinosaur builder. Ask them what they imagine this person does and ask them to look at the globe to see where he comes from.
- Read the words 1-5 to the students and ask them to repeat them. Correct their pronunciation where necessary.
- Ask students to read the meanings a-e and explain anything they don't understand.
- Ask students to do the task individually, but check as a class.

Answers

1b 2d 3e 4c 5a

While you watch

B

- Explain to students that they are now going to watch the video and do a task based on the information they hear.
- Ask students to read the statements 1-6 and ask them what they will learn about on the documentary (*about a person called Peter May who builds dinosaurs*).
- Explain anything in the statements that the students don't understand. Then ask them to think about which statements might be true and which ones might be false before they listen.
- Play the video all the way through without stopping and ask students to mark their answers. Ask students to compare their answers with a partner's and to justify any answers that are different. Play the video again so that they can check their answers.
- Ask students to do the task individually, but check as a class.

Answers

1	F	(Even before Hollywood's big hit dinosaur films, … fascinated children and adults alike.)	
			(00.09)
2	T		(00.53)
3	F	(… the museums of the world could come to him when they needed him)	(01.14)
4	F	(There aren't many courses about mounting dinosaurs)	(02.09)
5	F	(The unfortunate part of this puzzle … the entire skeleton can be thrown out of shape.)	(02.42)
6	T		(03.50)

After you watch

C

- Explain to students that this is a summary of the information they heard on the video.
- Read the words in the yellow box to the students and ask them to repeat them. Correct their pronunciation where necessary. Ask students to write N, Adj, Adv or V beside each of the words depending on whether it is a noun, adjective, adverb or verb.
- Explain to students that they should read the whole summary before writing any answers first to work out what part of speech is missing.
- Tell students to read back through the text once they have finished to check their answers.
- Ask students to do the task individually, but check the answers as a class.

Answers

1	constructs	5	fossils
2	career	6	incomplete
3	around	7	scientists
4	real	8	displays

Ideas Focus

- Ask students to read the instructions and make sure they understand what they have to do. Then ask them to read the three questions and answer any queries they might have.
- Ask students to work in pairs and explain that they should both give their opinions on all three questions.
- Go round the class monitoring students to make sure they are carrying out the task properly. Don't correct any mistakes at this stage, but make a note of any problems in structure and pronunciation.
- Ask each pair to answer one of the questions and repeat until each pair has had a turn.
- Write what most people look for in a job on the board and ask students to rank these depending on how important they are to them personally.

Answers

Students' own answers

103

10 Learn to Learn!

Reading:	multiple-choice, remembering what to do
Vocabulary:	education-related vocabulary
Grammar:	reported statements, reported questions, reported commands & requests, reporting verbs
Listening:	note-taking, completing sentences
Speaking:	talking about schools, subjects, education & skills, decision making, asking for clarification and rephrasing, requesting clarification
Use your English:	phrasal verbs, word formation, sentence transformation
Writing:	formal email, understanding different functions, choosing the right function, thanking, asking for information, making suggestions, making references, signing off

Unit opener

- Ask students to look at the title of the unit, the picture and its accompanying caption and ask them how they are related (*The monk is studying from the book as part of his education as a monk.*). Elicit that the unit will be about education.
- Ask students what kind of things they think this young monk might study and how his education might compare to their own.

Reading

A

- Ask students to look at the pictures on pages 122 and 123 and ask them what the animals are doing (*The dog is guiding its owner along a street, the monkey is washing the woman's face in one picture and putting on a CD in the other.*).
- Ask students to read the instructions and check that they understand what they have to do.
- Read the list of tasks to the students and explain anything they don't understand.
- Ask students to do the task in pairs to encourage discussion, but check as a class.

Suggested answers

bring someone a telephone	B
turn on the television	M
smell dangerous substances	D
warn people of danger	B
guide a blind person	D
wash someone's face	M

B

- Ask students to read the instructions and check that they understand what they have to do.
- Remind students that they don't have to read in detail as they will have another opportunity to read the text.
- Ask students to do the task individually, but check as a class.
- Once the answer has been checked ask students which of the tasks, that the monkeys are able to learn, they found to be the most impressive.

Answers

The monkeys' lifespan of 30-40 years allows them long careers as assistance animals. Because they are intelligent, adaptable and sociable, they make perfect partners to humans, lending a hand and offering companionship. They can do tasks that people with physical disabilities can't do, like using telephones, opening a bottle and pouring a drink, scratching an itch and picking up dropped objects. They can also be trained to operate electronic appliances.

Word Focus

- Ask students to look at the words in red in the text and to re-read the sentences they are found in. Remind students that when they don't know the meaning of a word, they should look carefully at the sentence it is found in to work out its meaning. Ask students to work in pairs to decide what each of the words mean.
- Ask students to read the *Word Focus* box to compare their answers with the definitions.

C

- Ask students to read the information in the *Exam Close-up* and ask a student to tell you what it says in his or her own words.
- Explain to students that when they come to do the task in D they should cover up the options for each question (except for item 1), read the question and match it with the relevant section of in the text. Then they should decide, in their own words, what the answer to the question is, then compare their answer with the options. The correct answer will be the one that is closest in meaning to their own answer.
- Ask students to read the six questions and match each of them to a section of the article.
- Ask students to do the task individually, but check as a class with students justifying their answers.

Answers

1 paragraph 2
2 paragraph 2
3 paragraph 3
4 paragraph 4
5 paragraph 5
6 paragraph 9

D

- Ask students to read the instructions and check that they understand what they have to do.
- Remind students of the advice in the *Exam Close-up* and encourage them to use the method outlined there as they do this task.
- Ask students to read the article again and underline information relevant to the questions.
- Ask students to do the task individually, but check as a class.
- If students seem interested, give them more information using the Background Information box below.

Answers

1d (*… all the monkeys used by Helping Hands are born and raised in the United States.*)
2a (*This species is quite small … lending a hand and offering companionship.*)
3b (*… each monkey masters simple everyday activities … picking up a dropped object.*)
4b (*Throughout their training, monkeys are encouraged to complete tasks … and small treats.*)
5d (*As the monkeys progress through the four distinct stages of their schooling, the training rooms gradually begin to resemble a home environment.*)
6c (*… designed to raise awareness among young people of the issues surrounding spinal cord injury. … The programme tries to persuade young people not to take risks …*)

Background Information

Helping Hands trained and placed the first capuchin monkey in 1979. It became a non-profit organisation in 1982 and its early research was supported by the Veterans Administration and the Paralysed Veterans of America. Initially, it was perceived that the majority of recipients would be those paralysed as a result of military involvement. Initial research included investigating what type of monkey would be best suited for this type of work. Today, the organisation also devotes time and resources to making monkeys' retirement as comfortable as possible.

E

- Ask students to look at the words in the yellow box and to scan the text again to find and underline them. Ask them to say each of the words after you and elicit that they are all verbs. Correct their pronunciation where necessary.
- Remind them that they should always try to work out the meaning of a word from its context and ask them to read the sentences in the text each word is in. Remind students this task is in two parts. Ask them to read all the definitions before matching them to a verb.
- Check answers first before students move on to the sentences.
- Encourage students to read all the sentences once before writing in any answers to work what form it should appear in.
- Ask students to do the task individually, but check as a class.

Answers

1 reward	a monitor
2 master	b mastered
3 graduate	c embark
4 support	d graduate
5 monitor	e support
6 embark	f rewarded

Ideas Focus

- Ask students to read the questions and explain anything they don't understand.
- Ask them to work in pairs to answer the questions and encourage them to use their own experience to help them support their opinions.
- Go round the class monitoring students to make sure they are carrying out the task properly. Don't correct any mistakes at this stage, but make a note of any problems in structure and pronunciation.
- As a class, ask each student to answer one of the questions and ask the others if they agree or whether they have anything else to add.
- Write any structural mistakes that students made on the board without saying who made them, and ask them to correct them. Deal with any problems in pronunciation that came up.

Answer

Students' own answers

Vocabulary

A

- Explain to students that in this task they are going to learn education-related words.
- Read the words in red to students and ask them to repeat them. Correct their pronunciation where necessary.
- Encourage students to read the whole sentence before circling any answers.
- Remind students to read back through the sentences once they have finished to check their answers.
- Ask students to do the task individually, but check as a class.

Answers

1 enrolled
2 retake
3 cheating
4 gives
5 repeat
6 get
7 raise
8 gets

B

- Read the words in the yellow box to students and ask them to repeat them. Correct their pronunciation where necessary. Elicit that they are all nouns that refer to people involved in education and training. Explain that most of these people are involved in teaching or training, but that they all work under different circumstances.
- Encourage students to read the whole sentence before filling in any answers to look for clues as to the situation.
- Remind students to read back through the sentences once they have finished to check their answers.
- Ask students to do the task individually, but check as a class.

Answers

1 counsellor
2 trainer
3 lecturer
4 instructor
5 coach
6 member
7 teacher
8 tutor

C

- Ask students to read the instructions and explain anything they don't understand.
- Ask them to read each sentence carefully without filling in any answers at this stage. Explain that they must use a different part of speech of the words given in capitals on the right of each sentence.
- Encourage students to underline the words immediately before and after the gaps and to think about what parts of speech they are as this will give them a clue as to what part of speech is missing from the gap.
- Remind students to read back through the sentences once they have finished to check their answers.
- Ask students to do the task individually, but check as a class.

Answers

1 progressing
2 praised
3 adapting
4 distractions
5 stages
6 assessment

D

- Ask students to read the instructions and check that they understand what they have to do.
- Read the words in the yellow boxes to the students and ask them to repeat them. Correct their pronunciation where necessary.
- Encourage students to read through both sentences in each pair before filling in any answers. Point out that the pairs of words are similar in meaning, but they are used for different circumstances.
- Ask students to do the task individually, but check as a class.

Answers

1 assessment, assignment
2 secondary, primary
3 go, attend
4 degree, certificate
5 subject, lesson
6 scholarship, apprenticeship
7 fees, payments
8 licence, permit

Grammar

- Write the sentences below on the board and ask students what the people would actually have said.
  - He said the course was a waste of time. ('The course is a waste of time.')
  - She said that the careers counsellor had given me good advice. ('The careers counsellor gave/has given you good advice.')
  - They said that introducing tuition fees might be a good solution. ('Introducing tuition fees may/might be a good solution.')
  - He said that he would help me pass the exam. ('I'll help you pass the exam.')
- Revise the changes that are made when changing direct speech to reported speech (tenses change to a tense further back in the past, many modal verbs and the Past Perfect stay the same, time and place references change and subject and object pronouns and possessive adjectives change).

A

- Read the sentences with the students and ask them to circle the verbs, time phrases and subject and object pronouns in the sentences in direct speech and to compare them with the words in bold in reported speech.
- Ask students to work in pairs to answer the questions to encourage discussion, but check as a class.

Answers

1 It changes/moves back.
2 Past Perfect
3 no
4 yes
5 yes

B

- Ask students to read the two sets of questions and ask them to underline the words that change in the reported questions. Ask them to explain in their own words what changes are made.
- Ask students to write two similar questions of their own in direct speech, then ask them to swap notebooks with their partner and write each other's questions in reported speech. Check their answers as a class.

Answers

if/whether, wanted; syntax changes
had studied; syntax changes

C

- Read the rules to the students and explain anything they don't understand.
- Encourage students to look back at the examples in B when filling in their answers.
- Ask students to do the task individually, but check as a class.

Answers

if
whether
question marks
statements

D

- Ask students to read the three sets of sentences and elicit which are commands *(the first and second set)* and which is a request *(the third set)*.
- Ask students to read the reported sentences once more and to underline the verb form in the reported part of the sentence.
- As a class, ask students to answer the question.

Answer

full infinitive

Now read the Grammar Reference on pages 172 & 173 (10.1 to 10.4) with your students.

E

- Ask students to read the instructions and check that they understand what they have to do.
- Encourage students to underline the mistakes in the sentences before they rewrite the sentences. Point out that they should look back at the information in A, B, C and D to help them here.
- Ask students to do the task individually, but check as a class.

Answers

1 The professor told us that he would see us the next day.
2 Albert asked me if/whether I liked complex mathematical problems.
3 We asked a local where we could find the observatory.
4 The librarian told me to stop talking in the library.
5 James asked the teacher how long the biology test was.

F

- Ask students to read the instructions and check that they understand what they have to do.
- Ask students to read the first sentence and ask them to rewrite it using the word in bold. Check the answer and discuss the changes made before moving on to the rest of the task.
- Ask students to do the task individually, but check as a class.

Answers

1 The teacher told his class (that) he would give them a test the following day.
2 Martin said (that) they were doing a chemistry experiment that morning.
3 The professor asked why I had applied for that course.
4 I asked Jason how the scanner worked.
5 I asked Tom if/whether he read science-fiction novels.
6 The secretary told me (that) my application form would be sent to me the following week/the week after.

Listening

A

- Ask students to read the instructions and check that they understand what they have to do.
- Ask students to read the sentences and to think about syntax and synonyms in them.
- Ask students to do the task in pairs to encourage discussion, but check as a class.

Answers

1 'Twice a year' is a phrase showing frequency, but there is already an adverb of frequency before the gap *(every)* so it must be wrong grammatically.
2 The word 'compete' is synonymous with 'take part' which appears immediately after the gap, so there is repetition.
3 The word 'Spanish' isn't necessary as it says 'from Spain'.
4 The words 'more than' before the gap mean 'over', so information is repeated and the answer isn't correct grammatically.
5 We can't use 'from' after 'including' so it's incorrect grammatically.

B

- Encourage students to think about what the answers might be before they listen.
- Play the recording once all the way through and ask students to mark their answers. Then ask students to discuss their answers with a partner and to justify any that are different.
- Play the recording again and ask students to check their answers and to complete any answers they haven't already completed.
- Check the answers as a class and ask students to justify their answers.

Answers

1 two years
2 over 50 countries
3 contestants
4 200,000
5 cake making

Teaching Tip

Once the answers have been checked in B, elicit that the student in A has written some numbers wrongly and that the numbers he or she wrote sound like the actual ones heard on the recording. Also, point out that some of the words which were unnecessary as they repeated ideas already in the sentence were words actually heard on the recording. Remind students that the sentences will paraphrase ideas heard on the recording so they have to be careful when selecting the exact words needed to complete each sentence.

C

- Ask students to read the information in the *Exam Close-up* and elicit the two main points made (*write no more than three words, check that answers make sense grammatically and don't repeat ideas already in the sentence*).
- Remind students that they should pay attention to prepositions, adverbs of frequency and verbs used in the sentences which may be expressed in other words on the recording.
- Ask students what they should not do (*repeat information that is given before or after the gap*).

D

- Ask students to read the instructions and check that they understand what they have to do.
- Ask students to read the sentences 1-10 carefully to work out what kind of information is missing from each gap.
- Elicit what the recording will be about (*a teenager called Ahmet's visit to WorldSkills in London*).
- Play the recording once all the way through and ask students to mark their answers. Then ask students to discuss their answers with a partner and to justify any that are different.

E

- Play the recording again and ask students to check their answers and to complete any answers they haven't already completed.
- Check the answers as a class and ask students to justify their answers.

Answers

1 floristry
2 sitting exams
3 make a choice
4 (truly) inspired
5 4/four days
6 motivated, committed
7 of different companies
8 (bridal) bouquet
9 group activities
10 2015

Speaking

A

- Ask students to read the three questions and answer any queries they may have about them.
- Ask students to work in pairs and take turns to ask and answer the questions about themselves.
- Go round the class monitoring students to make sure they are carrying out the task properly. Don't correct any mistakes at this stage, but make a note of any problems in structure and pronunciation.
- Ask each pair to ask and answer one of the questions and repeat until each student has had a turn.
- Write any structural mistakes that students made on the board without saying who made them, and ask them to correct them. Deal with any problems in pronunciation that came up.

B

- Ask students to read the instructions and check that they understand what they have to do.
- Ask students to quickly read the *Exam Task* in C and ask someone to tell you in their own words what they have to do.
- Play the recording once all the way through and ask students to mark their answers. Then ask students to discuss their answers with a partner and to justify any that are different.
- Play the recording again and ask students to check their answers and to complete any answers they haven't already completed.
- Check answers as a class.

Answers

1b 2c 3b 4b 5c

Useful Expressions

- Read the phrases in *Useful Expressions* to the students and explain anything they don't understand.
- Point out that these expressions will help them stay on track and complete the task appropriately and that they should avoid phrases like *I think … is boring, I wouldn't really like …, … doesn't really appeal to me*. Remind them that a personal response here is irrelevant to the task.
- If time allows, you could ask them to practise using these with a partner and complete the expressions with their own words before moving on to C.

C

- Ask students to read the information in the *Exam Close-up* and explain that in this kind of decision-making task they may be asked to decide which of the options is NOT appropriate/possible/a good idea. It's important therefore to listen to the instructions for the task very carefully indeed, and, if you're not 100% sure, ask the examiner to repeat them.
- Ask students to read the instructions and check that they understand what they have to do. Elicit that they have to discuss the pros and cons of offering such prizes to students and then decide which prize would not be a good idea.
- Encourage students to use the *Useful Expressions* to ask their partner to clarify what they mean or to express an idea clearly.
- Go round the class monitoring students to make sure they are carrying out the task properly. Don't correct any mistakes at this stage, but make a note of any problems in structure and pronunciation.
- Ask each pair to say which prize they decided would not be appropriate and to justify their choice
- Write any structural mistakes that students made on the board without saying who made them, and ask them to correct them. Deal with any problems in pronunciation that came up.

Ideas Focus

- Ask students to read the questions quickly and deal with any queries they may have.
- Ask students to work in pairs and take turns to answer the questions.
- Go round the class monitoring students to make sure they are carrying out the task properly. Don't correct any mistakes at this stage, but make a note of any problems in structure and pronunciation.
- Ask a student from each pair to answer one of the questions until each pair has had a turn. Ask other students if they agree or if they have something else to add.
- Write any structural mistakes that students made on the board without saying who made them, and ask them to correct them. Deal with any problems in pronunciation that came up.

Answer

Students' own answers

Grammar

A

- Read the information to the class and explain anything they don't understand.
- Point out that in task F on page 125 they had to rewrite the sentences using *say*, *tell* and *ask* as reporting verbs and ask them which other verbs could have been used in these sentences (*warned/informed/announced/enquired*, etc).
- Read the five sets of sentences to the students and ask them to circle the reporting verbs used in the reported sentences.
- Now ask students to underline the structures that immediately following the reporting verbs in each sentence.
- Check as a class.

Answers

to lend
me to fill in
taking
for losing
that clause

B

- Ask students to read the instructions and make sure they understand what they have to do.
- Ask students to answer the questions in pairs to encourage discussion, but check as a class.

Answers

1 gerund
2 *that* clause
3 object + full infinitive
4 full infinitive
5 preposition + gerund

Be careful!

- Read the information to students and explain anything they don't understand.
- Ask them to read the two sentences and ask a student to explain the difference in meaning between the two sentences.

Now read the Grammar Reference on page 173 (10.5) with your students.

C

- Ask students to read the instructions and check that they understand what they have to do.
- Ask students to read through the sentences and to think about which would be the most suitable reporting verb to use in each reported sentence. Encourage them to look back at A and B if they need help here.
- Remind students to read back through the sentences once they have finished to check their answers.
- Ask students to do the task individually, but check as a class. Elicit and accept any alternative correct answers.

Suggested answers

1 He accused me of taking his car and crashing it.
2 The doctor suggested eating less fatty food.
3 She reminded me not to forget to bring the things she had asked for.
4 The child apologised for damaging the bike.
5 The teacher accused Kevin of hitting John with his bag.
6 The judge ordered the jury to leave the courtroom immediately.

D

- Ask students to read the words in red and elicit that they are all reporting verbs.
- Ask students to read each sentence carefully and to underline the structures after the options in red to help them decide which one is correct in each sentence.
- Remind students to read back through the sentences once they have finished to check their answers.
- Ask students to do the task individually, but check as a class.

Answers

1 suggested	5 ordered
2 warned	6 claimed
3 promised to	7 persuaded
4 advised	8 recommended

Use your English

A

- Read the phrasal verbs 1-8 and ask students to repeat them. Correct their pronunciation where necessary.
- Explain that they have to consider the meaning of the verb + particle together and not just focus on the verb part. Ask them to read the definitions a-h on their own and explain anything they don't understand.
- Ask students to do the task individually, but check as a class.
- Encourage the students to copy the phrasal verbs and their definitions into their notebooks before moving on to B.

Answers

1h 2e 3a 4g 5c 6b 7f 8d

B

- Ask students to read the instructions and check that they understand what they have to do.
- Ask students to read through the sentences to work out the meaning of the missing phrasal verbs and to decide what form they should be in.
- Remind students to read back through the sentences once they have finished to check their answers.
- Ask students to do the task individually, but check as a class.

Answers

1 pick up, brush up	
2 breeze through, drop out	
3 hand in, go over	
4 figure out, look up	

C

- Read the words in capitals to the students and ask them to repeat them. Correct their pronunciation if necessary. Ask students what part of speech each word is (verbs: attend, correct, graduate; nouns: memory, graduate; adjectives: correct, absent) and which other parts of speech of these words they know.
- Ask students to read the sentences, without filling in any answers at this stage, to work out what part of speech is missing from each gap.
- Remind students to read back through the sentences once they have finished to check their answers.
- Ask students to do the task individually, but check as a class.

Answers

1 attendance	4 absence
2 corrections	5 graduation
3 memorise	

D

- Ask students to read the instructions and check that they understand what they have to do.
- Explain that they mustn't change the word in bold in any way in the second sentence.
- Ask students to read the two sentences in item 1. Then ask them to underline the part in the first sentence that is missing from the second sentence.
- Explain to students that in order to complete the second sentence they will have to make a structural change. Remind them to also count the number of words they have written. They should have between two and five words.
- Ask students to complete the first item and correct it before they move on to the rest of the task.
- Ask students to do the task individually, but check as a class.

Answers

1 not run	4 agreed to give
2 Listen to me	5 ordered us to sit
3 them if/whether they wanted	6 congratulated me on winning

Extra Class Activity

You could extend this task by setting up a debate on the advantages and disadvantages of boarding schools. Split the students into two teams, one for boarding schools and one against. Both teams should then spend time discussing the advantages and disadvantages of these schools – point out to students that if they are for boarding schools, they should touch on the disadvantages of them in their arguments in order to support their arguments for, and vice versa. When each team is ready, ask them to appoint a spokesperson who will present the group's arguments. The members of the opposite team can then ask questions which either the spokesperson or the other team members can answer.

Writing: a formal email

- Read the information on writing formal emails in the *Learning Focus* to the students and explain anything they don't understand.
- Ask students to look at the functions mentioned in the first bullet point and ask them which other functions they can think of (*enquire, complain, refuse, deny, express a preference*). Explain that in order to use the specific functions properly, they will have to use certain expressions and that they will cover common expressions for some functions later in *Useful Expressions*.

A

- Ask students to read the instructions and check that they understand what they have to do.
- Read the words in the yellow box and ask students to repeat them. Correct pronunciation if necessary.
- Ask students to read each sentence through without marking their answers and think which function is being represented in each statement.
- Ask students to do the task individually and then compare their answers with a partner. They should justify any differences in their answers.
- Check answers as a class.

Answers

1 thanking
2 advising
3 suggesting
4 apologising
5 describing
6 giving an opinion

B

- Ask students to read the instructions and the writing task, but not the email in response at this stage, and elicit who they are (*the teacher of a class that has been chosen to participate in an exchange programme*) and who they will write an email to (*the college principal*).
- Ask students to read the email from the principal and the questions that follow.
- Ask students to answer the questions individually, but check as a class.

Answers

1 the college principal
2 formal
3 b

C

- Ask students to read the instructions and check that they understand what they have to do.
- Ask students to read the example email through quickly, without marking any answers, and ask which functions are used in each paragraph (*thanking, asking for more information, suggesting, offering*).
- Ask students what tone should be used in the response to the principal (*formal*). Remind students to bear this in mind when choosing their answers.
- Ask students to complete the task individually, but check answers as a class.

Answers

1 Dear Mr Jones
2 I cannot thank you enough
3 Could I please have some
4 Regarding
5 please let me know
6 Kind regards

D

- Ask students to read the instructions and check that they understand what to do.
- Ask them to read the four statements and look again at the example email to mark their answers.
- Ask students to work individually and compare their answers with a partner.
- Check answers as a class.

Answers

Students should have ticked items 1 and 3

E

- Ask students to read the instructions and explain anything they don't understand.
- Ask students to read the example email again and underline the words that mean the same as the words 1-4. Remind them that the words are from the principal's email and Cindy has paraphrased these words in her email.
- Ask students to do the task individually and compare their answers with a partner. They should justify any different answers.
- Check answers as a class.

Answers

1 take part in
2 visit
3 suggestions
4 arrive

Useful Expressions

- Read the *Useful Expressions* to the class and explain anything they don't understand. Ask students in which part of the email the different categories of expressions would be found (*Thanking – 1st paragraph, Asking for information/Making references, Making suggestions – 2nd and 3rd paragraphs, Signing off – after the final paragraph*).
- Ask students which of these expressions Cindy Brady used in her email in C (*I cannot thank you enough …, Regarding …, could you …, Kind regards,*).

F

- Ask students to read the instructions and explain anything they don't understand.
- Ask them to read all the sentences before they rewrite any of them. Remind them they are too informal and they have to make them more formal. They can refer to the *Useful Expressions* for help and ideas.
- Complete the first item together so that they are aware of the other changes that might need to be made in each sentence, such as change the form of the verb *chose* to *choosing*. Ensure everyone has the sentence written correctly in their book.
- Ask them to do the rest of the task individually and then compare their new sentences with a partner. They should discuss any differences and make changes accordingly.
- Check answers as a class. Accept any answers that are formal and make grammatical sense, as well as in the context of the sentence.

Suggested answers

1. I cannot thank you enough for choosing our class for the programme.
2. One idea would be to take a trip to the park.
3. Could you tell me how long they are going to be here?
4. One idea would be to take them to the local discotheque.
5. Yours sincerely

G

- Ask students to read the information in the *Exam Close-up*.
- Remind students that they should bear these instructions in mind when they write their own emails.
- Ask students to read the instructions and the *Exam Task*, and ask them who they are and who they have to write to (*a teacher; the college principal*).
- Ask students to decide what functions each of the notes have (*thank, make suggestions, make references to their abilities, sign off*). Then ask what they have to thank the principal for, what they have to suggest and what they have to inform him/her of (*the reason why the person they are recommending is admired and why he/she would be a good choice*).
- If time allows, ask them to make a more detailed plan including the ideas they will use to deal with each of the notes.

- Encourage students to refer to the Writing Reference and checklist for formal emails on page 179 to help them with their email.

Suggested answer

From: Justin Thyme
Sent: 12th January
Subject: Re: Speaker for Careers Day
Dear Mrs Miller,
Thank you for your email. I cannot thank you enough for asking for my recommendation about someone who the students admire to speak at the Careers Day. Perhaps we could ask Ellie Simpson to speak at Careers Day. All the students know who she is and they all admire her and her success.
Concerning the reasons why I believe she is a good choice, she is an ex-student of the school. She proves that a good education and hard work can lead to success. She started her own fashion design business as soon as she left school and now sells her clothes all over the world.
If you need further suggestions, please let me know.
Yours sincerely,
Justin Thyme

10 Aquarium on Wheels

General Note

The National Geographic videos can be used as an interesting way to introduce your students to other cultures. They are authentic National Geographic videos, and it is not necessary for students to understand everything they hear to benefit from them. The videos have the option to play English subtitles so that students can read on screen exactly what is said in the documentary. This feature may help students with some of the tasks in the worksheets. The videos are also a good way to encourage your students to watch TV programmes and films in English so that they can get used to the sound of the language. The more students are exposed to English, the easier it will be for them to pick up the language.

Background Information

The 'Aquarium on Wheels' programme is run by the National Aquarium in Baltimore and is an after-school programme aimed at secondary school students of fourteen or over. The programme involves training and field trips designed to educate participants about aquatic organisms, provide them with co-operational skills and teaching techniques necessary to complete the programme. During the programme, participants create two original plays and two animal labs. They also give performances of their plays during summer at libraries in the city of Baltimore.

Before you watch

A

- Explain to students that in this lesson they are going to watch a video about an aquarium on wheels. Ask them what they imagine this might be and ask them to look at the globe to see which part of the world it comes from.
- Read the words 1-5 to the students and ask them to repeat them. Correct their pronunciation where necessary.
- Ask students to read the meanings a-e and explain anything they don't understand.
- Ask students to do the task individually, but check as a class.

Answers

1d 2b 3a 4e 5c

While you watch

B

- Explain to students that they are now going to watch the video and do a task based on the information they hear.
- Ask students to read the statements 1-6 and ask them who they will be introduced to in the documentary (*students taking part in the 'Aquarium on Wheels' project*).
- Explain anything in the statements that the students don't understand. Then ask them to think about which words might be correct before they listen.

- Play the video all the way through without stopping and ask students to mark their answers. Ask students to compare their answers with a partner's and to justify any answers that are different. Play the video again so that they can check their answers.
- Ask students to do the task individually, but check as a class.

Answers

1	employees	(00.51)	4	understand	(03.09)
2	goal	(01.11)	5	major	(03.37)
3	set	(02.12)	6	impact	(04.13)

After you watch

C

- Explain to students that this is a summary of the information they heard on the video.
- Read the words in the yellow box to the students and ask them to repeat them. Correct their pronunciation where necessary. Ask students to write N, Adv or Adj beside each of the words depending on whether it is a noun, an adverb or an adjective.
- Explain to students that they should read the whole summary before writing any answers first to work out what part of speech is missing.
- Tell students to read back through the text once they have finished to check their answers.
- Ask students to do the task individually, but check the answers as a class.

Answers

1	programme	5	future
2	presentations	6	advantageous
3	coordinator	7	satisfaction
4	skills	8	effect

Ideas Focus

- Ask students to read the instructions and make sure they understand what they have to do. Then ask them to read the two questions and answer any queries they might have.
- Ask students to work in pairs and explain that they should both give their opinions on both questions.
- Go round the class monitoring students to make sure they are carrying out the task properly. Don't correct any mistakes at this stage, but make a note of any problems in structure and pronunciation.
- Ask each pair to answer one of the questions and repeat until each pair has had a turn.

Answer

Students' own answers

Objectives

- To revise vocabulary and grammar from Units 9 and 10
- To practise exam-type tasks

Revision

- Explain to students that Review 5 revises the material they saw in Units 9 and 10.
- Remind students that they can ask you for help with the exercises or look back at the units if they're not sure about an answer, and stress that the review is not a test.
- Decide how you will carry out the review. You could ask students to do one task at a time and then correct it immediately, or ask students to do all the tasks and correct them together at the end. If you do all the tasks together, let students know every now and again how much time they have got left to finish the tasks.
- Ask students not to leave any answers blank and to try to find any answers they aren't sure about in the units.
- When checking students' answers to the review tasks, make a note of any problem areas in vocabulary and grammar that they still have. Try to do extra work on these areas so that your students will progress well.

Vocabulary Revision

- Play a word association game with words from Units 9 and 10. Say one word related to work or education and training and ask each student in turn to say another word which is related to these themes that they associate with the previous word, for example, *boarding school – dormitories – teacher – tutor*.
- Write the expressions below on the board and ask students to write sentences of their own with them.
  - learn a lesson
  - sit an exam
  - take the initiative
  - think on your feet
  - get a good mark
- Write the verbs *fill, take, hold, figure, brush, go* in one column and the particles *out, up, on, in, over, down* in another column on the board and ask students to match them up to form phrasal verbs they learnt in Units 9 and 10. Then ask them what each phrasal verb means.
- Write these words on the board and ask students what part of speech they are: *achieve, depress, produce, promote, rely, satisfy, work (verbs), suitable, satisfied, interesting (adjectives)*. Ask students to write down any other parts of speech of these words they know. Make sure that they revise the parts they will need to complete Part 3.
- Write the following sentences on the board and ask students to complete them using one word.
  - Students learn to respect each _____ at Summerhill. *(other)*
  - It feels _____ we've been working on this project for years! *(like)*
  - Can we depend _____ Dave to finish the report by Friday? *(on)*
  - Harsher punishments will prevent the students _____ breaking school rules. *(from)*

Grammar Revision

- Write these sentences on the board and ask students to correct them.
  - This is the city when I was born. *(where)*
  - That's the teacher told me to report to the head. *(who/that)*
  - The careers counsellor, that used to be a primary school teacher, was very helpful. *(who)*
  Revise the relative pronouns and adverbs that students learnt in Unit 9 and ask them to write sentences of their own with each one. Make sure they remember when we can use *that* instead of *who* or *which* and when we can omit the relative pronoun.
- Write these sentences on the board and ask students to rewrite them using participle clauses.
  - The student, who was standing at the window, shouted loudly at the teacher. *(Standing at the window, the student shouted loudly at the teacher.)*
  - The small boy was stuck in the games cupboard and started to cry. *(Stuck in the games cupboard, the small boy started to cry.)*
  - The report which was sent last week contained a number of errors. *(The report sent last week contained a number of errors.)*
  - Employees who work the night shift receive higher wages. *(Employees working the night shift receive higher wages.)*
- Write these sentences on the board and ask students to write them in reported speech. Then revise the changes that take place when we change direct speech into reported speech.
  - 'Sure, I'll give you a hand with your science project,' Barry said. *(Barry said that he would give me a hand with my science project.)*
  - 'This is the worst lecture I've ever attended,' Wendy said. *(Wendy said that that was the worst lecture she had ever attended.)*
  - 'You can't go out until you've finished your homework,' Mum told us. *(Mum told us that we couldn't go out until we had finished our homework.)*
  - 'There are two people waiting to be interviewed,' my assistant told me. *(My assistant told me that there were two people waiting to be interviewed.)*
  - 'You should enrol on a plumbing course,' the careers counsellor said. *(The careers counsellor said I should enrol on a plumbing course.)*
- Ask the students to rewrite the reported sentences using the reporting verbs *inform, warn, agree, advise* and *complain*.
  - *(Barry agreed to give me a hand with my science project.)*
  - *(Wendy complained that that was the worst lecture she had ever attended.)*
  - *(Mum warned us that we couldn't go out until we had finished our homework.)*
  - *(My assistant informed me that there were two people waiting to be interviewed.)*
  - *(The careers counsellor advised me to enrol on a plumbing course.)*

Part 1

- Ask students to read the instructions and check that they understand what they have to do.
- Ask students to read the title of the text and ask them what they think the text will deal with. Then ask them to skim read the text, without circling any answers at this stage, to find out what other companies can learn from Google (*If you treat employees well, they will work better and be more satisfied at work.*). Ask students if they would like to work for a company like Google and why.
- Point out to students that they should read all four options for each item before deciding which word best fits each gap. Remind them to pay attention to the whole sentence each gap is in as the general context will help them understand what word is missing.
- Remind students to read back through the text once they have finished to check their answers.

Answers

1D 2C 3A 4B 5A 6D 7C 8B 9C 10A 11B 12D

Part 2

- Ask students to read the instructions and check that they understand what they have to do.
- Ask students what continuous assessment is and whether their schools use this to assess their learning.
- Ask students to skim read the text, without filling in any answers at this stage, to find out how students can benefit from continuous assessment (*By having smaller tests after being taught small chunks of material, students' real progress can be assessed. Also, it can be very stressful for some students if everything rests on their performance in one exam, so continuous assessment can relieve the pressure and help them to perform better. It also helps them to work out what their strengths and weaknesses are so that they can improve.*).
- Encourage students to pay particular attention to the words immediately before and after each gap to work out what part of speech is missing. However, remind them that they have to take into consideration the general context of the sentence so that they understand which structure is being used.
- Remind students to read back through the text once they have finished to check their answers.

Answers

13 which	19 from
14 sit/take/do	20 few
15 teachers/schools	21 which/that
16 during/throughout	22 some
17 do	23 of
18 getting/receiving	24 out

Part 3

- Ask students to read the instructions and check that they understand what they have to do.
- Ask students to read the title of the text and ask them what they think it will be about. Ask them to skim read the text, without filling in any answers at this stage, to find out who can benefit from getting careers advice (*high school students, college/university students and graduates and adults who are unemployed or wish to change career*).
- Read the words at the side of the text to the students and ask them to repeat them. Correct their pronunciation where necessary.
- Ask students to read back through the text and to decide which part of speech is missing from each gap, and to complete the gaps using the correct form of the words given.
- Remind students to read back through the text once they have finished to check their answers.

Answers

25 counsellor	30 suitably
26 professionals	31 graduation
27 useful	32 unemployed
28 understanding	33 satisfaction
29 educational	34 advice

Part 4

- Ask students to read the instructions and check that they understand what they have to do.
- Ask students to read both sentences in each item and to underline the information in the first sentence that is missing from the second sentence. Then ask them to look at the word given to decide how the missing information could be inserted into the second sentence using this word. Remind students that they will have to use a different structure in order to keep the meaning the same.
- Remind students that they mustn't change the word given in any way.
- Encourage students to read back through the completed sentences once they have finished to check their answers.

Answers

35 the reason why he had
36 where I studied is/was
37 advised me against becoming/was against my becoming
38 reminded us (that) we had
39 whose mum is a
40 told us not to talk
41 the day when
42 agreed to help me

11 Wish You Were Here!

Reading:	multiple choice, understanding specific meaning
Vocabulary:	holiday- & travel-related vocabulary
Grammar:	comparison of adjectives & adverbs, gradable & non-gradable adjectives, adjective order
Listening:	multiple-choice, working with degree
Speaking:	using holiday vocabulary, comparing photographs, student A: timing the photo comparison, talking about holidays
Use your English:	phrasal verbs, prepositions, multiple choice questions
Writing:	story (2), prompts & tenses, writing effectively, talking about feelings, showing happiness, showing surprise, disbelief & fear

Unit opener

- Ask students to look at the title of the unit and explain that this is a common phrase in English. Then ask them where they think they are most likely to read this expression (on a postcard sent from someone on holiday).
- Ask students to look at the picture and its accompanying caption. Ask them what they think the woman is feeling and thinking in the picture and why she might be in this place. Ask them if they would like to be there and if this is the kind of place they usually go on holiday.
- Elicit that the unit will be about holidays and travelling and ask students to name as many different kinds of holidays as they can think of (eg beach holiday, city break, activity holiday, eco holiday, camping, etc.) and ask them which kind of holiday appeals to them most and why.

Reading

A

- Ask students to read the instructions and check that they understand what they have to do.
- Read the list of potential holiday problems to the students and ask them to repeat them. Correct their pronunciation where necessary. Explain any words they don't know.
- Give students a few minutes to tick any that have happened to them and then ask them to work with a partner to talk about their experiences. Ask them to discuss which item they think is the worst.
- As a class, conduct a survey to see which of these potential problems students think are the worst. Write the problems on to the board and ask for a show of hands for each one and note the number of students who think each problem is the worst. Discuss the results as a class.

B

- Ask students to read the instructions and check that they understand what they have to do.
- Explain to the students that they don't have to read the text in detail now as they will have another chance to read it later on.

- Encourage students to underline the reference to the problem when they come across it in the story.
- Ask students to do the task individually, but check as a class.

Answer

> She had her money stolen.

Word Focus

- Ask students to look at the words in red in the text and to read the sentences they are found in. Remind students that when they don't know the meaning of a word, they should look carefully at the sentence it is found in to work out its meaning. Ask students to work in pairs to decide what each of the words mean.
- Ask students to read the Word Focus box to compare their answers with the definitions given. Explain anything they don't understand.

C

- Ask students to read the information in the Exam Close-up and ask them which main idea it contains (a multiple-choice question could refer to a specific word or phrase in the text and its meaning; look at the context the word is used in, then choose from the options which word is closest in meaning to the way the word has been used in the text).
- Ask students to read the instructions and check that they understand what they have to do.
- Ask students to read the questions in the Exam Task and to underline the key words and phrases. Explain anything they don't understand.

D

- Ask students to read the instructions and check that they understand what they have to do.
- Encourage students to read the story again and underline information that relates to the ideas mentioned in the questions. Remind them that they won't find the exact same words.
- Ask students to do the task individually, but check as a class. Ask students to justify their answers by referring to where they found the answer in the text.

1a (*I was 19 and on my first ... independence, hooray!*)

2d (*First-time flyers? Perhaps.*)

3a (*How was that possible? I mean, they were going to ROME. Why weren't they as excited as I was?*)

4b (*I'm ashamed to admit that I began to cry; ... I was overcome by the problem.*)

5a (*And that's when I got the biggest shock of all. ... and his real name was Nigel Waters, an Englishman from Manchester!*)

6d (*I realised I should never trust a stranger.*)

E

- Ask students to look at the words in the yellow box and to scan the text again to find the words. Ask them to say each of the words after you and elicit that they are all nouns. Correct their pronunciation where necessary.
- Remind them that they should always try to work out the meaning of a word from its context and ask them to read the sentences in the text each word is in.
- Ask students to read the instructions and check that they understand what they have to do. Encourage them to read all the sentences in E once before writing in any answers to work out the meaning of the missing words.
- Ask students to do the task individually, but check as a class.

Answers

1 tip
2 terminal
3 monument
4 guide book
5 destination
6 insight

Ideas Focus

- Ask students to read the questions and answer any queries they have about them.
- Ask students to do the task in pairs and encourage them to draw on their own experience as much as possible.
- Go round the class monitoring students to make sure they are carrying out the task properly. Don't correct any mistakes at this stage, but make a note of any problems in structure and pronunciation.
- Ask each pair to answer one of the questions and ask other students if they have anything else to add.
- Write any structural mistakes that students made on the board without saying who made them, and ask them to correct them. Deal with any problems in pronunciation that came up.

Answer

Students' own answers

A

- Ask students to read the instructions and check that they understand what they have to do.
- Read the words in the yellow box to students and ask them to repeat them. Correct their pronunciation where necessary.
- Ask students to read the sets of words in 1-8 to work out how they are connected. Point out that the part of speech is the same for all words in each set so this should give them a clue about which word completes each group.
- Ask students to do the task individually, but check as a class.

Answers

1 abroad	**5** shuttle
2 runway	**6** isolated
3 quay	**7** ship
4 hostel	**8** bay

B

- Write the words *travel agent*, *package tour* and *departure lounge* on the board. Ask students what they mean and what they have in common (*They all have two parts.*). Explain to students that these are compound nouns as they are made up of two words. Point out that this task introduces them to other travel-related compound nouns and that they should choose the correct answers depending on which of the two options can collocate with the previous word or the word that follows.
- Ask students to read the whole sentence before circling their answers.

Answers

1 excess	**4** crew
2 pass	**5** compartment
3 gate	**6** in-flight

Teaching Tip

Explain to students that compound nouns like these need to be learnt by heart. Explain that although the other options were fairly similar in meaning and that they would be understood if they used the wrong options instead of the correct ones, a native speaker would never use these words. Encourage students to copy the compound nouns and their meanings into their notebooks and ask them to write sentences of their own with these words if time allows.

C

- Ask students to read the instructions and check that they understand what they have to do. Point out that they will have to change the form of the verb in some sentences.
- Read the words in the yellow box to students and ask them to repeat them. Correct their pronunciation where necessary.
- Ask students to read all the sentences first to work out the meaning of the missing verb and which form it should go in.

- Remind students to read back through the sentences once they have finished to check their answers.
- Ask students to do the task individually, but check as a class.

Answers

1	declare	4	board
2	ground	5	landed
3	cancelled	6	delayed

D

- Read the words in capitals to the students and ask them to repeat them. Correct their pronunciation if necessary. Ask students what part of speech each word is *(nouns: nerve, shop; verbs: miss, eat, hire, perform, shop)* and which other parts of speech of these words they know.
- Ask students to read the sentences without filling in any answers at this stage, to work out what part of speech is missing from each gap.
- Remind students to read back through the sentences once they have finished to check their answers.
- Ask students to do the task individually, but check as a class.

Answers

1 nervous
2 missing
3 eaten
4 hired
5 shopping
6 performers

Grammar

- Ask students to look back at the Reading to find examples of comparative and superlative adjectives and adverbs *(Paragraph 1: the best; Paragraph 2: the best, as excited as; Paragraph 3: less noisy than).*

A

- Ask students to read the instructions and check that they understand what they have to do.
- Ask students to read each sentence or question through first, before they underline anything.
- Ask students to do the task individually, but check as a class.

Answers

1 The more, the more
2 as beautiful as
3 more politely than
4 the most interesting
5 as fast as
6 better than
7 the slowest

Now read the Grammar Reference on pages 173 & 174 (11.1 to 11.3) with your students.

B

- Ask students to read the instructions and check that they understand what they have to do.
- Ask students to read the questions and to look back at the underlined parts of the sentences in A.
- Ask the students to do the task with a partner to encourage discussion, but check as a class.

Answers

a 3, 6
b 4, 7
c 2, 4, 6
d 3, 5, 7
e 6
f 2
g 1

C

- Read the rules to the students and explain anything they don't understand.
- Encourage students to look back at the examples in A and B when filling in their answers.
- Ask students to do the task individually, but check as a class.

Answers

comparative, more
superlative, most

D

- Ask students to read the instructions and check that they understand what they have to do.
- Ask students to read each sentence through before they read the words in brackets and to note if they need to use the comparative or superlative form.
- Remind students to read the sentences through again once they have written their answer to check they are correct.
- Ask students to do the task individually, but check as a class.

Answers

1 best
2 more healthy/healthier
3 more comfortable
4 more difficult
5 the strictest
6 naughtier
7 the most delicious
8 more careful

E

- Ask students to read the instructions and check that they understand what they have to do.
- Ask students to read the text, without finding any errors at this stage, to find out where dinosaurs roamed (*Dinosaur Ridge, USA*).
- Ask students to underline the errors in the text and write the correct answers above them.
- Ask students to do the task individually, but check as a class.

Answers

1 more interesting *from* should be *than*
2 the famous should be the *most* famous
3 *so* wonderful should be *such* wonderful
4 *the good* known should be the *best*-known
5 earliest should be *the* earliest
6 *the* old as should be *as* old as
7 hot *enough* should be *too* hot
8 the *earliest* should be the *earlier*
9 *too* popular should be *so* popular

Listening

A

- Ask students to read the instructions and check that they understand what they have to do.
- Give each pair enough time to discuss all of the phrases. Encourage them to put them into sentences which demonstrate their differences if necessary.
- As a class, ask each pair to explain the difference in meaning between one of the sets and ask the others if they agree or have anything else to add.

Answers

1 'House swapping' is when you stay at someone else's house for an agreed amount of time while they stay at your house, whereas 'house sitting' is when you look after someone else's house while they are away somewhere.
2 'Have a lot in common' means that people are similar in many ways as they have the same tastes and interests in many things, whereas 'have one thing in common' means they are mainly different and have the same taste or interest in only one thing.
3 'For next to nothing' means that you pay a small amount of money for something, whereas 'absolutely free of charge' means that you don't pay anything at all for something.
4 'Browse a property' usually means to look at photographs and read descriptions of a building or piece of land online, whereas 'visit a property' means to go and see a building or piece of land up close.
5 'Not very often' means rarely, whereas 'more often than not' means usually.

B

- Ask students to read the instructions and check that they understand what they have to do.
- Ask students to read sentences 1-4 and to discuss with a partner the differences in meaning between the two options.
- Play the recording once all the way through and ask students to mark their answers. Then ask students to discuss their answers with a partner and to justify any that are different.
- Play the recording again and ask students to check their answers and to complete any answers they haven't already completed.
- Check the answers as a class and ask students to justify their answers.

Answers

1 any time soon
2 most
3 part of the holiday
4 extremely

C

- Ask students to read the information in the *Exam Close-up* and explain that these adverbs can often be the difference between a right and a wrong answer. Sometimes most of the information in an option can match what the speaker says, but a wrong adverb of degree or frequency can make the whole answer wrong. For example, you may hear *We usually go abroad once a year.*, but the option may read *The speaker says they always visit a foreign country once every year*. Here the words *usually* and *always* alter the meaning of what the speaker says.
- Ask students to tell you what they should pay careful attention to (*adverbs of degree, adverbs of frequency, comparatives and superlatives*).
- Explain to students that adverbs are key words in multiple-choice options and that they should always underline them in options.

D

- Ask students to read the instructions and check that they understand what they have to do. Ask students what they expect to hear on the recording.
- Ask students to read items 1-7 and to underline key words in the stems and the options. Encourage them to think about how the three options in each item are different.
- Play the recording once all the way through and ask students to mark their answers. Then ask students to discuss their answers with a partner and to justify any that are different.

E

- Play the recording again and ask students to check their answers and to complete any answers they haven't already completed.
- Check the answers as a class and ask students to justify their answers.

Answers

1b 2a 3c 4a 5a 6c 7b

Teaching Tip

Use the idea of house swapping as the basis for a class discussion. Ask students to comment on whether or not they think it's a good idea, whether they would be prepared to do it and what they think the advantages and disadvantages of it would be.

Speaking

A

- Ask students to read the three questions and answer any queries they may have about them.
- Ask students to work in pairs and take turns to ask and answer the questions about themselves.
- Go round the class monitoring students to make sure they are carrying out the task properly. Don't correct any mistakes at this stage, but make a note of any problems in structure and pronunciation.
- Ask each pair to ask and answer one of the questions and repeat until each student has had a turn.
- Write any structural mistakes that students made on the board without saying who made them, and ask them to correct them. Deal with any problems in pronunciation that came up.

B

- Ask students to read the instructions and check that they understand what they have to do. Explain that they should present the idea they support in a favourable way and comment on the drawbacks of the opposing idea.
- Read the topics to students and explain anything they don't understand.
- Ask students to work in pairs and to decide who will support the red ideas and who will support the blue ideas. Give the students time to prepare and give them any help they may need with vocabulary. Remind them they only have 40 seconds to speak.
- Go round the class monitoring students to make sure they are carrying out the task properly and within the time limit. Don't correct any mistakes at this stage, but make a note of any mistakes in structure and pronunciation.
- Ask each pair to speak in front of the class. Time them. Make sure that all pairs take a turn and that all the topics are covered.
- Write any structural mistakes that students made on the board without saying who made them, and ask them to correct them. Deal with any problems in pronunciation that came up.

C

- Ask students to read the information in the *Exam Close-up* and remind them that in the kind of task they have in C, both students are given a set of pictures to talk about for one minute and that they are asked a question about their partner's picture. Remind them that they should reply in about twenty seconds to the question on their partner's picture, so they should be to the point.
- Read the expressions in *Useful Expressions* to the students and ask them to repeat them. Correct their pronunciation and intonation if necessary. Explain anything students don't understand.
- Ask students to look at the two pairs of pictures in C and elicit which expressions could be used to discuss each picture.
- Ask students to read the instructions and check that they understand what they have to do.
- Ask students to decide who will be Student A and who will be Student B. Then ask them to read the instructions and questions for their part.
- Give students about a minute to prepare their answers and remind them of the time limits for each part of the task.
- Go round the class monitoring students to make sure they are carrying out the task properly. Don't correct any mistakes at this stage, but make a note of any problems in structure and pronunciation.
- Ask two pairs of students to carry out the task in front of the class and ask the others if they have anything else to add.
- Write any structural mistakes that students made on the board without saying who made them, and ask them to correct them. Deal with any problems in pronunciation that came up.

Ideas Focus

- Ask students to read the questions quickly and deal with any queries they may have.
- Ask students to work in pairs and take turns to answer the questions.
- Go round the class monitoring students to make sure they are carrying out the task properly. Don't correct any mistakes at this stage, but make a note of any problems in structure and pronunciation.
- Ask a student from each pair to answer one of the questions until each pair has had a turn. Ask other students if they agree or if they have something else to add.
- Write any structural mistakes that students made on the board without saying who made them, and ask them to correct them. Deal with any problems in pronunciation that came up.

Answer

Students' own answers

Grammar

- Write the sentences below on the board and ask students to find and correct the mistakes. Elicit why the words are wrong (*They have been collocated with the wrong kind of adjective.*).
  - I'm absolutely tired. (*really/very/quite*, etc) or (*exhausted*)
  - These ticket prices are very ridiculous. (*absolutely/ utterly*, etc) or (*expensive*)
- Read the information on gradable and non-gradable adjectives to students and explain anything they don't understand.
- Elicit that in the sentences above, *tired* and *expensive* are gradable and *ridiculous* and *exhausted* are non-gradable.

A

- Ask students to read the instructions and explain anything they don't understand.
- Ask students to look at the adjectives and think about whether they are gradable or non-gradable.
- Ask students to do the task in pairs to encourage discussion, but check as a class.

Answers

1G 2N 3G 4N 5G 6G 7N 8N

B

- Read the information in *Be careful!* to students and ask them to write sentences of their own with these adverbs and the adjectives *astounding, stunning, reasonable, angry* and *disappointed* which are based on the theme of travel and tourism.
- Ask students to read the instructions and check that they understand what they have to do.
- Ask students to look back at the adjectives in A and the answers they wrote as to whether they are gradable or non-gradable. They should also look back at the information before task A.
- Ask students to do the task individually and then compare their answers with a partner. Check answers as a class.

Suggested answers

1 slightly/fairly/rather/very/extremely/really/fairly/ pretty/quite hungry
2 absolutely/almost/utterly/really boiling
3 slightly/fairly/rather/very/extremely/really/fairly/ pretty/quite cold
4 absolutely/utterly furious
5 slightly/fairly/rather/very/extremely/really/fairly/ quite/pretty hot
6 slightly/fairly/rather/very/extremely/really/fairly/ pretty/quite angry
7 absolutely/almost/utterly freezing
8 absolutely/really starving

C

- Ask students to read the instructions and check that they understand what they have to do.
- Ask students to underline the adjectives and then compare their answers with a partner.
- Check answers as a class.

Answers

fantastic new red Italian
big old leather

D

- Read the rule to students and explain anything they don't understand.
- Ask students to look back at the sentences in C to help them complete the rule.
- Ask students to do the task individually, but check as a class.

Answers

opinion, age, material

Now read the Grammar Reference on page 174 (11.4 to 11.6) with your students.

E

- Read the words in red to students and elicit which are adjectives (*options in 1, 2, 3, 4 & 8*) and which are adverbs (*options in 5, 6 & 7*).
- Encourage students to read the whole sentence and to note whether adverbs are grading or non-grading and whether adjectives are gradable or non-gradable before circling their answers.
- Remind students to read back through the sentences once they have finished to check their answers.

Answers

1 good	5 quite
2 hungry	6 extremely
3 freezing	7 reasonably
4 annoyed	8 impossible

F

- Ask students to read the instructions and check that they understand what they have to do.
- Encourage students to read the adjectives before the sentences to decide what each adjective tells us about the noun it describes. Explain that they should look back at D for help if necessary.
- Remind students to read back through the sentences once they have finished to check their answers.
- Ask students to do the task individually, but check as a class.

Answers

1 pretty blue wooden
2 comfortable wide leather
3 rusty old metal
4 cool green Swiss
5 ugly red plastic
6 ridiculous big designer

11 Wish You Were Here!

Extra Class Activity

Make a holiday brochure with your students. Ask students to write an advert for their favourite holiday destination on a piece of paper. Encourage them to use comparative and superlative adjectives and adverbs, gradable and non-gradable adjectives wherever possible. Remind students that the main purpose of the advert should be to inform readers about the main features of the place and attract them to go there. If you have Internet access and a printer, ask students to find and print a photo of their destination to include in their advert. If not, ask students to draw a picture of the place or of something they associate with the place.

Use your English

A

- Ask students to read the instructions and check that they understand what they have to do.
- Read the phrasal verbs in the yellow box to students and ask them to repeat them. Correct their pronunciation where necessary.
- Remind students that they should read the whole sentence and think about the meaning of the particle as well as the verb when deciding which phrasal verb is missing from each sentence.
- Remind students to read back through the sentences once they have finished to check their answers.
- Ask students to do the task individually, but check as a class.
- Give students time to copy the phrasal verbs and their meanings into their notebooks before moving on to B.

Answers

1 make for	4 check out
2 set off	5 see ... off
3 book into	6 check in

B

- Ask students to read the instructions and check that they understand what they have to do. Point out that they will have to change the form of the verb in some sentences.
- Ask students to read all the sentences first to work out the meaning of the missing phrasal verb and which form it should go in.
- Remind students to read back through the sentences once they have finished to check their answers.
- Ask students to do the task individually, but check as a class.

Answers

1 made for	4 set off
2 check out	5 checked in
3 book into	6 saw ... off

C

- Ask students to read the instructions and check that they understand what they have to do.
- Ask students to read the prepositions in the yellow box and elicit that some prepositions will be used more than once.
- Ask students to read the sentences before they fill in any answers and to pay attention to the words either side of the gaps. Explain that the prepositions are part of common expressions in English.
- Remind students to read back through the sentences once they have finished to check their answers.
- Ask students to do the task individually, but check as a class.

Answers

1 on	5 at
2 within	6 on
3 in	7 in
4 on	8 by

D

- Ask students to look at the picture and to imagine that they want to go on holiday to the place shown. Ask them how they could arrange to go there.
- Ask students to look at the title of the text and ask them to skim read the text, without circling any answers at this stage, to see how it relates to the text (The text talks about how we can arrange holidays these days in comparison to in the past, so 'Getting there' is an appropriate title.).
- Read the words in the options in 1-8 to students and ask them to repeat them. Correct their pronunciation where necessary. Explain anything they don't understand.
- Remind students that they should consider all four options before circling their answers.
- Remind students to read back through the text once they have finished to check their answers.
- Ask students to do the task individually, but check as a class.

Answers

1a 2c 3d 4a 5c 6d 7b 8d

Writing: a story (2)

- Read the information on writing stories in the *Learning Focus* to students and explain anything they don't understand.
- Ask students to look at the picture and ask them to write a sentence based on it that could be the start of a story. Point out that their sentences should generate a certain emotion in readers. Then ask students to read their sentences to the class and ask the others to say what emotion is generated by each sentence.

- Remind students that we use past tenses when narrating a story. Elicit that we use the Past Simple to narrate events that take the story forward, the Past Continuous for descriptions and the Past Perfect tenses to talk about events that happened before the time of the narrative. Remind students that we only use the present tenses in direct speech in stories.

A

- Ask students to read the instructions and check that they understand what they have to do.
- Elicit different emotions from the students and make a list of them on the board, for instance, *suspense, fear, anxiety, joy, anticipation, sadness, loneliness, relief.*
- Read the first sentence as a class and elicit which emotion it generates. Check the answer before moving on to the rest of the task.
- Ask students to do the task in pairs to encourage discussion, but check as a class.

Suggested answers

1 mystery, suspense	4 sadness
2 urgency	5 excitement
3 surprise, shock	6 fear

B

- Ask students to do the task in pairs to encourage discussion, but check as a class. Point out that they should only choose one sentence.
- Ask students to think about which sentence probably wouldn't make sense without such an explanation.
- Ask students to do the task in pairs to encourage discussion, but check as a class.

Answers

Prompt 5: the writer would have to explain what the experience was, how it had come about, how it had affected him/her, ie to discuss events that led up to the prompt. You would use a Past Perfect tense.

C

- Ask students to read the instructions and the writing task to find out who the story will be about and when and where it will be set (*A person called Cathy is the main character and the story will be set at night in a city that she doesn't know very well.*).
- Ask students which emotions this sentence generates (*suspense, fear, uncertainty*).
- Ask students to answer questions 1-3 in pairs to encourage discussion, but check as a class.

Answers

1 scared, worried
2 *completely lost, dark streets* and *strange city*
3 find her way, get directions

D

- Ask students to read the instructions and check that they understand what they have to do. Explain that their introduction should be able to replace the one in the example story in such a way that the rest of the story still makes sense.
- Ask students what they think will happen in the story then ask them to read through it to find out. Ask them if the plot is what they expected.
- Give students about five minutes to write their paragraphs and then ask them to swap with a partner. Point out that they should look out for mistakes in spelling, use of vocabulary and tenses as they edit each other's work.
- Ask several students to read out their paragraphs to the class.

E

- Ask students to read the instructions and the three questions and check that they understand what they have to do. Explain anything in the three questions that they don't understand.
- Encourage students to underline relevant parts of the text in order to help them answer the questions.
- Ask students to do the task individually, but check as a class.

Answers

1 Cathy needed to ask for directions and headed towards a light which turned out to be a shop./ She found an old man who spoke English and she explained that she was lost./The old man told her where her hotel was.
2 Present Simple
3 She was relieved because she had found her hotel, and felt foolish because it was nearby.

F

- Ask students to read the instructions and check that they understand what they have to do. Explain that they should write sentences like the ones in E1.
- Point out to students that their stories should also be based on the introductory sentence in the writing task in B, but that the plot should be completely different from the one in the example story.
- Give students time to think about how they could develop the story and to write their sentences.
- As a class, ask students to read out their three sentences and to explain how their stories are different from the model.

G

- Ask students to read the instructions and check that they understand what they have to do.
- Elicit that if they use direct speech, they should use present tenses and appropriate punctuation.
- Remind students that they should use the basic idea of the sentence they wrote in F in their paragraphs.
- Give students time to write their paragraphs and then ask them to swap with a partner to edit each other's paragraphs.
- As a class, ask several students to read their paragraphs to the class.

H

- Ask students to read the instructions and check that they understand what they have to do. Ask them to quickly re-read the conclusion in the example story to see how the writer has linked it to the rest of the story and brought the story to an end.
- Remind students that their own conclusions should be able to follow on logically from the ideas in the sentences they wrote in F and the paragraph they wrote in G.
- As a class, ask several students to read out their conclusions, making sure students who didn't read out their paragraph in G have a chance to read theirs out this time.

I

- Ask students to read the information in the *Exam Close-up* and elicit that the writer of the example story has done all of these things.
- Remind students that they can use the points here as a checklist when writing their own stories.
- Ask students to also look at the paragraph plan to help them. Read the note under the plan to the class and explain anything they don't understand.

Useful Expressions

- Read the *Useful Expressions* to students and ask them to repeat them. Correct their pronunciation and intonation if necessary.
- Ask students to find expressions from here in the example story (*Cathy had never felt so …*).
- Remind students that they can use these expressions in their stories, but that they shouldn't overuse them.

J

- Ask students to read the instructions and the *Exam Task* and ask them to answer the questions below.
  - Who will the story be about? (*a person called Joe*)
  - How do you think Joe was feeling at the start? (*panicked*)
  - What words indicate that he had reason to feel this way? (*realised his passport was gone*)
  - What do you think Joe would try to do? (*find his passport, report it missing*)
- Ask students to think up as many different situations as possible that Joe might be in, how he could resolve the problem and how things could turn out in the end.
- Encourage students to use the *Useful Expressions* to express what the characters in your story are feeling. Ask students to read the paragraph plan again. If time allows, ask them to make a more detailed plan by writing one sentence for each paragraph to summarise the main ideas.
- Encourage students to refer to the Writing Reference and checklist for stories on page 181 to help them with their stories.

Suggested answer

Joe put his hand into his pocket and realised his passport was gone. Panicking, he ran back to the duty-free shop, sure that he had last used it there. Joe didn't have time to wait in the huge queue. Although he didn't want to seem rude, there was nothing else he could do but push past all the customers loaded down with last-minute shopping before boarding.

'Excuse me,' Joe said to the cashier, 'I think I may have left my passport here.' The cashier casually glanced at the area round the till. 'Sorry,' came the reply, 'There's no passport here.'

Joe's heart sank. His flight was leaving in just over an hour. Just then he remembered that his friend had used his identity card when travelling abroad. He rummaged in his bag only to find that his passport was tucked inside a pocket.

As he dashed to the check-in desk, he felt a bit cross with himself as he was always doing silly things like that. 'I must learn to concentrate more', he said to himself as he handed over his ticket and passport.

11 Gliding Across the Gobi

General Note

The National Geographic videos can be used as an interesting way to introduce your students to other cultures. They are authentic National Geographic videos, and it is not necessary for students to understand everything they hear to benefit from them. The videos have the option to play English subtitles so that students can read on screen exactly what is said in the documentary. This feature may help students with some of the tasks in the worksheets. The videos are also a good way to encourage your students to watch TV programmes and films in English so that they can get used to the sound of the language. The more students are exposed to English, the easier it will be for them to pick up the language.

Background Information

The Gobi Desert, which is the world's fifth largest desert, is located in the north and northwest of China and southern Mongolia. It is currently over 1,600 km in length and 800 km in width. However, the desert is growing at an alarming rate due to the process of desertification. This process is due to human activities such as deforestation. The Gobi is a desert of extremes, with winter temperatures as low as -40° C and summer temperatures as high as 50° C. Temperatures in the desert can fluctuate greatly and can even change by as much as 35° C in 24 hours.

Before you watch

A

- Explain to students that in this lesson they are going to watch a video about paragliding across the Gobi Desert. Ask them to look at the globe to see which part of the world the Gobi is in.
- Read the deserts 1-5 to the students and ask them to repeat them. Correct their pronunciation where necessary.
- Ask students to read the locations on their own.
- Ask students to do the task individually, but check as a class.

Answers

1e 2c 3a 4d 5b

While you watch

B

- Explain to students that they are now going to watch the video and do a task based on the information they hear.
- Ask students to read the statements 1-5 and ask them who they will be introduced to on the documentary (a person called Lao Ji).
- Explain anything in the statements that the students don't understand. Then ask them to think about which statements might be true and which might be false before they listen.
- Play the video all the way through without stopping and ask students to mark their answers. Ask students to

compare their answers with a partner's and to justify any answers that are different. Play the video again so that they can check their answers.

- Ask students to do the task individually, but check as a class.

Answers

1T	(00.36)
2F *(He was born and raised …)*	(01.11)
3T	(02.05)
4F *(By the third day the sand dunes are over 1,000 feet high.)*	(02.30)
5F *(… get photos of the Gobi Desert from a bird's eye view.)*	(05.42)

After you watch

C

- Explain to students that this is a summary of the information they heard on the video.
- Read the words in the yellow box to the students and ask them to repeat them. Correct their pronunciation where necessary. Ask students to write *N, Adv, V* or *Adj* beside each of the words depending on whether it is a noun, an adverb, a verb or an adjective.
- Explain to students that they should read the whole summary before writing any answers first to work out what part of speech is missing.
- Tell students to read back through the text once they have finished to check their answers.
- Ask students to do the task individually, but check the answers as a class.

Answers

1 explorers	**5** paraglide
2 arid	**6** attempts
3 safely	**7** takes off
4 shade	**8** lives

Ideas Focus

- Ask students to read the instructions and make sure they understand what they have to do. Then ask them to read the three questions and answer any queries they might have.
- Ask students to work in pairs and explain that they should both give their opinions on all three questions.
- Go round the class monitoring students to make sure they are carrying out the task properly. Don't correct any mistakes at this stage, but make a note of any problems in structure and pronunciation.
- Ask each pair to answer one of the questions and repeat until each pair has had a turn.
- On the board, write what we gain from our holidays and ask students which things are more important to them personally.

Answer

Students' own answers

Reading:	missing sentences, getting it right
Vocabulary:	food- & health-related vocabulary
Grammar:	unreal past: *wish & if only, had better & It's (about/high) time, would prefer, prefer & would rather; be used to & get used to,* inversion
Listening:	multiple-choice, , conquering the exam
Speaking:	talking about health care & fitness facilities, health & well-being, decision making, remembering to collaborate , answering questions
Use your English:	phrasal verbs, word formation, collocations & expressions, prepositions
Writing:	review, using the right language, planning your review, starting paragraphs, what I liked & disliked, food, cost, popularity

Unit opener

- Ask students to read the title of the unit and elicit what the theme of Unit 12 is *(health & fitness)*. Ask students why it's important to be fit for life and how people can stay in good shape throughout their lives. Make sure they cover following a sensible diet and taking regular exercise in their discussion.
- Ask students to look at the picture and its accompanying caption and ask them how they relate to the unit title *(It shows middle-aged people doing yoga during part of an expedition in the Himalayas. This shows that they find it important to keep fit even though they are at an age when many people want to take life easy.)*.
- Allow students to discuss their opinions on how these people have chosen to spend their free time.

Reading

A

- Ask students to read the instructions and check that they understand what they have to do.
- Read the words in the labels to students and ask them to repeat them. Correct their pronunciation where necessary.
- Ask students to work in pairs to encourage discussion. Encourage students to discuss which things they, and people in their country in general, eat, which things people from other countries might eat and why they would or would not eat any of these things.
- As a class, ask students which things you can eat and discuss the question.
- If students seem interested, give them further information using the Background Information box.

Answers

All of these things can be eaten.
We don't eat certain foods because of our culture, religion, or, how we were brought up. Also, the appearance, colour and smell of certain foods may put us off eating them.

Background Information

Ants, scorpions and seaweed are all popular foodstuffs in many Asian countries. Century eggs are usually found in China, where duck, chicken or quail eggs are preserved in a mixture of clay, ash, salt, lime and rice hulls for weeks or months. Sea urchins, oysters and snails are popular in many countries around the world. Exotic fruits, beans and blue cheese may be the most easily-recognisable foodstuffs here to westerners, however, they are foods which many people either don't eat or won't try either due to their appearance or smell.

B

- Ask students to read the instructions and check that they understand what they have to do.
- Ask students to look at the title and the accompanying picture and ask them what they think the text will be about *(strange foodstuffs)*. Elicit that far-out means strange or unusual.
- Ask students to underline and make a note of all the foodstuffs that are mentioned in their notebooks as they read.
- Remind students that they don't need to read in detail as they will have another chance to read the text.
- Ask students to do the task individually, but check as a class.

Answers

fruit and vegetables, sugar, salt, insects, lemon, bacon, grasshoppers, waterbugs, termites, peanut butter, chocolate, durian fruit, strawberry, garlic, manioc, fugu, fish

Word Focus

- Ask students to look at the words in red in the text and to read the sentences they are found in. Remind students that when they don't know the meaning of a word, they should look carefully at the sentence it is found in to work out its meaning. Ask students to work in pairs to decide what each of the words mean.
- Ask students to read the *Word Focus* box to compare their answers with the definitions given. Explain anything they don't understand.

C

- Ask students to read the information in the *Exam Close-up* and ask a student to tell you what it says in his or her own words. Remind students to look out for linking words and expressions, subject, object and possessive pronouns, adverbs that show sequence and synonyms of key words found immediately before or after the gaps.
- Ask students to look at sentences F and H and to try to work out what the words *cup* and *process* refer to by looking back at the text (*cup refers to the poisonous juice which is strained out of manioc, process refers to the careful preparation of manioc required in order to make it edible*).
- Ask students to look at all the sentences and read them carefully to underline the key words in each one.
- Ask them to compare what they have underlined with a partner and discuss any differences they have.

D

- Ask students to read the instructions and check that they understand what they have to do.
- Ask students to read the sentences A-I again and pay particular attention to the key words they have already underlined. Remind them to look out for the features mentioned in the notes in the *Exam Close-up*.
- Point out that the sentences must fit in both with the information before and after the gap in order to be correct.
- Ask students to read back through the text once they have finished to check their answers and check that the sentence they haven't used doesn't make sense.
- Ask students to do the task individually, but check as a class.

Answers

1E 2A 3I 4C 5D 6H 7F 8B

Extra Class Activity

Ask students to look at all the pictures and accompanying captions surrounding the text. Ask them to discuss as a class which of these foods they would be more tempted to try in light of what they have just read, and which they would be less tempted to try. Ask them to justify their answers. Finish off the discussion by asking students how far they agree or disagree with Wade Davis' opinions on the subject.

E

- Ask students to look at the words in the yellow box and to scan the text again to find and underline them. Ask them to say each of the words after you and elicit that they are all adjectives, except for *consume* and *processed*, which are verbs. Correct their pronunciation where necessary.
- Remind them that they should always try to work out the meaning of a word from its context and ask them to read the sentences in the text each word is in.
- Ask students to read the instructions and check that they understand what they have to do. Encourage them to read all the sentences in E once before writing in any answers to work out the meaning of the missing words.
- Ask students to do the task individually, but check as a class.

Answers

1	balanced	4	consume
2	fatal	5	conservative
3	processed	6	beneficial

Ideas Focus

- Ask students to read the questions and answer any queries they have about them.
- Ask students to do the task in pairs and encourage them to draw on their own experience as much as possible.
- Go round the class monitoring students to make sure they are carrying out the task properly. Don't correct any mistakes at this stage, but make a note of any problems in structure and pronunciation.
- Ask each pair to answer one of the questions and ask other students if they have anything else to add.
- Write any structural mistakes that students made on the board without saying who made them, and ask them to correct them. Deal with any problems in pronunciation that came up.

Answer

Students' own answers

Vocabulary

A

- Ask students to read the instructions and check that they understand what they have to do.
- Read the words in the yellow box to students and explain that they are all substances found in food.
- Ask students to read through all sentences before filling in any answers.
- Remind students to read back through the sentences once they have finished to check their answers.
- Ask students to do the task individually, but check as a class.

Answers

1	fat	4	fibre
2	protein	5	dairy
3	carbohydrates	6	minerals

B

- Ask students to read the instructions and check that they understand what they have to do.
- Read the words 1-6 and ask them to repeat them. Correct their pronunciation where necessary. Elicit which words are adjectives (*poisonous, natural, obese*), which are phrasal verbs (*work out*) and which are nouns (*cure, allergy*).
- Ask students to read through all the definitions before matching any answers.
- Remind students to read back through their answers once they have finished to check they are correct.
- Ask students to do the task individually, but check as a class.

Answers

1c 2f 3e 4b 5a 6d

C

- Ask students to read the instructions and check that they understand what they have to do.
- Read the words in the yellow box to students and ask them to repeat them. Correct their pronunciation where necessary. Elicit which words are adjectives (*allergic to, immune to, sick of*), which are verbs (*benefit from, operate on, suffer from*) and which are nouns (*cure for, lack of*).
- Ask students to read through all the sentences before filling in any answers. Point out that they should work out whether a noun, verb or adjective is missing from each gap.
- Remind students to read back through the sentences once they have finished to check their answers.
- Ask students to do the task individually, but check as a class.

Answers

1	lack of	5	allergic to
2	suffer from	6	operate on
3	cure for	7	benefit from
4	sick of	8	immune to

D

- Ask students to read the instructions and check that they understand what they have to do.
- Ask students to look at the pictures and invite them to tell you what each picture represents without unscrambling the words in the box yet.
- Ask students to look at the scrambled words and unscramble them to form correctly spelled words that mean the same as what they can see in each picture.
- Ask students to do the task individually, but check as a class.

Answers

1 braces
2 contact lenses
3 first-aid kit
4 hot water bottle
5 stethoscope

Grammar

A

- Ask students to read the instructions and check that they understand what they have to do.
- Ask students to read the sentences and underline the verbs, then ask them the questions below about each of the sentences in order.
  - Is the person fit and healthy? (*no*)
  - Did the person take the doctor's advice? (*no*)
  - Does he eat a lot of junk food? (*yes*)
- Ask students what they notice about the verb tenses in the sentences and how they are different from those used in the questions above.

Answers

Students should underline the following: *were, had taken, wouldn't eat*
The past tense *were* is used to talk about an unreal present situation, *had taken* is used to talk about an unreal past situation and the hypothetical form *wouldn't eat* is used to criticise someone's actions in the present.

B

- Read the rules to students and explain anything they don't understand.
- Encourage students to look back at the sentences in A if they need help here.
- Ask students to do the task individually, but check as a class.

Answers

Past Simple, Past Perfect, *would*

C

- Ask students to read the instructions and check that they understand what they have to do.
- Ask students to read the sentences and underline the verbs, then ask them which modal verbs could replace these structures (*must, should, ought to*).
- Ask students to do the task in pairs to encourage discussion, but check as a class.

Answers

Students should underline the following: *change, not skip, started.*
We use *had better/I'd better* + bare infinitive, *It's (high/about time)* + Past Simple.

D

- Read the rules to students and explain anything they don't understand.
- Encourage students to look back at the sentences in C if they need help here.
- Ask students to do the task individually, but check as a class.
- Once the answers have been checked, ask students to look back at the article in Reading to find an example of these structures (*Paragraph 6 – you had better be careful*).

Answers

had better, Past Simple

E

- Ask students to read the instructions and check that they understand what they have to do.
- Ask students to do the task in pairs to encourage discussion, but check as a class.

Answers

Students should underline the following: *to eat, riding, cook, you didn't go.*
would prefer + full infinitive
prefer + gerund
would rather + bare infinitive or object + Past Simple

F

- Read the rules to students and explain anything they don't understand.
- Encourage students to look back at the sentences in E if they need help here.
- Ask students to do the task individually, but check as a class.

Answers

full infinitive, gerund, bare infinitive, Past Simple

Now read the Grammar Reference on pages 174 & 175 (12.1 to 12.5) with your students.

G

- Ask students to read the instructions and check that they understand what they have to do.
- Ask students to read through all the sentences, without filling in any answers at this stage, to underline the structures before each gap.
- Encourage students to look back at A, C and E to check which verb form follows after each structure.
- Remind students to read back through the sentences once they have finished to check their answers.
- Ask students to do the task individually, but check as a class.

Answers

1 had had	**4** wearing
2 eat	**5** started
3 hadn't gone out	

H

- Ask students to read the instructions and check that they understand what they have to do.
- Ask students to read the two sentences in item 1 and to underline the information in the first sentence that is missing from the second. Then ask them to think how this information could be expressed using the word in bold. Check the answer to item 1 before moving on to the rest of the task.
- Remind students to read back through the sentences once they have finished to check their answers.
- Ask students to do the task individually, but check as a class.

Answers

1 only we'd had
2 you didn't sneeze
3 wishes she had trained
4 had better see
5 wish you wouldn't eat

Listening

A

- Ask students to read the instructions and check that they understand what they have to do.
- Ask students to read the four topics and, with a partner, choose which one they would prefer to talk about.
- Ask them to take turns with their partner to talk for about a minute on their chosen topic. Go round the class monitoring students to make sure they are carrying out the task properly. Don't correct any mistakes at this stage, but make a note of any problems in structure and pronunciation.
- When finished, invite random students to repeat what they talked about to the class.
- Write any structural mistakes that students made on the board without saying who made them, and ask them to correct them. Deal with any problems in pronunciation that came up.

B

- Ask students to read the instructions and check that they understand what they have to do.
- Ask students to look at the picture on the left and invite them to tell you where the people might be. Encourage everyone to give their opinion.
- Ask students to work with a partner to continue discussing this picture and then discuss the second one.
- Go round the class monitoring students to make sure they are carrying out the task properly. Don't correct any mistakes at this stage, but make a note of any problems in structure and pronunciation.
- When finished, invite random students to repeat what they discussed to the class.
- Write any structural mistakes that students made on the board without saying who made them, and ask them to correct them. Deal with any problems in pronunciation that came up.

C

- Ask students to read the information in the *Exam Close-up* and ask a student to tell you what it means in his/her own words.
- Ask students what is important to do before listening *(underline the key words in the Exam Task)*.
- Ask students to read the *Exam Task* instructions and then each of the questions. Then go through the questions again and underline the key words.
- Ask students to do the task individually and then compare what they have underlined with a partner.

D

- Ask students to read the instructions and check that they understand what they have to do. Remind students that it's important they always underline the key words and think of words they might expect to hear.
- Ask students to look again at the questions and to ask you anything they're still not sure about before they listen.
- Play the recording once all the way through and ask students to mark their answers. Then ask students to discuss their answers with a partner and to justify any that are different.

E

- Play the recording again for students to mark any answers they have missed and to check their other answers.
- Check the answers as a class and ask students to justify their answers. If necessary, replay each conversation as you check the answers.

Answers

1b 2c 3a 4c 5b 6a 7b 8c

Speaking

A

- Ask students to read the three questions and answer any queries they may have about them.
- Ask students to work in pairs and take turns to ask and answer the questions about themselves.
- Go round the class monitoring students to make sure they are carrying out the task properly. Don't correct any mistakes at this stage, but make a note of any problems in structure and pronunciation.
- Ask each pair to ask and answer one of the questions and repeat until each student has had a turn.
- Write any structural mistakes that students made on the board without saying who made them, and ask them to correct them. Deal with any problems in pronunciation that came up.

B

- Ask students to read the instructions and check that they understand what they have to do.
- Ask students to read the *Exam Task* in D and then the questions in B. Answer any queries they might have.
- Play the recording once all the way through and ask students to answer the questions and then to discuss their answers with a partner. Play the recording a second time if necessary for students to check their answers or mark any they have missed.
- Check the answers as a class and ask students to justify their answers.

Answers

1A 2B 3C 4B 5B 6B 7C

C

- Ask students to read the instructions and check that they understand what they have to do.
- Ask students to read the questions and answer any queries they might have.
- Play the recording once all the way through and ask students to circle the expressions they hear and then to discuss their answers with a partner.
- Check the answers as a class.

Answers

1 Shall we start with ...?
2 What do you think?
3 Do you really think so?
4 Let's move on to ...
5 I know what you mean.
6 That's a good point.

Useful Expressions

- Read the *Useful Expressions* to the students and ask them to repeat them. Correct their pronunciation and intonation if necessary.
- Remind them that the students in B and C, who were very successful, used these expressions and encourage them to use them when carrying out the *Exam Task*.

D

- Ask students to read the information in the *Exam Close-up*. Point out that they should be aiming to perform like the students in B and C. Make sure they realise that both of them are responsible for how well the task is carried out and whether it is completed properly.
- Point out that it is a conversation, so they should both talk and not rely on one of them doing all the talking. They should give their opinion and ask if their partner agrees or disagrees.
- Remind them they have to discuss the advantages and disadvantages of each one, as well as reach agreement on two activities that would be best for a group to do.
- Encourage students to use some of the words from the *Useful Expressions* to help them hold a conversation with their partner.
- Go round the class monitoring students to make sure they are carrying out the task properly. Don't correct any mistakes at this stage, but make a note of any problems in structure and pronunciation.
- Ask each pair to say which two options they chose to see which were the most popular with the class.
- Write any structural mistakes that students made on the board without saying who made them, and ask them to correct them. Deal with any problems in pronunciation that came up.

Ideas Focus

- Ask students to read the questions quickly and deal with any queries they may have.
- Ask students to work in pairs and take turns to answer the questions.
- Go round the class monitoring students to make sure they are carrying out the task properly. Don't correct any mistakes at this stage, but make a note of any problems in structure and pronunciation.
- Ask a student from each pair to answer one of the questions until each pair has had a turn. Ask other students if they agree or if they have anything else to add.
- Write any structural mistakes that students made on the board without saying who made them, and ask them to correct them. Deal with any problems in pronunciation that came up.

Answer

Students' own answers

Grammar

A

- Ask students to read the instructions and check that they understand what they have to do.
- Ask students to read the sentences and ask them to underline the structures that follow *be used to* and *get used to*.
- Ask students to work in pairs to encourage discussion, but check as a class.
- Once the answers have been checked, ask students to look back at the article in Reading to find examples of these structures (*Paragraph 2 – is used to meeting, Sentence I – are used to eating*).

Answer

They both have the same structure.
We use *be used to* + noun or gerund to say that someone has done something or experienced something so often that it is no longer strange or difficult for them. We use *get used to* + noun or gerund to talk about situations or states that are or are becoming usual or familiar.

B

- Ask students to read the instructions and check that they understand what they have to do.
- Ask students to read the sentences and to underline the main verbs and their subjects.
- Ask students to work in pairs to encourage discussion, but check as a class.
- Once the answers have been checked, ask students to look back at the article in Reading to find examples of inversion (*Paragraph 4 – Not only are these creepy crawlies tasty, but they are a good source of protein., Rarely are you far from a potential snack!; Paragraph 5 – Not only is it high in fibre, but it's packed with carbohydrates …; Paragraph 7 – Only after they have trained for as long as seven years, do they become experts.*).

Answer

They use the question form.

Note

- Read the information in the note to the students and explain anything they don't understand.
- Write the sentences below on the board and ask students to rewrite them replacing the *if*-clause.
  - If you had eaten less at lunchtime, you wouldn't feel sick now. (*Had you eaten less at lunchtime, you wouldn't feel sick now.*)
  - If you see the coach, tell him I'll be late for training. (*Should you see the coach, tell him I'll be late for training.*)

Now read the Grammar Reference on page 175 (12.6 & 12.7) with your students.

C

- Ask students to read the instructions and check that they understand what they have to do.
- Encourage students to read the whole sentence to work out what meaning of *used to* appears in each one. Remind them to look back at the sentences in A if they need help here.
- Remind students to read back through the sentences once they have finished to check their answers.
- Ask students to do the task individually, but check as a class.

Answers

1	got	4	am
2	are	5	will
3	got		

D

- Ask students to read the instructions and check that they understand what they have to do.
- Ask students to read the two sentences in item 1 and to underline the information in the first sentence that is missing from the second. Then ask them to think how this information could be expressed using the word in bold. Check the answer to item 1 before moving on to the rest of the task.
- Remind students to read back through the sentences once they have finished to check their answers.
- Ask students to do the task individually, but check as a class.

Answers

1 Not only does Sally
2 Little did we know/realise that
3 Never have I been
4 Had he kept exercising
5 Under no circumstances

E

- Ask students to read the instructions and check that they understand what they have to do.
- Read the words in the yellow box to the students and elicit that they can all be used in inverted forms. Encourage students to look back at B and the Note if they need help here.
- Ask students to read the text, without filling in any answers at this stage, to work out how the picture is related to the text (*It is a picture of a bag of crisps, and part of the text is about how the first crisps came to be made.*).
- Remind students to read back through the sentences once they have finished to check their answers.
- Ask students to do the task individually, but check as a class.

Answers

1	Little	4	sooner
2	only	5	than
3	but	6	Had

12 Fit for Life

Use your English

A

- Read the phrasal verbs 1-5 and ask students to repeat them. Correct their pronunciation where necessary.
- Explain that they have to consider the meaning of the verb + particle together and not just focus on the verb part. Ask them to read the definitions a-e on their own and explain anything they don't understand.
- Ask students to do the task individually, but check as a class.
- Encourage the students to copy the phrasal verbs and their definitions into their notebooks before moving on to B.

Answers

1b 2c 3a 4e 5d

B

- Ask students to read the instructions and check that they understand what they have to do.
- Ask students to read through the sentences to work out the meaning of the missing phrasal verb and to decide what form it should be in.
- Remind students to read back through the sentences once they have finished to check their answers.
- Ask students to do the task individually, but check as a class.

Answers

1 come round
2 fight off
3 pass out
4 get over
5 come down with

C

- Ask students to look at the title of the text and the accompanying picture. Elicit what the 'food pyramid' is and how it can help us (*The food pyramid is a way of arranging the four major food groups in a way that shows the amount and frequency with which we should consume various foods. For example, our diet should consist mainly of the foods in the bottom two tiers of the pyramid, with the foods in the top two tiers appearing occasionally. It can help us maintain a balanced and healthy diet.*).
- Ask students to read the text, without filling in any answers at this stage, to find out what else we should do to have a healthy body (*at least half an hour of exercise each day*).
- Read the words in capitals to students and ask them to repeat them. Ask students which words are nouns (*balance, essence, season, process*), which are verbs (*balance, contribute, process, recommend, depend*) and which are adjectives (*nutritious*). Ask students which other forms of these words they know.
- Remind students to read back through the text once they have finished to check the answers.
- Ask students to do the task individually, but check as a class.

Answers

1 balanced
2 essential
3 nutrition
4 contributor
5 seasonal
6 processed
7 recommendations
8 dependent

D

- Remind students that collocations are phrases made up of two or more words that go naturally together.
- Encourage students to read the whole sentence before circling any answers.
- Remind students to read back through the sentences once they have finished to check their answers.
- Ask students to do the task individually, but check as a class.

Answers

1 made
2 skip
3 lost
4 lay
5 took
6 fill
7 apply
8 catch

E

- Ask students to read the instructions and check that they understand what they have to do.
- Read the phrases in the yellow box to students and ask them to repeat them. Correct their pronunciation where necessary.
- Ask students to read through the sentences and to think about the meaning of the phrases in bold.
- Remind students to read back through the sentences once they have finished to check their answers.
- Ask students to do the task individually, but check as a class.

Answers

1 under the weather
2 up and about
3 in bad shape
4 in agony

Writing: a review

- Read the information on writing reviews in the *Learning Focus* to the students and explain anything they don't understand.
- Ask students to underline the things mentioned that a review can be about (*a book, a play, a restaurant*) and ask them if they can add to this list (*a film, a holiday resort/hotel, an art exhibition, a cultural festival*, etc). Then ask them what the main functions of reviews are (*to describe, to express an opinion and to recommend*).
- Ask students how reviews are different from reports (*They are more friendly and chatty.*).
- Ask students if they have ever read a real review. If so, ask them what it was for, if it was favourable or unfavourable and whether they were influenced by it.

A

- Ask students to read the instructions and check that they understand what they have to do.
- Point out to students that they should bear in mind the tone of the sentences when making their decision.
- Ask students to read the sentences and explain anything they don't understand.
- Ask students to work in pairs to encourage discussion, but check as a class.

Answers

Report – 1, 3, 5: They are more impersonal in tone and offer a dry description.
Review – 2, 4, 6: They use contractions and have a chattier style.

B

- Ask students to read the instructions and check that they understand what they have to do.
- Ask students to read the writing task and to underline what information they should include in their review.
- Ask students to answer the questions in pairs to encourage discussion, but check as a class.

Answers

Five paragraphs: introduction, equipment, staff, fees, conclusion/recommendation

C

- Deal with each of the questions one step at a time.
- Ask students to read question 1 and the options and explain anything they don't understand. Explain to students that they should be able to justify their answers.
- Check the answers to question 1 before moving on to 2.
- Ask students to read question 2 and then read the adjectives in the yellow box and the nouns below to students and ask them to repeat them. Correct their pronunciation if necessary. Point out that they should match one adjective to each noun. Remind students that in their reviews they should use adjectives to help give more information about the place or thing being reviewed.
- Check the answers to question 2 before moving on to question 3.
- Ask students to read question 3 and to work in pairs to come up with as many adjectives as possible.
- Check the answers as a class.

Answers

1 name of the gym; address; how long you've been a member; how long it has been in business
2 convenient location; helpful staff; spotless changing rooms; reasonable fees; brand new equipment
3 location: inconvenient, easy to get to
staff: qualified, knowledgeable, rude
changing rooms: neat, filthy, spacious, cramped
fees: affordable, high equipment: state of the art, old

D

- Ask students to read the instructions and check that they understand what they have to do.
- Ask students to read the review and then to discuss the style in pairs. Explain that they should justify their answers with specific examples from the text.
- As a class, ask students to answer the question and to provide examples that justify their answers.

Answers

It is personal in tone as the writer addresses the reader directly (*You won't be disappointed, you'll definitely get fit*); there are a few contractions (*I've been, there's*), and some colloquial/informal language (*Then there's the staff., I've never come across, Nothing is too much trouble*).

E

- Ask students how many things the task asks them to do (*three – say how the writer has linked the main paragraphs, write the phrases and come up with alternative phrases*).
- Ask students to work in pairs to encourage discussion, but check as a class.

Answers

The first thing to mention … (*instead of saying Firstly/First of all/To begin with*); Then there's the staff (*as a way of saying Next/Secondly*); For such great service and equipment (*refers back to the previous two sentences; could have used Finally*).

F

- Ask students to read the instructions and check that they understand what they have to do.
- Elicit from students that the example review is very favourable.
- As a class, discuss what someone who is not pleased with the gym might say about the equipment, staff and fees. Then ask students to decide which of these features they will write their paragraph about.
- Give students enough time to write their paragraphs and ask them to read back through them once they have finished to edit them.
- As a class, ask students to read their paragraphs to the rest of the class and discuss any alternative ways of discussing the features.

Useful Expressions

- Read the *Useful Expressions* to students and ask them to repeat them. Correct their pronunciation and intonation if necessary.
- Remind students that they can use these expressions in their reviews in order to deal with each point appropriately.

133

G

- Ask students to read the information in the *Exam Close-up* and explain that the writer did all these things in the model review.
- Remind students that they can use these points as a checklist when they write their own review.
- Ask students to read the instructions and the *Exam Task* and ask them to underline the main points that their review should focus on.
- Ask students how many paragraphs they should write and what they should be about *(five paragraphs – introduction, review of service, review of food, review of prices, conclusion/recommendation).*
- As a class, discuss all the positive and negative things a reviewer could write about the three main points mentioned in the task. Create a list on the board of related nouns and ask students to collocate them with suitable adjectives and to say whether each adjective is negative or positive.
- Ask students to think about a restaurant they will review and to decide whether it will be positive, negative or a mixture of positive and negative features. Then ask them to look at the paragraph plan and to make more detailed notes for each paragraph.
- Encourage students to refer to the Writing Reference and checklist for reviews on page 183 of the Student's Book to help them with their reviews. They should also look again at the *Useful Expressions* to help them when they write their review.

Suggested answer

Everyone had been raving about Moufara Restaurant, so I decided to check it out for myself. It's in the middle of the main square, so it has a major advantage over its competitors: location.

However, that's where the advantages begin and end. For a start, I wasn't impressed by the service. There was only one waiter for twenty tables and I waited almost half an hour for a menu. To make matters worse, the waiter was extremely rude on several occasions.

As far as the food was concerned, well, what can I say? It's the first time I've been served cold soup and melted ice cream. My main course, chicken risotto didn't taste at all fresh.

Regarding the prices, they seemed reasonable enough when I looked at the menu. However, given the standard of the service and the quality of the food, I'd say it's definitely not worth the money.

I wouldn't recommend Moufara Restaurant. The prices may be reasonable, but the poor service, along with the disappointing food make it a place you can afford to miss.

12 Living in the Slow Lane

General Note

The National Geographic videos can be used as an interesting way to introduce your students to other cultures. They are authentic National Geographic videos, and it is not necessary for students to understand everything they hear to benefit from them. The videos have the option to play English subtitles so that students can read on screen exactly what is said in the documentary. This feature may help students with some of the tasks in the worksheets. The videos are also a good way to encourage your students to watch TV programmes and films in English so that they can get used to the sound of the language. The more students are exposed to English, the easier it will be for them to pick up the language.

Background Information

Greve in Chianti, which has a total population of around 14,000, is situated in Tuscany close to Florence and Siena. This wine-producing area is very popular with tourists and travellers due to the fact that it is a quaint town.

Before you watch

A

- Explain to students that in this lesson they are going to watch a video about taking a slow approach to life. Ask them to look at the globe to see which part of the world they will learn about the locals' way of life (Tuscany, Italy).
- Ask students to read the instructions and the three questions and explain anything they don't understand.
- Ask students to work in pairs to ask and answer the questions.
- Go round the class monitoring students to make sure they are carrying out the task properly. Don't correct any mistakes at this stage, but make a note of any problems in structure and pronunciation.
- As a class, ask students at random to answer each of the questions and ask the others if they agree or have something to add.
- Write any structural mistakes that students made on the board without saying who made them, and ask them to correct them. Deal with any problems in pronunciation that came up.

Answers

1 taking a relaxed approach to life without creating any extra stress for yourself
2 Students' own answers
3 Students' own answers

While you watch

B

- Explain to students that they are now going to watch the video and do a task based on the information they hear.
- Ask students to read the statements 1-6 and ask them what they imagine the Slow City and the Slow Food movements might be.

- Explain anything in the statements that the students don't understand. Then ask them to think about which words might be correct before they listen.
- Play the video all the way through without stopping and ask students to mark their answers. Ask students to compare their answers with a partner's and to justify any answers that are different. Play the video again so that they can check their answers.
- Ask students to do the task individually, but check as a class.

Answers

1	regions	(00.20)	5	product	(03.42)
4	hand-moulded	(02.47)	3	moved	(02.16)
2	developed	(01.24)	6	rushing	(04.08)

After you watch

C

- Explain to students that this is a summary of the information they heard on the video.
- Read the words in the yellow box to the students and ask them to repeat them. Correct their pronunciation where necessary. Ask students to write N, V or Adj beside each of the words depending on whether it is a noun, a verb or an adjective.
- Explain to students that they should read the whole summary before writing any answers first to work out what part of speech is missing.
- Tell students to read back through the text once they have finished to check their answers.
- Ask students to do the task individually, but check the answers as a class.

Answers

1	population	5	manage
2	official	6	example
3	quality	7	sheep
4	preserve	8	dying out

Ideas Focus

- Ask students to read the instructions and make sure they understand what they have to do. Then ask them to read the three questions and answer any questions they might have.
- Ask students to work in pairs and explain that they should both give their opinions on all three questions.
- Go round the class monitoring students to make sure they are carrying out the task properly. Don't correct any mistakes at this stage, but make a note of any problems in structure and pronunciation.
- Ask each pair to answer one of the questions and repeat until each pair has had a turn.

Answer

Students' own answers

Objectives

- To revise vocabulary and grammar from Units 11 and 12
- To practise exam-type tasks

Revision

- Explain to students that Review 6 revises the material they saw in Units 11 and 12.
- Remind students that they can ask you for help with the exercises or look back at the units if they're not sure about an answer, and stress that the review is not a test.
- Decide how you will carry out the review. You could ask students to do one task at a time and then correct it immediately, or ask students to do all the tasks and correct them together at the end. If you do all the tasks together, let students know every now and again how much time they have got left to finish the tasks.
- Ask students not to leave any answers blank and to try to find any answers they aren't sure about in the units.
- When checking students' answers to the review tasks, make a note of any problem areas in vocabulary and grammar that they still have. Try to do extra work on these areas so that your students will progress well.

Vocabulary Revision

- Write the following on the board and ask students to fill in the missing letters to write travel-related words. b _ _ _ _ _ g, d _ _ _ _ _ _ _ _ _ n, t _ _ _ _ _ a _ _ _ _, a _ _ _ _ d, f _ _ _ _ _ n, h _ _ _ _ l (booking, destination, travel agent, abroad, foreign, hostel)
- Write the words, baker, chef and doctor on the board and ask students to write sentences of their own using these words explaining where these people work and what they do. Try to revise bakery/baker's and dishes.
- Ask students to explain the difference between the following pairs: processed food/food which is high in vitamins, a runny nose/a blocked nose, fight off an illness/suffer from an illness.
- Write the words below on the board and ask students to fill in the missing prepositions.
  _____ search _____, allergic _____, benefit _____, rich _____, contribute _____, _____ the distance, _____ a cruise
  (in/of, to, from, in, to, in, on)
- Write these words on the board and ask students what part of speech they are: allergy, process, mistake (nouns). Then write tiny, normal and unconscious and ask what part of speech they are (adjectives). Then write bake, suffer, react and run and ask what part of speech they are (verbs). Ask students to write down any other parts of speech of these words that they know. Make sure that they revise the parts that they will need to complete Part 3.

Grammar Revision

- Ask students to complete these sentences with one word. Then revise the various forms of comparison of adjectives and adverbs.
  - Ian is a _____ experienced doctor than Harriet. (more/less)
  - What is _____ busiest time of the year for the tourist industry? (the)
  - Is Toronto _____ cold as Alaska? (as)
  - The more I travel, the _____ I want to see new places. (more)
  - The journey to Singapore is shorter _____ the journey to Sydney. (than)
- Write the adjectives below in a mixed up order on the board and ask students to put them into two columns: gradable and non-gradable. Then ask them to collocate them with appropriate grading (extremely, fairly, rather, slightly, very) or non-grading (absolutely, utterly, extremely) adverbs.
  - gradable – cold, hungry, warm, good, annoyed
  - non-gradable – freezing, ridiculous, extortionate, furious, boiling, starving
- Ask students to write sentences of their own with the following sets of adjectives then revise the correct order for adjectives: (cotton, brown, old), (glass, lovely, Chinese), (ancient, huge, round).
- Ask students to write sentences of their own with I wish/If only, had better, It's time, would prefer, prefer and would rather. Revise the meanings of these phrases and the various structures that they are followed by. Encourage students to write sentences that are related to travel and tourism or health and fitness.
- Write the sentences below on the board and ask students what the difference in meaning between them is (get used to talks about the process of something strange becoming familiar/usual, whereas be used to means that something that used to be strange is no longer strange). Then revise the structures used after these expressions (gerund or noun).
  - I'm getting used to working in a busy hospital.
  - Kelly is used to travelling long distances each day.
  - The tourists aren't used to the heat.
  - We soon got used to eating squid when we were in Greece.
- Write the sentences below on the board and ask students to find and correct the mistakes.
  - No sooner than had we arrived, it started to rain. (No sooner had we arrived than it started to rain.)
  - Under any circumstances must you panic the patient. (Under no circumstances must you panic the patient.)
  - If had I known you were a doctor, I would have asked for help. (Had I known/If I had known you were a doctor, I would have asked for help.)
  - Seldom I have seen such a beautiful sunset. (Seldom have I seen such a beautiful sunset.)
  - Not only did she realise she had lost her tickets. (Only then did she realise she had lost her tickets.)

Part 1

- Ask students to read the instructions and check that they understand what they have to do.
- Ask students to read the title of the text and ask them what they think it means. Then ask them to skim read the text, without circling any answers at this stage, to find out what kind of travellers cooking classes appeal to *(those who are looking for something different to do on holiday)*. Ask students if they would like to go on such a course and to say why.
- Point out to students that they should read all four options for each item before deciding which word best fits each gap. Remind them to pay attention to the whole sentence each gap is in as the general context will help them understand what word is missing.
- Remind students to read back through the text once they have finished to check their answers.

Answers

1D 2A 3B 4C 5C 6D 7B 8C 9A 10A 11D 12B

Part 2

- Ask students to read the instructions and check that they understand what they have to do.
- Ask students if they know what superfoods are and why they might be *nature's wonder drugs*.
- Ask students to skim read the text, without filling in any answers at this stage, to find as many examples of superfoods as possible *(beans, blueberries, broccoli, chocolate, oats, oranges, salmon, spinach, tomatoes, walnuts and yoghurt)*.
- Encourage students to pay particular attention to the words immediately before and after each gap to work out what part of speech is missing. However, remind them that they have to take into consideration the general context of the sentence so that they understand which structure is being used.
- Remind students to read back through the text once they have finished to check their answers.

Answers

13 of
14 high/rich
15 fight
16 to
17 live
18 while/though/although
19 few
20 those
21 has
22 blood
23 better
24 benefit

Part 3

- Ask students to read the instructions and check that they understand what they have to do.
- Ask students to read the title of the text and ask them what someone might have a nasty reaction to. Elicit the word *allergy* and discuss the various things people can be allergic to and what the various symptoms of allergies are. Ask them to skim read the text, without filling in any answers at this stage, to find out what Kelly Bracks is allergic to and what happens to her if she consumes this foodstuff *(peanuts – she becomes unconscious)*.
- Read the words at the side of the text to the students and ask them to repeat them. Correct their pronunciation where necessary.
- Ask students to read back through the text and to decide which part of speech is missing from each gap, and to complete the gaps using the correct form of the words given.
- Remind students to read back through the text once they have finished to check their answers.

Answers

25	allergic	30	sufferers
26	tiniest	31	mistakenly
27	Normally	32	reaction
28	processed	33	runny
29	baker's/bakery	34	unconscious

Part 4

- Ask students to read the instructions and check that they understand what they have to do.
- Ask students to read both sentences in each item and to underline the information in the first sentence that is missing from the second sentence. Then ask them to look at the word given to decide how the missing information could be inserted into the second sentence using this word. Remind students that they will have to use a different structure in order to keep the meaning the same.
- Remind students that they mustn't change the word given in any way.
- Encourage students to read back through the completed sentences once they have finished to check their answers.

Answers

35 I wish I did not
36 only we had seen
37 it is time you took
38 was such a beautiful view
39 is not as popular as/less popular than
40 am used to travelling
41 had her blood pressure taken
42 had better not eat

Unit 1 Personally Speaking

TRACK 1.1

N: Listening, Unit 1, Page 10, A

1 <u>I can't believe he chickened out</u> of the competition.

2 Try and <u>look on the bright side!</u>

3 His behaviour is <u>irrational</u>.

4 The film really <u>let me down</u>.

TRACK 1.2

N: Listening, Unit 1, Page 10, B

N: 1: You will hear a boy speaking to his mother.

Mum, why do I have to do the washing–up every evening? You know how much I hate it! Why can't we all do chores that we enjoy? I like watering the plants, but Jody's always complaining about doing it, and says she'd prefer the dishes any day. I don't understand why we haven't got a dishwasher anyway like everyone else has. I wouldn't mind so much if all I had to do was load the dishwasher and press a button.

N: 2: You will hear a head teacher speaking to a student.

Hi Anne, in you come. Now, what I want to talk to you about this morning is your grades. I'm concerned about them as they've fallen quite dramatically this term. Now, I know you've been absent quite a lot due to your operation, but I'm not entirely sure that's the only reason for such poor performance. You don't really seem interested in school these days and most of your teachers say you can't concentrate in class. Is there anything we can do to help?

TRACK 1.3

N: Listening, Unit 1, Page 10, D

N: You will hear people talking in six different situations. For questions one to six, choose the best answer (a, b or c).

N: 1: You hear a woman talking about a phobia she has.

I've been afraid of the dentist for years now, and <u>I'm not really sure what brought it on. There doesn't seem to be any logical reason for it.</u> Of course, it doesn't stop me going for a check-up every year. I know that if I put it off, things will only get worse. It's not like I freak out or do anything embarrassing while I'm in the dentist's chair. <u>I can't explain it</u>; I just seem to tense up and my palms go all sweaty. <u>But it's weird though</u> because I wasn't always like that and I know that nothing can happen to me.

N: 2: You hear a man talking about his driving test.

I've been taking a crash course in driving for over a month now, and my instructor is keen for me to take the test soon. I'm not sure I'm ready psychologically, though. It's not that I don't know how to drive; I'm pretty sure I'd pass. The course has been very intense and I've managed to do a lot of driving in such a short length of time. The thing is, I don't react very well in stressful situations like tests. <u>I suppose what worries me most is that I'll chicken out of the test at the last minute.</u> What a waste of time and money that'd be!

N: 3: You hear a woman talking about horror films.

I love watching horror films. They usually make me laugh. I mean, the storylines are normally so predictable it's unbelievable, and the special effects are very often a bit of a joke really. But I got a film last night from my local DVD shop which had got good reviews, and to my amazement, <u>I was absolutely terrified! It had me on the edge of my seat from start to finish.</u> It really deserved the glowing reviews it got.

N: 4: You hear a woman talking to her daughter.

I know you must be very upset that you didn't make it to the finals. But it's not the end of the world! I admit Dad and I haven't always been that supportive in the past. I guess we didn't think you'd make it this far, and we were annoyed when you left college to play tennis professionally. But you've certainly proved us wrong, haven't you? <u>Try and look on the bright side.</u> You were the runner-up after all, and your sponsorship has been renewed.

N: 5: You overhear two people talking on a plane.

F: What's up, Rob? You've hardly even touched your meal. Isn't it up to your usual gourmet standards?

M: No, it's perfectly fine. <u>It's just that I can't eat when I'm crammed into such a small space.</u>

F: You should have asked for extra legroom.

M: Well, that's just it, you see! <u>I even paid more for extra legroom, but there was some mix-up and I was given an ordinary seat in the end. I feel really let down by the airline.</u> Normally, they're very reliable, but I guess they're more interested in making money than making sure passengers enjoy the flight.

N: 6: You hear a man talking about living alone.

I can remember being so enthusiastic when I first moved in. I'd never lived on my own before, so I was looking forward to some peace and quiet. Having been brought up on a farm with nine brothers and sisters, I just wanted to do my own thing and come and go when I wanted. And I do mostly, but <u>I must admit I do miss them and their company when I come home to a cold, dark, empty house.</u> That's when I realise how alone I am. My mum took it really hard when I first told her I was moving out. She burst into tears. She was scared that I wouldn't be safe living on my own in a big city, I suppose.

TRACK 1.4

N: Speaking, Unit 1, Page 11, C

N: A I think <u>if I could choose something, I'd like to try a new sport,</u> umm, for example, something a bit risky, like scuba diving or para gliding.

N: B I don't know. <u>Maybe a lawyer.</u> My dad's a lawyer.

N: C Yes, I have. Last summer <u>I went to Ireland</u> with my family and <u>I spoke English a lot</u> because my mum and dad can't speak it very well.

N: D Well, <u>I usually go home, then I have lunch and do my homework.</u> But after that I like to relax so I watch TV or play video games with my younger brother.

N: E Um, the summer, yes, <u>I like the summer best.</u>

Unit 2 One World

TRACK 2.1

N: Listening, Unit 2, Page 22, A

If you happen to be <u>in Berlin and you want to go on a walking tour</u> of the city, then head for Museum Island. Museum Island has built a reputation for itself as <u>a cultural centre</u> in the German capital. Built on a small island on the Spree River, the island <u>is home to five of Berlin's most visited museums</u>. Each museum was custom-built to house the specific collections they contain. These impressive buildings <u>were constructed between 1824 and 1930</u>. The collections, such as the gold of Troy, are of immense historical value. It has been said that they trace the development of civilisations throughout the ages. As a result, Museum Island <u>was designated a World Heritage Site</u> by UNESCO in 1999.

TRACK 2.1

N: Listening, Unit 2, Page 22, D

N: You will hear part of a radio report about a cultural festival. For questions one to seven, complete the sentences with a word or short phrase.

I've always been intrigued by the way in which customs, lifestyles and habits spread from one country to the next. These days, people can travel from one country to another with relative ease. They can also access information about foreign countries and their customs at the touch of a button. Both of these <u>play an important role</u> in the exchange of knowledge concerning what's happening elsewhere.

The Long Night of the Museums in Berlin is an example of how good local ideas can catch on in other parts of the world and end up becoming an international phenomenon. The event, which started in Berlin in 1997, is simply paradise for culture vultures. The Long Night takes place twice a year, at the end of January and then again at the end of August. During the event participating museums, palaces and exhibitions remain open from six in the evening till two in the morning. For a measly 15 euros, Berliners and visitors to the city can purchase a special pass which allows them unrestricted access to all participating institutions. This pass also entitles them to rides on special shuttle buses which ferry them from museum to museum.

The event started on a small scale with around a dozen museums opening their doors late into the night on the designated days. The original idea arose in order to attract the general public to museums which they might not have known about or visited previously. Today, over 120 institutions take part in The Long Night, and other cultural events, such as concerts, dance performances and film viewings, also take place at the same time.

What is really interesting is that the event hasn't only expanded to include other museums, but it has also extended to other cities. You can find similar festivals in cities such as Aachen, Munich, Stuttgart and Cologne to mention a few German examples. On a global level, The Long Night has in recent years become a common occurrence in other cosmopolitan cities such as Barcelona and Buenos Aires.

However, some say the concept of having such cultural events late into the night has its roots elsewhere and dates to before Berlin's Long Night. It is possible the idea migrated from Russia, and in particular from Saint Petersburg, where the White Nights Festival has been held annually since 1993. Unlike the Berlin event, however, the Saint Petersburg festival doesn't last only one night, nor does it happen twice a year. It is a series of cultural events and performances that take place from May to July. At this time of year, days are exceptionally long in this part of the world. Around the summer solstice in mid-June, sunset is as late as 10 pm and twilight lasts almost all night. As a result, the locals make the most of this extra light by attending classical ballet performances as well as concerts and operas.

Unit 3 Star Quality

TRACK 3.1

N: Listening, Unit 3, Page 36, B

… but the idea of what it means to be a celebrity is one that is forever changing. For example, Cleopatra reached celebrity status as a member of the Egyptian royal family. In the twentieth and twenty-first centuries, celebrities have more often than not been people from the world of show business. However, after years of obscurity, young royals are now once again being pronounced idols. Having been seen as dull and boring for decades, the new young glamorous royals have been pushed into the limelight. Barely a day goes past without seeing the faces of the Duke and Duchess of Cambridge, or those of Zara Phillips and Princesses Eugenie and Beatrice in the press. It seems that the British public can't get enough of them these days.

TRACK 3.2

N: Listening, Unit 3, Page 36, E

N: You will hear five people talking about meeting celebrities. For questions one to five, choose from the list A-H what each person says about the experience. Use the letters only once. There are three extra letters which you do not need to use.

N: Speaker 1

It all happened by accident really. There I was looking through the bargain bin at my local supermarket, when someone tugged on the T-shirt I was picking up. I looked up, ready for an argument about who had seen the T-shirt first, when I realised I was looking at that actor from CSI. You know, the one who plays the computer nerd. It was really quite embarrassing because I blurted out something like 'Oh, I didn't expect to see you here,' and he replied 'I didn't expect to see you here either!' I'm glad he saw the funny side of it.

N: Speaker 2

It was towards the end of the summer holidays and I wanted to find out from the university administration if the dates for the September resits had come out. I'd been touring Europe all summer and had lost all contact with the others on my course. As I was approaching the campus, I felt that something wasn't quite right. The street signs had been changed and there were lots of American-looking cars on the road. Before I knew what was happening I saw this Brad Pitt lookalike running across the street. Then when I tried to get into the university they told me it was closed to the public all week due to shooting for the Hollywood film *World War Z*. It actually had been Brad Pitt running across the street. How cool is that?

N: Speaker 3

I'm a receptionist in a five-star hotel, so I get to meet all sorts of rich and famous people. I've got used to it over the years, and I usually don't bat an eyelid when celebrities check in. Most of them are pretty low-key and don't want to draw too much attention to themselves. It must get tiring being in the limelight constantly. But I'll never forget the time Brian Ingram, the singer with the Simpletons, came to stay. I had been dreading him turning up because he's got this reputation as being a bit of a 'wild child' who always gets into fights with photographers. But in reality he was really very sweet. I even saw him carrying this old lady's suitcases for her when there was no porter available.

N: Speaker 4

My dad's got a season ticket for Sheffield. He's always been a huge fan and never misses a game. I'm not particularly interested in football myself, but I went with him to the cup final, to keep him company. After the game, Dad wanted to go to the Members' Club for a bite to eat. When we got there, there was a crowd of people gathered in a corner. One of the team's top players, still wearing his strip and everything, was signing autographs for the fans! It wasn't a surprise really because the press are always going on about how he really appreciates his fans. It was good to see that they were right. I mean, so many celebrities take their fans for granted these days.

N: Speaker 5

The nearest I've ever come to meeting anyone famous was when I was a teenager – about fifteen years ago. My friend Tracey brought round her cousin Bobby one day to hang out with us. She was babysitting him for her aunt. He was only about two at the time. He made our lives a right misery that day, chucking stuff on the floor, spilling drinks and writing on the walls. My mum had a fit when she saw it. But anyway, I was watching *Top of the Pops* one day last week when I got a call from Tracey. The guitarist in the band that was playing at the time was none other than Bobby.

Unit 4 City Living

TRACK 4.1

N: Listening, Unit 4, Page 48, B

F: When I first moved to Brighton what really impressed me was that I had all the facilities that a city can offer with the seaside as an added bonus. I was brought up in a small fishing village in Ireland, so being near the sea is very important to me. I'd hate to live in a city further inland.

M: I know what you mean, but I feel that way about cities in general. They're just too crowded and noisy. I much prefer the peace and quiet of the countryside to the noise pollution and stress of cities. I left my childhood home – a little village – when I was twenty because there just wasn't any work there. I might have found a good job here in Brighton and everything, but I get really homesick here.

F: Before I moved to Brighton I thought I'd be stressed out all the time, you know, rushing from one place to another. But in fact, the pace of life is just right for me here. I feel I've got the best of both worlds. The people here are very friendly too. And I like the fact that I've got to know people here from all walks of life.

TRACK 4.2

N: Listening, Unit 4, Page 48, E

N: You will hear an interview with a psychologist called Karen Black, who's talking about the effects of city living on health. For questions 1 to 6, choose the best answer (a, b or c).

INT: And now let me introduce my next guest, psychologist Karen Black, who's currently doing research into how living in big cities can affect our mental health. Karen, why is there a need for this kind of research?

KAREN: Well, it's estimated that <u>by the year 2050, around 70 per cent of the world's population will be permanently resident in urban areas.</u> People are attracted to the bright lights of big cities for various reasons. For some, it's a conscious decision based on certain lifestyle choices: the promise of a prestigious job with a high salary, improved health care systems and schools, as well as easier access to entertainment and cultural facilities. Sadly, for others, it's a matter of necessity. Lack of employment opportunities in rural areas leave a great number of people with no choice but to head for cities in the hope of finding a job of any description in order to survive. But whatever the reason, <u>there's no doubt that those who live in the city experience higher levels of stress than those in rural areas.</u>

INT: What can this be put down to?

KAREN: There are various factors involved, really. The pace of life is much faster in cities, the noise pollution is incomparable to the noise levels in smaller towns and villages, even the greater distances to be travelled on an everyday basis all put pressure on city dwellers. Add to that the fact that most big cities today are overcrowded, which means there's less personal space for everyone, and that <u>crime is on the increase</u>, it's not difficult to see why life is stressful in urban areas.

INT: What about those who live in residential areas in the suburbs, do they suffer from less stress than those in inner-city areas?

KAREN: Not necessarily, you see the majority of suburban residents travel into city centres for work, entertainment, shopping, etc.

on a regular, if not daily, basis. <u>This means that they are just as exposed to the factors causing urban stress as those who live in inner-city areas despite living in areas with better amenities and a higher quality of life.</u>

INT: So what is the link between stress and mental health?

KAREN: Well, *past research* has shown us that city dwellers are 21 per cent more likely to suffer from anxiety disorders like phobias and panic attacks than those in country areas. They are also almost 40 per cent more likely to suffer from severe mood swings. <u>But the research that I'm currently involved in has brought to light some interesting new findings about why this is the case. Our studies have shown that the brains of people living in cities actually work in a different way to those in rural areas.</u> Our tests showed that the part of the brain that controls the emotions and anxiety – the amygdala – is overstimulated in city-dwellers. This is due to their senses constantly being bombarded with information. We believe that this overstimulation is responsible for increased mental health problems.

INT: In what way can these studies help those living in the cities?

KAREN: Firstly, <u>those responsible for city planning should take the results into consideration when designing cities.</u> Recognising that current city design can negatively affect mental health is the first step. The next step is to use this knowledge to redesign cities so that they become more functional and better places to live in. But that on its own isn't enough. We also need to see improved health care facilities for those suffering from poor mental health in cities.

Unit 5 Tied to Technology

TRACK 5.1

N: Listening, Unit 5, Page 62, B

M: Do you fancy going to the computer fair on Saturday? It's the opening day.

W: Yeah, why not? Oh, hold on! I forgot Aunt Maggie's coming on Saturday. It'll have to be Sunday.

M: No problem. I'll pick up the tickets on the way home from work on Friday.

TRACK 5.2

N: Listening, Unit 5, Page 62, D

N: **You will hear eight short conversations. After each conversation, you will be asked a question about what you heard. The answer choices are shown as pictures (a, b and c).**

Circle the letter of the correct answer. You hear each conversation only once.

N: **Number 1**

M: Have you seen that huge box sitting in reception? It must be a new fridge.

W: Actually, it's the new vending machine they promised us.

M: Pity, because we really need a fridge. The old one's broken.

W: That reminds me, I need to arrange for my washing machine at home to be repaired.

N: **What does the man think is in the box?**

N: **Number 2**

M: What's wrong with this computer? It keeps shutting down every time I try to print out a document.

W: Have you tried switching it off, unplugging it and plugging it back in again?

M: I've done that twice already.

W: If I were you, I'd consult the instruction manual.

N: **What should the man do?**

N: **Number 3**

M: Hey, isn't that man over there the guy who hosts *Crazy Inventions* on Delta Channel?

W: Who Keith Theroux? No, he's got medium-length blond hair, not short brown hair.

M: He might have changed his style.

W: But how do you explain the glasses? Keith Theroux's always boasting on the show about how great his vision is!

N: **Who are they looking at?**

N: **Number 4**

M: Come on! We're going to miss the start of the sci-fi movie. It starts at ten to nine.

W: What's the big rush? It's only 7.45.

M: Yeah, but we need to catch the eight o'clock train to get downtown in time.

N: **What time is it now?**

N: **Number 5**

W: I saw a great sewing machine at the store today. I might get it for mum for her sixtieth birthday.

M: I'm getting her a smart phone because I can never reach her when I need to.

W: I usually leave a message on her answering machine when she's out. She always gets back to me right away.

N: **What will the man buy?**

N: **Number 6**

M: I can't get this device to work. I've tried pressing the button several times.

W: You need to pull the lever down first.

M: OK, let's see. That's no good. The lever's stuck.

W: You'll need to unscrew the front part then.

N: **What did the man do first?**

N: **Number 7**

W: Have you seen that information pack they sent us for recycling household appliances?

M: I left it on the bookshelf above the CD player. Isn't it still there?

W: No, I put it on my desk next to the computer earlier. But it's not there anymore.

M: Oh, there it is on top of the printer! The cleaner must have moved it.

N: **Where did the woman put the information pack?**

N: **Number 8**

M: Did you hear about the fire at the recycling plant? I wouldn't be surprised if it was due to a lightning bolt during last night's electric storm.

W: I read about it online this morning. <u>Reports say it was caused by sparks from a faulty high voltage cable.</u>

M: Well, at least it wasn't arson.

N: What caused the fire?

TRACK 5.3

N: Speaking, Unit 5, Page 63, A

M: Now I'd like you to talk about something together. Here are some things which have had an effect on <u>our everyday lives</u>. First talk to each other about <u>the advantages and disadvantages</u> of these <u>aspects of technology.</u>

(Pause) Now you have one minute to decide which of these things <u>has improved our lives</u> the most.

Unit 6 Fun, Fun, Fun!

TRACK 6.1

N: Listening, Unit 6, Page 74, B

Announcer: Following the release of their <u>sixth album</u> and to celebrate their tenth anniversary, the Charming Rascals will be appearing live in Manchester. Their latest album - <u>Basically Zero</u> - has shot to number one in the charts with sales of over <u>150,000</u> on the first day alone. Concert tickets for the <u>July</u> 17th and 18th shows due to go on sale on <u>May 28th</u>. Those wishing to purchase tickets are advised to do so early as promoters predict a sell-out for both dates. Tickets cost £60 and are <u>half price</u> for students.

TRACK 6.2

N: Listening, Unit 6, Page 74, E

N: You will hear a radio interview with Barry Gribbs about a youth festival. For questions 1 to 10, complete the sentences with a word or short phrase.

Presenter: Good evening and a warm welcome from the fifth International Youth Festival. Tonight is the festival's Opening Showcase

and we're reporting live from the <u>Athletics Stadium</u>, the venue for the event every year. With me tonight is Barry Gribbs, one of the festival organisers. Welcome, Barry. What have we got to look forward to?

Guest: I think this year promises to be the biggest and best ever. <u>Ten fun-filled days and nights</u> of young performers from all corners of the globe showing off their talents and, like every year, it <u>kicks off</u> tonight with the Showcase, where some of the top acts participating in the festival will entertain us.

Presenter: Ah yes, the Showcase. There's something different about it this year, isn't there?

Guest: Indeed there is. The festival has <u>too many</u> acts to appear in one show, so we've chosen only home grown talent for the Showcase. So tonight, spectators in the stadium, and TV viewers and radio listeners at home, will be able to watch and listen to local singers, dancers and musicians and get a sneak preview of what they'll be doing for the rest of the week.

Presenter: What about the rest of the acts? The ones we won't be seeing tonight.

Guest: Don't worry; the festival catalogue has a comprehensive list of performances, as well as their venues, <u>dates and times</u>.

Presenter: So what have we got this year?

Guest: What haven't we got?! There's everything <u>from African</u> dance troupes to Norwegian choirs. There'll be theatre productions from <u>local schools</u> as well as students from some of the most prestigious academies of music and drama in the world.

Presenter: And where will the events be held?

Guests: They'll be held <u>throughout the city</u>, not just here at the athletics stadium. Just check the catalogue for details.

Presenter: I know the organisers have tried to keep the cost down, so how much are we looking at for tickets?

Guest: You can see some shows for as little as eight dollars. The most expensive shows are <u>fifteen</u>. But there are several <u>festival passes</u> that you can purchase which offer huge discounts. For example, a twenty-show pass costs a mere eighty dollars. That works out at four dollars a show!

Presenter: Well, that certainly is affordable, Barry … [fade]

Unit 7 Right or Wrong?

TRACK 7.1

N: Listening, Unit 7, Page 88, A

N: **Speaker 1**

Look at all these broken shop windows! It's an absolute outrage.

N: **Speaker 2**

I couldn't care less if he ends up in prison.

N: **Speaker 3**

My heart goes out to the victims of violent crimes.

N: **Speaker 4**

Guess what! I was given a ride in a police car at the open day yesterday!

N: **Speaker 5**

Oh, my goodness, it's the police! I hope Jenny isn't in trouble again.

N: **Speaker 6**

Oh no, not another case! I thought we'd heard the last one.

N: **Speaker 7**

Yuck! This cell is absolutely filthy!

TRACK 7.2

N: Listening, Unit 7, Page 88, C

N: **You will hear people talking in seven situations. For questions one to seven, choose the best answer (a, b or c).**

N: **1: You will hear part of a lecture about dealing with organised crime.**

Organised crime nowadays is a very complicated and widespread phenomenon. It is no longer the work of certain groups of people or gangs in a particular geographical area. Instead, networks of organised criminals now operate across nations and continents, as well as in cyberspace. In this respect, it can be seen as a product of globalisation. This makes it extremely difficult for the authorities to deal with. With laws varying from country to country, as well as the added problem of distance, capturing those involved in organised crime can sometimes seem like an impossible task.

N: **2: You will hear a woman talking to her son.**

I can't believe you've broken the law again! Last time it was graffiti, now it's carjacking! When is it all going to end? Can't you see you're ruining your life? Your father was right; we shouldn't have let you hang around with Sam. With an armed robber in the family, he's hardly had a proper upbringing, has he? But you, you always had the best of everything. I just don't understand it. Where did we go wrong?

N: **3: You hear a teenager talking about a crime she witnessed.**

I mean, I was just walking down the road thinking about all the maths homework I had for the next day when suddenly I heard screaming behind me. I turned round and this middle-aged lady was being mugged by a masked man. He had grabbed her bag and hit her quite hard on the head. Luckily, I had my mobile on me, so I called the police and an ambulance. The poor woman was in a right state, so I stayed with her until help arrived. I even had to make a statement to the police. I hope they catch him; I'd hate to think that he'd get away with something like that. By the time I got home, I was in no state to do my homework, I can tell you.

N: **4: You hear a youth worker talking about juvenile crimes.**

I suppose in areas like ours, it's taken for granted that adolescents are going to be involved with the police at some point. My heart really goes out to them because most of these kids come from broken homes or from families who've had to live with long-term unemployment. Quite often their grandparents and great-grandparents were also unemployed. So, <u>they've not really had a chance in life</u> and to some extent they're angry and reacting against a system which couldn't care less about them. They're constantly treated as outsiders by society at large. I guess leading a life of crime becomes second nature to them.

N: 5: You hear two friends talking about a neighbour who was found guilty of a crime.

M: Did you hear that Olivia Paterson was found guilty of shoplifting last week?

W: No! I knew that she'd been arrested, but I didn't know the court case had taken place. Did she get a prison sentence?

M: No. Because it was her first offence they gave her a fine.

W: A fine? Is that all? <u>They could at least have given her community service. That'd be more likely to stop her doing it again.</u>

N: 6: You hear a police officer talking about a special crime-prevention event.

This year's Bolton Against Crime Festival is going to be great. It's going to be in Overton Park this time and I'm sure young people are going to love it. We've even arranged for police cars, motorbikes, and vans used to transport criminals to and from prison to be on display. Members of the public can even get a short ride in the vehicles. The chief is trying to get permission to land one of the helicopters in the middle of the park, but that still needs clearance with health and safety. <u>My division will, of course, be riding into the park and the public will have the chance to see our horses up close.</u>

N: 7: You will hear a radio announcement about a trial verdict.

And next up, Lewisham man, Gary Cale, was sentenced to five years' imprisonment for computer hacking. Twenty-one-year-old Cale, who has ten previous convictions for online fraud, was described by the judge on passing sentence as a menace to society. Due to his criminal record, Cale was given the maximum prison sentence available for this crime. <u>The judge commented that since previous punishments such as fines and disabling</u>

<u>Cale's Internet connection had failed</u> to make him law-abiding, <u>she had no choice but to remove his freedom in this instance.</u>

Unit 8 Environmental Affairs

TRACK 8.1

N: Listening, Unit 8, Page 100, B

N: 1

The workshop organizers do not recommend the use of chemical fertilizers and <u>will be advising</u> the use of environmentally-friendly, organic alternatives instead.

N: 2

<u>Don't throw that plastic bag</u> into the river <u>under any circumstances</u>!

N: 3

<u>Most likely Mary will cancel at the last minute</u> and not show up to our clean-up-the-beach day.

N: 4

<u>I'd think again</u> about buying an electric car <u>if I were you.</u>

N: 5

<u>I was the one who notified the police</u> about the neighbours' cruelty to animals.

TRACK 8.2

N: Listening, Unit 8, Page 100, C

N: You will hear five people talking about environmental issues. For questions one to five, choose from the list A to H what each person is doing. Use the letters only once. There are three extra letters which you do not need to use.

N: Speaker 1

<u>Well, there are many ways we could make a difference right here in our own back garden.</u> Have you seen that poster for the permaculture seminar at the end of September? It looks pretty

interesting. They'll be showing participants various techniques for cultivating land using methods like crop rotation so that valuable minerals and stuff aren't overused or washed out with rainwater. And they'll be concentrating on growing fruit, vegetables and herbs that are suitable to our particular climate without the use of chemical pesticides. Just think of the benefits to the environment, and we'd be able to produce our own food. I'd sign up for it if I were you.

N: Speaker 2

Yes, but what you have to realise is that when the people of this town elected you to office it was because you promised to tackle green issues in our area. Not only has no positive action been taken so far, but your administration has allowed our finest beach to become a rubbish dump. It's an absolute disgrace. What happened to the recycling plant that citizens were promised before the elections? We haven't even seen as much as a recycling bin being put in place in the whole town. It's time you accepted your responsibilities and honoured the promises that brought you to power in the first place.

N: Speaker 3

We put in a bank of photovoltaic panels on our land last year, and we've been amazed at the savings we've made on our energy bills. I know the initial outlay for the equipment was quite high, but judging by how much we've saved this year alone, it should pay for itself in the future. And it's really satisfying to know that we're doing our bit for the environment by using solar energy. But what I wanted to ask you about was whether you're aware of any possible health concerns. I'm no expert, but I was wondering if it's 100% safe to live so close to where electricity is generated and stored.

N: Speaker 4

Now, I know we've been lying here a very long time and nothing whatsoever has happened, but I promise you, you are about to witness one of the most remarkable sights on Earth. The grasslands, which are the lion's natural habitat, offer just the camouflage we need to get as close to these magnificent animals as possible. It'll be dark soon so they will start to hunt down the prey that will make their next meal. Unlike other cats, lions work in groups called prides. Each pride hunts together and the lions fan out in order to stop the prey getting away from them. What is particularly interesting is that it is the females who do the hunting, with the males patrolling the area to offer security. Once the prey has been caught, however, the male will take the 'lion's share' of the food.

N: Speaker 5

Well, it's just that I'm not sure that it's such a good idea to take the kids to the zoo. I understand what you're saying about zoos playing an important role in protecting endangered species and everything. And that it's a chance for the kids to see animals up close that they've never seen before. But do we really want them to see animals in captivity, being kept in conditions that have no relation to their natural habitat? No, I think you should reconsider the trip. The kids will be disappointed at first, but they'll understand why it's been cancelled if you point out to them why they shouldn't go.

Unit 9 And What Do You Do?

TRACK 9.1

N: Listening, Unit 9, Page 114, B

I left college in 2007, but it wasn't until two years later, in 2009, that I landed my first real job. I got off to a good start and had only been there for a year when I was promoted to head of sales. This was a highly responsible position where you have to be able to communicate effectively with other departments and clients, as well as have the courage to take decisions without consulting others when necessary. I enjoyed this aspect of it and the constant contact with others. I could never have worked in the editorial department where so much time is spent on intricate detail. I'm just not patient enough for that sort of job, I guess.

But the hardest part about the job came when I was responsible for nominating employees for redundancy. The company hadn't been doing well for three years, so they had to reduce the workforce. In many ways, I think it's easier to sack someone because he or she has done something wrong and has been responsible for getting the sack. But it's a different matter with redundancies.

Anyway, I was lucky because a month after redundancies were announced, <u>a competitor approached me and said they had a vacancy, and was I interested. I jumped at the chance.</u> It was even more convenient because <u>it was on the outskirts of town,</u> a short bus ride away from my neighbourhood. Previously, I had to commute all the way into the town centre. But what made a very good impression on me was that when I arrived for the interview, the owner showed me round and introduced me to all my potential new colleagues. He even introduced me as 'their next line manager'!

N: 1 When did the man graduate?

2 What qualities did the man not require for his previous job?

3 Why did the man leave his previous job?

4 Where is the man's new job?

TRACK 9.2

N: Listening, Unit 9, Page 114, E

N: **You will hear part of a television programme about a careers fair. For questions one to six, choose the best answer (a, b or c).**

Good evening, and welcome to tonight's show. Tonight we'll be discussing what visitors to this year's careers fair can expect to see. <u>The main target group is final year college students and recent graduates.</u> But it'll also appeal to the long-term unemployed who need advice about getting themselves back into the jobs market. Also, people who're looking to change jobs attend the fair. These employees may be dissatisfied with their current position, looking for a promotion or interested in retraining and changing field altogether. This year promises to be the biggest and best event to date! <u>Over 200 companies interested in taking on new staff have applied for a stand.</u> That's a 50% rise on last year when a total of 133 companies turned out. Visitors should go round the stands focusing on companies they are more interested in. Apart from stands, <u>there will also be talks at certain times by careers officers</u> and representatives of top companies participating in the fair. <u>They will be followed by workshops</u> designed to help job-hunters put

together a professional CV and develop essential interview skills, as well as discussions on the kind of behaviour expected in the workplace. The fair is over four days <u>from January</u> 6 through January 10. That's Friday through Monday. Doors open 9.30 am and <u>the last visitor will be allowed entry at 8 pm.</u> Doors close at 10 pm. Go as early as possible because from noon on, it'll be extremely crowded. Oh, and for those planning to spend all day at the fair, there will be various refreshment stands selling snacks and drinks and a specially designated area for those who want to bring their own food to eat. Eating and drinking is prohibited in the main exhibition area, however.

Unit 10 Learn to Learn!

TRACK 10.1

N: Listening, Unit 10, Page 126, B

WorldSkills International is a remarkable event held every <u>two years,</u> where young people from <u>over 50 countries</u> compete in vocational skills competitions. The event dates back to 1950 when the first competition took place in Spain with 12 <u>contestants</u> from Spain and 12 from Portugal. The last event involved over 1,000 competitors and saw around <u>200,000</u> visitors pass through the doors of the ExCel London Exhibition and Conference Centre in the city's Docklands. Young people competed in 46 skill areas ranging from <u>cake making</u> to spray-painting cars.

TRACK 10.2

N: Listening, Unit 10, Page 126, D

N: **You will hear a radio interview with a teenager. For questions one to ten, complete the sentences with a word or short phrase.**

INT: In the studio today is London teenager, Ahmet Khan, who's here to tell us about how he decided on his chosen vocational training course. Ahmet, you've just signed up for a college course in <u>floristry</u>. But you didn't always have the ambition to work in this particular field, did you?

AHMET: No, in fact, a few months ago I didn't really know what I wanted to do when I left school. I've always hated sitting exams and I knew that I didn't have the brain to do something academic. But everyone kept going on at me to make up my mind. I just felt there was a lot of pressure on me to decide, but at the same time I wasn't getting anything in the way of useful, practical assistance to help me make a choice.

INT: But you attended an event that gave you a brainwave.

AHMET: That's right. Last autumn, my form teacher announced that she was taking us all on a trip to WorldSkills International. At first I thought 'boring' – I'd always found school trips really dull and could never see the point in them. But I was truly inspired by the visit.

INT: In what way?

AHMET: Well, for a start it was an extremely well organised event aimed at bringing young people from all over the world to compete in skills competitions in national teams. It was kind of like the Olympics and it even had spectacular opening and closing ceremonies. WorldSkills took place over four days and you had teams of construction trainees doing things like bricklaying and plumbing; beauticians doing people's hair and nails; and even carers doing first aid. I guess I was struck by the talent of these people. They all seemed really motivated and committed to their tasks. I realised right there and then that I wanted to do something creative with my hands.

INT: So why floristry?

AHMET: I don't know really, by chance I suppose. As well as the competitions, they also had what they called 'Have a go'. You could try your hand at all sorts of things at stalls organised by lots of different companies. There was some really wacky stuff like building your own bedroom burglar alarm and chocolate welding. There were huge crowds at most stands. The floristry one was practically empty, though. I went over to have a look and before I knew it I was making up a bridal bouquet. It was great fun, and the trainer told me I was a natural.

INT: So what was the next step?

AHMET: My teacher was dead impressed with the bouquet I'd made and suggested that maybe I should become a florist. She was given information packs on gaining vocational skills and we worked through them in class throughout that term. I reckon it was the most important term I've ever had at school. We did a lot of group activities discussing the vocational skills needed for all the occupations we were interested in and how we could go about getting them. I guess seeing how jobs are really done and getting hands-on experience of them at WorldSkills helped us all to figure out what we wanted to do with our lives and made us realise it was up to us to make sure we got the proper training.

INT: An invaluable lesson indeed. So would you attend WorldSkills again?

AHMET: I can't hide the fact that I'm holding out hopes of being a competitor at a future event. Of course, it'll take a lot of hard work and dedication, but I'm raring to go. I won't make it to the next event in 2013, but I've got my eyes set on the 2015 event. By that time, I'll be well into my training …

TRACK 10.3

N: Speaking, Unit 10, Page 127, B

M: I'd like you to imagine that a school or college is planning to offer a prize to a group of students who have worked very hard all year and got good results. Here are some of the prizes they are thinking about giving them. Talk to each other about the advantages and disadvantages of giving prizes like this to students. [pause] Now you have about one minute to decide which prize would not be a good idea.

Unit 11 Wish You Were Here!

N: Listening, Unit 11, Page 140, B

N: 1

The last time I visited the island, I was really let down. It had become run-down and the locals obviously weren't interested in making the tourists happy. It's such a shame because I used to love going there year after year. Some people were saying they wouldn't go back again. It'll certainly be a long while before I go back again.

N: 2

But the good thing was that I went straight up to the check-in desk. There were no long queues to wait in like there usually are. Never have I had such a relaxing journey.

N: 3

There we were walking along the beach in Phuket, when, who do we run into but Bob and Maureen from number 17! They were into their last week in Thailand. You know what great company they are, so we had an absolutely fantastic time with them for a few days. Overall, it was a holiday to remember, but it just wasn't the same when they left.

N: 4

And when I stepped into the room, argh, I practically fainted. It was the filthiest hotel room you could imagine. I couldn't believe that they seriously expected us to sleep there. The sheets hadn't been changed and there were cockroaches everywhere! I even saw a rat running under the bed.

TRACK 11.2

N: Listening, Unit 11, Page 140, D

N: **You will hear part of a television programme about house swapping. For questions one to seven, choose the best answer (a, b or c).**

INT: And next up, those of you who've seen the film *The Holiday* will be familiar with the idea of house swapping. In the film, two women who live on opposite sides of the Atlantic have one thing in common: failed relationships. In order to escape from their lives, the two women arrange online to swap houses over Christmas. Amanda, played by Cameron Diaz, suddenly finds herself in a small cottage in England, whereas Iris, played by Kate Winslet, is transported to a luxury villa in Hollywood. Now, if that all seems a bit far-fetched, you might be surprised to learn that house swapping is becoming more common these days. I'm joined in the studio by Alex Forsyth, the founder of House Swap International. Alex …

ALEX: Hello.

INT: Alex, why would anyone want to house swap?

ALEX: It's simple really; many people like to travel regularly, but don't want to pay the high prices of holiday accommodation. So house swapping allows them to travel to the destinations of their dreams and stay in someone else's house for next to nothing while the other person stays in their house.

INT: Is it really as simple as that, though? I mean, how do swappers get in touch with one another?

ALEX: That's where House Swap International comes in. A few years ago, my brother and I decided to set up a company which would allow people to arrange swaps. For an annual fee, members can advertise their home on our website and browse the properties that other members from all over the world have listed. At the moment there are over a thousand properties listed on the site. We encourage our members to upload recent photographs of their home and include details like how many people can stay there, whether or not pets are welcome and how far it is from local amenities. They also fill in a chart giving information about the local area such as good restaurants, museums and local sights as well as activities that are available in the region. That gives people a fuller picture of a place they might be interested in visiting, without having to research various websites.

INT: So, say I've browsed the properties and I've picked out a home I'd be interested in swapping for my own for a few weeks, what's the next stage? Do I send the owner an email or ring them up?

ALEX: Oh no, you wouldn't have access to their email address or phone number. Our members' personal details remain confidential until an arrangement is made. At first, members get in touch with each other through the site's secure messaging system. That way, members can communicate safely and easily so that they can arrange when their house swap will take place and ask and answer any questions they might have about the house and area they will be visiting.

INT: What tips would you give those planning to swap their house?

ALEX: It's important that both sides are 100 per cent happy with the deal. That's why communication is the key to success. The more you are in contact with the other owner before you arrive at your destination, the more likely you are to get what you're looking for. A nice touch would be to stock the kitchen with essential supplies so that your guest feels welcome. Also, it's extremely important that your home is as tidy and clean as possible for your guests, and that at the end of your holiday, you leave the other person's house as you found it. Finally, you will have to arrange for the keys to be collected in as convenient a way as possible. You might need the assistance of a friendly neighbour, relative or friend to make sure that the keys are available when the holidaymakers arrive.

INT: Do members always expect a home similar to their own?

ALEX: Not always. It's surprising how different their choices can be. People travel to different places for different reasons and more often than not they want something different to what they have at home. For example, the owner of a luxurious villa with a pool in Malibu might be interested in a small flat in central Paris in order to see the sights. So you see, all sorts of tastes are catered for on our site, and there's plenty to choose from …

Unit 12 Fit for Life

TRACK 12.1

N: Listening, Unit 12, Page 152, D

N: **You will hear people talking in eight different situations. For questions one to eight, choose the best answer (a, b or c).**

N: **1: You hear two friends talking about an accident.**

A: That's a bad burn on your arm. What happened?

B: Yes, it's nasty, isn't it? Stupidly, I scalded myself with some hot water earlier as I was washing the dishes. Really, I should have been more careful.

A: Shouldn't you do something about it?

B: I already have. I ran it under the tap for ten minutes and put some ice on it, but it's still really red.

A: Maybe you should apply some cream to it.

B: Perhaps I will.

A: Does it hurt?

B: Actually, it's starting to hurt quite badly …

N: **2: You hear a doctor giving a talk.**

There's a very good reason why people say breakfast is the most important meal of the day. After six, seven or, if you're lucky, eight hours of sleep, your body and brain need some fuel to power up and prepare them for the day ahead. Like a car, you can't run on an empty fuel tank; you need some petrol.

Plus, breakfast is good for you. According to researchers, those who eat breakfast are less likely to have blood sugar problems. Also, some breakfast foods such as grains, seeds and dried fruit provide vitamins and minerals that are hard to find in other foods.

N: **3: You hear a sports commentator at a football game.**

Suarez is taking the ball from the referee. He's placing it carefully. I think he's hoping to strike it. He's having a word with his captain, Gerrard. The captain is nodding his head, so Suarez will take the penalty. If he scores, Liverpool will lead 2 to 1, and they desperately need a win after their shock defeat at Fulham last weekend to keep their title hopes alive … back to Suarez now … he kicks the ball and … <u>OH! … he's missed! He's furious and he's shouting!</u> But what's this? The referee is showing him a yellow card for unsportsmanlike behaviour! Oh dear …

N: 4: You overhear a woman talking about her weight loss.

A: So how did you drop all that weight?

B: <u>Not in the usual way, that's for sure.</u> There was no diet or exercise for me. <u>I got a tummy bug out in Africa and I lost my appetite.</u> Not only was the thought of food disgusting, but whenever I did eat – and only just the tiniest amount – I would become violently ill and throw up. Honestly, I have never felt so wretched in all my life. And the antibiotics took ages before they had any effect. I was so tempted to get on the first plane out of there, but I would have let the others down if I'd done that …

N: 5: You hear two friends talking about their favourite teams.

A: The Reds are going to win it this year, you just watch!

B: Don't be ridiculous. You haven't won the basketball title in years and nothing's going to change now.

A: Why not? We've bought some great players, <u>and spent a lot of money actually.</u>

B: <u>That's true, you have,</u> but are they the right players? Expensive doesn't necessarily mean good. Take my team … the Greens have spent less money than any other major club in Europe and we're still the champions.

A: You will never let me forget that, will you? But one day … ohhhh … one day … we'll be holding up that trophy. Just you wait and see.

N: 6: You hear a girl telling a friend about her ambitions.

I was doing a degree in pharmacy at first. Why? Because I had an interest in chemistry and health care, and wanted to become a research scientist. As a young child, I was attracted to the idea of putting on a white coat and mixing chemicals in a lab. It seemed really brainy and important work. And it is, but I changed. I discovered that I really enjoyed communicating with people and solving

their problems. <u>I was very good at this and began to realise that a career in medicine would be better for me.</u> So now I'm applying to become a doctor.

N: 7: You hear a radio interview about a winter activity.

A: Meet 78-year-old Elsie Smith. She's a very brave lady. Elsie thinks nothing of taking a dip in freezing cold water. Why not, Elsie?

B: Oh, it's very refreshing. <u>It clears your head and helps you to concentrate.</u> Plus, I wear a wetsuit, so I don't get the full impact of the cold water.

A: What advice would you give to anyone thinking of taking up winter swimming?

B: Well, firstly, be sensible about where you swim and never swim alone. Enter the water in stages, not all at once as that can shock your body. Oh, and never, ever attempt it if you have a heart condition.

N: 8: You overhear two friends in a restaurant.

A: Some interesting items on the menu, don't you think? Pork with pineapple and celery … Twice-fried chips … I bet they're delicious!

B: Aren't you supposed to avoid fried food?

A: I can eat small amounts, no problem. <u>It's dairy I have to be careful about.</u> I've got an allergy.

B: That must make life a bit difficult. I mean, dairy's in everything! What do you do if you're invited to dinner?

A: I just eat what I can and leave the rest. I'm used to it now.

B: Does it bother you if someone's eating it in front of you?

A: No, not at all.

B: In that case, I'll have the cheeseburger!

TRACK 12.2

N: Speaking, Unit 12, Page 153, B

Andrea: <u>So, shall we start with this photo?</u> Playing football could be a good idea because it keeps you fit and you can play in a team together, and the friends want to do something as a group. <u>What do you think?</u>

Carlo: Yes, it's a good idea, <u>I agree.</u> And you learn a lot by playing team sports, you know, how to get on with other people…<u>but do you think all the friends will like this activity?</u> I mean, some girls might not…

Andrea: …do you really think so? <u>I know girls who play for school football teams and are in to that type of sport. Anyway, let's move on to this photo… I think learning how to cook is a good idea for a group of friends.</u> It's a useful skill…

Carlo: …hmmm, <u>I'm not sure I agree.</u> It depends on what you cook as it might not be good for your health…yeah, and young people usually prefer eating fast food, so they'll probably make hamburgers or chocolate cakes…

Andrea: [laughing a bit] I know what you mean, that's a good point <u>but I don't really agree.</u> I think it's very important to learn how to cook and it could be fun as a group.

Carlo: <u>Well, how about this photograph?</u> I think swimming is…

WORKBOOK B2 KEY

Unit 1

Reading
A
Student's own answer

B
1c 2a 3b 4b 5c 6a

Vocabulary
A
Student's own answer

B
1	dissatisfied	4	confidence
2	loneliness	5	anxious
3	disgusting	6	happy

C
1e 2d 3a 4f 5b 6c

D
1	irrational	4	affect
2	express	5	shame
3	amazed	6	miserable

Grammar
A
1 We go to the beach every day.
2 Why are you always complaining about the weather?
3 These roses smell lovely.
4 They usually have a test at the end of each term.
5 Do neurons send messages to the brain?
6 What are you staring at?
7 I am looking for the station. Can you tell me where it is?
8 She's getting more and more excited about her birthday every day.

B
1 does, take off
2 Does, belong
3 shows, goes
4 take
5 looks
6 is, bursting into
7 freaks out
8 am not seeing

Listening
A
Student's own answer

C
1b 2a 3c 4a 5c 6b

Grammar
A
1 haven't, cleaned
2 has been giving
3 have never been
4 have just met
5 Has, been running
6 has asked
7 have, been staying
8 haven't given

B
1 has been hitting
2 has dated
3 has/have, given
4 has, met
5 has been getting
6 has made
7 has ended
8 have parted

Use your English
A
1 is the first time
2 has been travelling
3 I have ever
4 was at a loss for
5 have never been
6 have known Sue since

B
Student's own answer

C
1 to
2 at
3 is
4 happiness
5 and
6 feel
7 expressing
8 on
9 insight
10 us

Writing
A
1 why she didn't go to Jack's party
2 how Joy managed to spill a drink on Kate's dress
3 what Joy should do to get back on good terms with Kate
4 Joy sending her photos of the party
5 Student's own answer

B
The following should be circled:
right! (paragraph 1)
party! (paragraph 1)
off! (paragraph 3)

The following should be underlined:
You're (paragraph 1)
haven't (paragraph 1)
didn't (paragraph 1)
club's (paragraph 1)
we've (paragraph 1)
you've (paragraph 2)
I'm (paragraph 2)
she'll (paragraph 2)
She's (paragraph 2)
she'll (paragraph 2)
Don't (paragraph 3)

The following should be highlighted:
You're right! We haven't seen each other for ages. (paragraph 1)
Well, hope to catch up with you soon, (paragraph 4)

C
Student's own answer

Unit 2

Reading
A
Student's own answer

B
1A 2B 3D 4C 5C 6B 7D 8A

Vocabulary
A
1	company	4	canal
2	exchange	5	lifestyles
3	move	6	departed

B
1	custom	4	concept
2	knowledge	5	influence
3	phenomenon		

C
Student's own answer

D
1	Egyptian	5	occurrence
2	civilisation	6	international
3	global	7	professional
4	American	8	beliefs

Grammar

A
1 started
2 used to
3 was searching
4 would go
5 built
6 collected
7 was staying
8 used to watch

B
1 use
2 was
3 Did
4 Were
5 would
6 were
7 Was
8 did

C
Student's own answers

Listening

A
Student's own answer

C
1 Melbourne, Australia
2 different school
3 third term
4 public transport network
5 European
6 (extremely) lucky
7 customs and traditions

Grammar

A
1 Have, been
2 flew
3 spent
4 have, had
5 did, do
6 visited
7 have enjoyed
8 had

B
When the group (1) has set out -> set out for the mountains that morning, they didn't realise what an ordeal lay ahead of them. They (2) have planned -> planned to be back before dusk and asked the inn-keeper to prepare an evening meal for them. The idea was to walk up to the highest peak and ski down the north face. However, four hours into their hike, snow (3) has started -> started to fall heavily. The closer they got to the peak, the heavier it fell. The group leader, Franz, (4) has seemed -> seemed worried. 'This is the first time I (5) climbed -> have climbed in such bad conditions,' he (6) has told -> told the others in a worried voice. 'I (7) didn't ski -> haven't skiied before in such thick snow. We should turn back.' But

just as they (8) have turned back -> turned back, they realised that the path they (9) have followed -> were following up the mountain was now buried under the snow! The other members of the group panicked. They would be stuck on the mountain until the snow cleared. To make matters worse, darkness was falling. 'I (10) was -> have been in more dangerous situations than this,' Franz thought to himself. 'I can get us back safe and sound'. Just then the sound of an engine could be heard in the distance. It was a rescue helicopter. Luckily, the inn-keeper, who sensed the group was in danger when they didn't return in time, had sent for help.

Use your English

A
1 Swiss
2 amazement
3 civilisations
4 international
5 eagerness
6 confidence
7 occurrences
8 professional
9 anxiety
10 loneliness

B
1 is
2 have
3 on
4 take
5 never/not
6 in
7 are
8 to
9 used
10 the
11 has
12 thinking

Writing

A
1T 2F 3T 4F 5F 6T 7F 8T

B
1d 2c 3a 4b

C
Student's own answer

Review 1   Units 1 & 2

Vocabulary

A
1c 2a 3b 4a 5d 6b 7a 8c 9a
10c 11c 12b 13c 14d 15d 16b
17a 18c 19a 20c 21c 22b 23b
24c 25a 26a 27d 28b

Grammar

B
1c 2b 3c 4d 5a 6b 7a 8c 9a
10b 11c 12d 13a 14d 15c 16a
17a 18c 19b 20b 21c 22d 23b
24a 25c 26b 27d 28d

Unit 3

Reading

A
Student's own answer

B
1F 2C 3G 4B 5E 6A

Vocabulary

A
1 rumour
2 personality
3 gossip
4 accomplishment
5 shame
6 account
7 character
8 disgrace

B
1 astonishment
2 representative
3 servants
4 inspiration
5 location
6 privacy
7 publicity
8 stylish

C
1 qualified
2 reputation
3 break
4 notorious
5 money
6 influential
7 scandal
8 figure

Grammar

A
1 They had been staying
2 had he starred in
3 She had been watching
4 had represented
5 He had never visited
6 The star had been walking

B
1 had been staying
2 had been getting
3 hadn't been
4 had never played
5 Had, been nosing about
6 hadn't asked

C

1	had	5	was
2	been	6	just
3	had	7	already
4	were	8	had

Listening

A

Student's own answer

C

1D 2F 3B 4C 5A

Grammar

A

1 had been having, walked
2 Had, been acting, offered
3 had been playing, ended
4 had never belonged, joined
5 went, had been writing/wrote/had written
6 had changed, was

B

1 had never met
2 once she had shaken
3 because she had seen/saw
4 had not/never played
5 she died
6 had been touring for

Use your English

A

1 At
2 well
3 his
4 on
5 for
6 would
7 by
8 get
9 With
10 was
11 had
12 able

B

1b 2d 3b 4a 5b 6a 7d 8b 9b
10b

C

1 didn't look down on
2 had been living for
3 Shall we go
4 wouldn't name drop
5 out of nowhere
6 will have been
7 had finished/ended by
8 a lot of tension

Writing

A

1 begin   3 positive
2 Celia   4 past

B

1 had arrived   5 uncontrollably
2 ecstatic   6 appeared
3 blue   7 asked
4 slumped   8 was floating

C

Student's own answer

Unit 4

Reading

A

Student's own answer

B

1A 2A 3B 4A 5C 6C 7C 8B 9D
10B

Vocabulary

A

1 speed bump
2 outskirts
3 landlord/landlady
4 concrete jungles
5 flatmates
6 districts

B

1b 2c 3a 4c 5b 6a 7a 8c

C

1 away   5 paint
2 into   6 walks
3 lead   7 space
4 out

Grammar

A

1 Shall we go
2 Sharon will have left
3 I will come
4 they will create
5 you arrive
6 residents will be using

B

1 will have finished
2 won't run
3 Shall … give
4 are going to crash into
5 am going to paint
6 will have lived/been living
7 will improve
8 Will … help

Listening

A

Student's own answer

C

1c 2c 3b 4a 5c 6c

Grammar

A

1 furniture, table
2 jewellery, brooch
3 chair, hair
4 firefighter, school children, fire
5 job, experience
6 glass, bin
7 milk, cereal
8 chocolate, chocolates

B

1 Many   6 paper
2 lot of   7 slice
3 some   8 trips
4 no   9 Is
5 Lots of   10 was

Use your English

A

1 more
2 in
3 was
4 when
5 to
6 since
7 which
8 had
9 used
10 were

B

Student's own answer

C

1b 2c 3a 4c 5d 6b 7d 8a 9b
10a

Writing

A

Students should tick: 1, 3, 5 & 7

B

1 by asking questions and providing examples and descriptions
2 provided a possible answer to it
3 building houses in suburbs, creating efficient transport systems, making green roofs on buildings compulsory
4 Student's own answer

C

Student's own answer

Review 2 Units 3 & 4

Vocabulary
A
1c 2a 3c 4a 5d 6b 7d 8c 9a
10c 11d 12c 13a 14b 15b 16c
17b 18c 19d 20a 21c 22c 23a
24c 25d 26a 27c 28a

Grammar
B
1b 2d 3c 4c 5b 6d 7a 8b 9c
10b 11a 12a 13c 14d 15b 16a
17b 18a 19d 20a 21c 22d 23b
24c 25d 26b 27c 28d

Unit 5

Reading
A
Student's own answer

B
1d 2b 3b 4c 5d

Vocabulary
A
1	excursion	4	limited
2	researcher	5	precise
3	intelligent	6	fact

B
1	interactive	5	simulation
2	originate	6	technological
3	appliances	7	Exposure
4	exhibition	8	stimulation

C
1	time machine	4	measure
2	ability	5	lose
3	miss	6	generate

Grammar
A
1	Could	5	can't
2	can't	6	couldn't
3	shouldn't	7	needn't
4	be able to	8	ought

B
1 ought/has/needs
2 able
3 can't
4 Can/Might/May/Should/Must
5 have/need
6 can't
7 Could
8 must/should

Listening
A
Student's own answer

C
1b 2c 3a 4c 5c 6c 7a 8b 9b
10b

Grammar
A
1a 2c 3b 4a 5a 6c

B
1 You needn't have got
2 They ought to/should have told
3 Jan can't/couldn't have caused
4 Should I have asked
5 The customers must have been impressed
6 Mark would have repaired

Use your English
A
1 as
2 in
3 across
4 on
5 soon
6 ever
7 there
8 of
9 are
10 in

B
1a 2c 3d 4d 5a 6a 7b 8a 9d
10a

C
1 had better assemble
2 must have been
3 didn't remember to switch
4 ought to have stayed
5 grab/have a bite to eat
6 can't have been
7 can/is able to seat
8 can't have been

Writing
A
1 How modern means of communication have affected our relationships.
2 3
3 My opinion on how people communicate, how modern communications affect relationships, what negative effects modern means of communication can have.
4 Yes, because it says in the task 'What do you think'.

B
Students should cross out the following:
1	According to	5	Even though
2	For example	6	such
3	Although	7	Even so
4	In spite of	8	Though

C
Student's own answer

Unit 6

Reading
A
Student's own answer

B
1b 2d 3c 4a 5d 6b 7c 8a 9d
10a

Vocabulary
A
1 jogging
2 basketball/backgammon
3 aerobics
4 windsurfing
5 cards
6 athletics
7 gymnastics
8 sailing

B
1	alley	5	track
2	course	6	net/Internet
3	record	7	court
4	time	8	bite

C
1b 2c 3a 4c 5a 6b 7c 8b

Grammar
A
1	to get	5	go
2	Jogging	6	to have
3	playing	7	to wash
4	buy	8	to give

B
1 talking
2 to have escaped
3 to take
4 get
5 knowing
6 to go
7 hurry
8 driving

Listening

A

Student's own answer

C

1 most
2 has
3 than
4 with
5 out
6 after
7 its
8 war
9 within
10 accommodation

Grammar

A

1 would like to know
2 you mind taking me
3 don't suppose you know
4 if/whether you could lend me
5 like to ask you
6 wonder if/whether you could help

B

1d 2e 3g 4h 5c 6a 7b 8f

Use your English

A

1 have
2 be
3 any/enough
4 which
5 order
6 able
7 in
8 have/need
9 the
10 could/would

B

1b 2a 3d 4c 5d 6a 7b 8c 9a
10c

C

1 interactive
2 beginners
3 participants
4 addiction
5 collections
6 exhibitions
7 equipment
8 exposure
9 stimulation
10 ability

Writing

A

1F 2F 3T 4T 5T

B

a Introduction
b Sports offered
c Cost of Membership
d Facilities
e Conclusion

1 my findings are presented below
2 In particular, members are keen to have classes in tai chi and yoga.
3 The most popular suggestion was to
4 Regarding
5 there are not enough
6 I would therefore suggest that membership fees be more affordable

C

Student's own answer

Review 3   Units 5 & 6

Vocabulary

A

1c 2b 3a 4d 5b 6c 7d 8a 9d
10c 11d 12c 13a 14b 15a 16c
17a 18b 19c 20b 21a 22a 23c
24c 25a 26d 27c 28d

Grammar

B

1c 2d 3b 4a 5b 6c 7a 8d 9a
10b 11c 12c 13a 14c 15b 16d
17a 18a 19b 20d 21a 22a 23d
24b 25c 26b 27c 28b

Unit 7

Reading

A

Student's own answer

B

1b 2c 3d 4a 5d 6b

Vocabulary

A

1d 2e 3a 4b 5f 6c

B

1 case
2 criminals
3 goods
4 clothes
5 court
6 act
7 service
8 duty

C

1a 2b 3c 4a 5c 6c

Grammar

A

1 was/has been sentenced
2 was started
3 will/is going to be printed
4 has been broken into
5 are called
6 is being arrested
7 be released
8 was knocked down

B

1 were
2 been
3 opened/searched/taken
4 was
5 had
6 woken
7 being
8 was
9 been
10 by

Listening

A

Student's own answer

C

1c 2a 3b 4c 5a 6b 7b

Grammar

A

1e 2c 3a 4f 5b 6d

B

1 will have had the police station decorated
2 gets his lawyer to check/has his lawyer check
3 did … have hidden cameras installed
4 is having his cell searched
5 got the bank robber to put down
6 have had our garden table stolen

Use your English

A

1a 2b 3d 4b 5b 6b 7a 8c

B

1 masked
2 armed
3 statement
4 robbers
5 deadly
6 criminal
7 mugger
8 hardened
9 tried
10 service

C

1 were evacuated by
2 being pulled down
3 was questioned by
4 is having numbers engraved
5 was found not guilty by
6 are releasing/will release him from
7 wasn't aware of
8 had my car stolen

Writing

A

1 They have started up a Neighbourhood Watch scheme to help combat crime locally.
2 Because of the high crime rates in the area.
3 Should residents get involved in police work?
4 specific examples
5 Students' own answers

B

1 I read your article about the Neighbourhood Watch scheme that has been set up by the residents of Blackton.
2 However, I disagree that ordinary citizens should get involved in police work.
3 I disagree with the view that if the police cannot reduce crime, the local people should help out.
4 In short, I believe that creating groups like the one in Blackton is not the best way to tackle neighbourhood crime.

C

Student's own answer

Unit 8

Reading

A

Student's own answer

B

1F 2H 3C 4G 5A 6B 7E

Vocabulary

A

1 from   5 deforestation
2 with   6 moisture
3 wears   7 on
4 on   8 torrential

B

1 endangered species
2 victims
3 climate change
4 resulted

5 conservation
6 wiped
7 ecosystems
8 objected

C

1 wind turbine   4 flames
2 cycle   5 current
3 gust   6 sea level

D

1 rise   5 exposed
2 respect   6 pessimistic
3 organic   7 evaporate
4 unleaded 8 forces

Grammar

A

1 I would sign
2 appear
3 they wouldn't have been injured
4 If the utilities company pays
5 If they ban OR there would be
6 had risen OR the ice caps will melt
7 Would you have studied OR if they offered
8 If we recycled OR we will help

B

1 don't, know   5 will use
2 will notice   6 want
3 consume   7 proves
4 would be   8 will save

Listening

A

Student's own answer

C

1D 2F 3A 4C 5E

Grammar

A

Possible answers:
1 the fire wouldn't have started
2 the fire will get out of control
3 we'll have to plant more
4 the fire will spread to other areas
5 they won't survive the fire
6 the earth will be polluted

B

1 wouldn't   5 hadn't
2 give   6 will be
3 had protected 7 had been
4 was   8 would

C

1 provided/providing
2 Supposing
3 would

4 had
5 long
6 on

Use your English

A

1 emissions
2 burst
3 renewable
4 coastal
5 blocked
6 erosion
7 freezes
8 solar

B

1b 2a 3c 4a 5c 6a 7c 8c 9b 10a

C

1 will
2 be
3 is
4 if
5 in
6 rode/used
7 would/could
8 on
9 than
10 take

Writing

A

1F 2F 3T 4T 5T

B

1 though   5 For instance
2 indeed   6 Also
3 However   7 To sum up
4 In fact   8 Nonetheless

C

Student's own answer

Review 4   Units 7 & 8

Vocabulary

A

1c 2b 3c 4a 5d 6c 7d 8a 9b
10c 11a 12a 13d 14a 15b 16d
17b 18c 19b 20a 21a 22c 23c
24a 25a 26c 27d 28d

Grammar

B

1c 2a 3b 4c 5a 6a 7c 8c 9a
10d 11b 12d 13a 14c 15d 16c
17d 18a 19b 20b 21a 22a 23a
24b 25c 26b 27b

Unit 9

Reading

A
Student's own answer

B
1B 2C 3D 4B 5B 6D 7C 8A 9C
10A

Vocabulary

A
1 satisfaction   5 punctual
2 productive   6 promotion
3 contract   7 working
4 freelance   8 colleagues

B
1 openings   5 availability
2 supervisor(s)   6 applicants
3 permission   7 employees
4 attendant   8 profitable

Grammar

A
1 the man that/- Gina
2 factory where I work
3 The woman whose briefcase
4 The desk where you
5 the accountant who/that deals
6 the application form that/which/-
   you
7 Do you know why he
8 The year when I

B
1 who   5 which/that
2 who/that   6 where
3 why   7 whose
4 which   8 when

Listening

A
Student's own answer

C
1c 2d 3d 4a 5b 6a
    b   c   c

Grammar

A
1 Waiting   5 handing
2 Disappointed   6 trained
3 Being   7 handled
4 Wearing   8 arriving

B
1 Working   6 requiring
2 starting   7 organising
3 Attending   8 Employed
4 travelling   9 Taking
5 made   10 Exhausted

Use your English

A
1 is where
2 the girl whose father
3 that we ate last night
4 was when
5 is why
6 the kidnapper who escaped

B
1d 2b 3a 4b 5d 6c 7b 8a 9d
10d 11b 12c

C
1 availability
2 applicants
3 depressing
4 dissatisfied
5 suitably
6 vacancies
7 possess
8 permission
9 employees
10 satisfaction

Writing

A
1 a letter of application
2 school bus driver for kindergarten
3 taking under sixes to and from
   kindergarten
4 a clean driving licence
5 They should be friendly,
   outgoing, responsible and good
   with children.

B
1 Stirling Moss
2 thirty years old
3 professional driving licence, clean
   driving licence
4 worked as a taxi driver and mini-
   bus driver for a holiday company
5 yes
6 hard working, honest, punctual,
   friendly, gets on well with
   children

C
Student's own answer

Unit 10

Reading

A
Student's own answer

B
1b 2c 3a 4b 5a 6d 7b 8c

Vocabulary

A
1d 2a 3f 4e 5b 6c

B
1 tutor   5 Cheating
2 scholarship   6 assignment
3 tournament   7 discipline
4 graduation   8 fees

Grammar

A
1 cheating wouldn't help me
2 I had been absent
3 me to hand in my
4 if/whether she could sit
5 the teacher had given them
6 to put our bags there

B
1 if Joe wants   5 told
2 had graduated   6 previous
3 me   7 not to
4 had to   8 would

Listening

A
Student's own answer

C
1 music high schools
2 1988
3 over/more than 70
4 general lessons
5 theory
6 in June
7 video clips
8 newest member
9 English teacher
10 rehearsals

Grammar

A
1 refused to help me with my
   homework
2 agreed to let me/us do the
   experiment in the lab
3 denied cheating in the exam
4 reminded me to enrol on the
   course in time
5 apologised for spilling coffee on
   my notebook
6 offered to teach my son English
   free of charge
7 advised us to revise regularly
8 admitted that he had stolen/to
   stealing Brian's research

B
National plant a tree week
Schools throughout the UK are
busy preparing for National Tree

Week. From 26th November to 4th December all schools in the UK are encouraged to plant trees on their school grounds. Head teacher at a primary school in Devon, Isa Green, has decided **(1)** giving -> to give children at her school a break from ordinary lessons in order to plant elm trees at the school entrance. She agreed **(2)** for -> to plant these trees when she heard about the project, which is run by The Tree Council. She explained **(3)** to -> that the trees are provided by The Woodland Trust, a national charity. She persuaded all classroom teachers at the school **(4)** getting -> to get involved. She also **(5)** advised to -> advised them to make use of the 70-page activity booklet issued free to schools by The Woodland Trust to help them prepare for the event. She encouraged them **(6)** about using -> to use activities such as building sculptures out of pine cones, leaves and other materials that students could collect from a nearby forest. At first, some teachers were worried that students might destroy the trees. Green, however, warned students **(7)** about not to harm -> about harming OR not to harm the trees. She even announced **(8)** to -> that students would be severely punished if they did.

Use your English
A
1 of
2 who
3 where
4 when
5 no
6 their
7 ~~in~~ since
8 the
9 whose
10 from
11 Although
12 why

B
1 warned us that she/he would
2 whose dad is
3 if/whether she could see
4 reason why Shelley didn't
5 was the person who
6 advised/told me to be punctual
7 the woman (who is dressed)
8 suggested playing

Writing
A
Students should tick the following:
2, 4, 5, 7 & 9

B
1c 2e 3d 4b 5a

C
Student's own answer

Review 5   Units 9 & 10

Vocabulary
A
1d 2c 3b 4d 5b 6a 7c 8d 9a
10b 11c 12d 13a 14b 15d 16b
17a 18d 19d 20a 21b 22c 23d
24d 25a 26d 27a 28a

Grammar
B
1a 2c 3d 4b 5d 6a 7b 8c 9b
10a 11b 12c 13d 14c 15a 16b
17c 18a 19c 20b 21c 22a 23a
24c 25d 26d 27d 28d

Unit 11

Reading
A
Student's own answer

B
1d 2c 3b 4a 5d

Vocabulary
A
1 retreat   4 itinerary
2 vessel   5 international
3 yacht   6 coves

B
1 agent
2 tour/holiday/that
3 advance
4 pass
5 departure
6 reservation/booking
7 air
8 airlines

Grammar
A
1 the busiest
2 more/less popular
3 dangerous
4 easier
5 the best
6 earlier
7 the most/least interesting
8 the worst

B
1 the   5 so
2 than   6 cheaper/better
3 as   7 such
4 more   8 so/too

Listening
A
Student's own answer

C
1c 2b 3a 4c 5a 6c 7a

Grammar
A
1b 2a 3c 4a 5a 6b

B
1 wonderful   5 rather
2 new   6 fully
3 Absolutely   7 decorated
4 Dutch   8 velvet

Use your English
A
1 on
2 on
3 in
4 in
5 within
6 in

B
1a 2d 3c 4c 5d 6b 7a 8c 9d
10c 11b 12a

C
1 the most beautiful hotel
2 only we could go
3 is getting used to
4 rather you didn't
5 isn't as popular as
6 wish I had gone
7 no circumstances should you
8 sooner had he dived

Writing
A
1 alone, departure lounge, Bob, about to, a life-changing journey
2 mystery, fear, excitement
3 a passenger called Bob
4 in an airport departure lounge, sitting waiting for his flight to board
5 It will happen after.
6 He could have a terrible journey/ be involved in a crash. He could meet somebody who would become a good friend. etc.

B

1	read	6	quizzed
2	pushed	7	had applied
3	smiled	8	answered
4	was walking	9	had arranged
5	thought		

C

Student's own answer

Unit 12

Reading

A

Student's own answer

B

1E 2H 3A 4C 5B 6G 7D 8F

Vocabulary

A

1	braces	4	allergic
2	prescription	5	beneficial
3	poisonous	6	operation

B

1	allergic	4	work
2	carbohydrates	5	minerals
3	fibre	6	obese

C

1	protein	5	bitter
2	balanced	6	suffer
3	solution	7	essential
4	filling	8	opt for

Grammar

A

1	could	5	to eat
2	joined	6	tell
3	hadn't broken	7	playing
4	suffer	8	started

B

1	had taken	5	drinking
2	to book	6	to go
3	wasn't	7	do
4	tell	8	opened

Listening

A

Student's own answer

C

1b 2c 3a 4b 5b 6a 7a 8b

Grammar

A

1	only	5	Should/If
2	used	6	has
3	Under	7	Little
4	to	8	sooner

B

1b 2c 3a 4b 5a 6c 7c 8a

Use your English

A

1 prefer
2 used
3 Little
4 had
5 more
6 than
7 of
8 for
9 well
10 getting
11 only
12 but

B

1 natural
2 solution
3 beneficial
4 advisors
5 recommendation
6 Nutrition
7 contributor
8 plentiful
9 dependent
10 sensibly

C

1 no circumstances should you ring
2 sooner had he dived
3 Little did she know
4 Had he kept practising French,
5 Never have I been so tired
6 Under no circumstances are you allowed

Writing

A

1 a health spa you visited recently
2 the spa's facilities, the staff and the prices
3 swimming pools, Jacuzzis, beauty treatment, massage parlours, etc
4 either as the task leaves it open
5 readers of 'Your Health' magazine

B

1 Option b is the most appropriate answer as it covers the second point in the task (the staff). Without mentioning the staff, the writer wouldn't have answered the task properly. Also, it speaks about the staff in a positive way, which means that 'The only thing I didn't find impressive' in the next paragraph follows on well. For this reason option a is wrong as it talks about the staff in a negative way. Option c is not a good choice as it deals with another one of the facilities, so it would mean 'staff' wouldn't be covered in the review.
2 Option d is the best answer as it generally recommends the spa after reviewing it mainly positively, but also mentions the aspect that the writer was disappointed with. Option e is too negative and blows the expense involved out of proportion given that the first paragraphs are positive. Option f, on the other hand, is too positive as it ignores the feature the writer was disappointed with.

C

Student's own answer

Review 6   Units 11 & 12

Vocabulary

A

1b 2a 3d 4c 5a 6b 7c 8c 9b
10a 11c 12d 13b 14a 15d 16d
17a 18d 19b 20c 21b 22b 23d
24a 25b 26a 27c 28c

Grammar

B

1c 2d 3b 4a 5a 6d 7a 8a 9c
10d 11b 12a 13d 14b 15a 16a
17d 18a 19b 20d 21a 22b 23a
24c 25a 26d 27b 28a